Praise for
THE MEN BEHIND THE TRIDENT
SEAL Team One in Vietnam

"This book manages to do what other books on Vietnam-era SEALs have not: illuminate the daily lives of SEALs in Vietnam. These true oral histories give the men a chance to tell their own stories unfettered by sensationalism."
—*Dale Andrade, author and historian,*
Center for Military History

"An outstanding work . . . I felt as if I were in the room with these men as they told their stories."
—*Barry Enoch, SEAL veteran of three Vietnam tours, winner of the Navy Cross and two Silver and Bronze stars*

THE MEN BEHIND THE TRIDENT

SEAL Team One in Viet Nam

Dennis J. Cummings

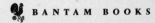 BANTAM BOOKS

New York Toronto London Sydney Auckland

This edition contains the complete text of the original hardcover edition. NOT ONE WORD HAS BEEN OMITTED.

THE MEN BEHIND THE TRIDENT
A Bantam Book

PUBLISHING HISTORY
Naval Institute Press hardcover edition published in 1997
Bantam mass-market edition / May 1998

Library of Congress Catalog Card Number: 96-52042

ISBN 0-553-57928-2

Published simultaneously in the United States and Canada

Bantam Books are published by Bantam Books, a division of Bantam Doubleday Dell Publishing Group, Inc. Its trademark, consisting of the words "Bantam Books" and the portrayal of a rooster, is Registered in U.S. Patent and Trademark Office and in other countries. Marca Registrada. Bantam Books, 1540 Broadway, New York, New York 10036.

PRINTED IN THE UNITED STATES OF AMERICA
OPM   0 9 8 7 6 5 4 3

This book is dedicated to the Teams.
May they always remember the lessons
of the past and their teammates who have
gone before, both the living and those
who have made the ultimate sacrifice.

Contents

Acknowledgments

This book on the combat experiences of SEAL Team One operators in Vietnam came about, as does anything involving the Teams, through teamwork. Foremost I would like to thank the SEAL Team One veterans who agreed to talk openly about their experiences as SEALs in Vietnam. Without their time, patience, and insight this book would not exist.

Over the years many members of the UDT/SEAL community have assisted in gathering background material, such as photographs, slides, film footage, and personal anecdotes on SEAL operations in Vietnam. I would like to thank the following for their help in this regard: Gary Parrott, Gary R. Smith, Mike Walsh, Alan Yutz, Scott Lyon, Tipton Ammen, Al Starr, George "Doc" Thomas, Clint Majors, Sam Birky, Terry Bryant, Bob Schaedler, and Gordon Clisham.

I also thank Chip Maury for the photograph of Barry Enoch, Lou Hyatt for providing the group shot of Echo Platoon, and Jim La Vore for his photo of Tom Leonard.

While conducting interviews for this work, I was afforded the hospitality of several families. In recognition I would like to thank John, Jimmie, and Jennifer Ware; Gilbert "Espi" Espinoza, Rose, and their children; Darryl "Willy" Wilson and Darlene; Hal and

Denise Kuykendall; Dwight and Kate Daigle; and Steve and Kathy Felstein. In opening their homes to me they made my trips around the country far more pleasant than they would otherwise have been. Their kindness will always be remembered.

Others who were not in the Teams also made significant contributions. Mike Rush assisted with the spelling of names, SEAL platoon rosters, and background information on the LDNN. SOG historian Harvey Saal spent hours on the telephone with me to make sure that my information on the Studies and Observations Group was accurate. Don Muschany spent many days behind the wheel of my car as we drove across the country, conducting interviews. Janine Henry deserves my thanks for her help in setting up the second interview with her husband, Bob, while he was in the hospital. I must also thank Anna Keyes, who used her considerable photographic skills to reproduce many of the original photographs used in this book. Victor Clayton has my appreciation for his assistance in scanning the photographs used in the manuscript. Dyan Yutz provided computer-generated art for the cover of the original manuscript, for which I am grateful.

Another person who deserves more than my thanks is Mark Gatlin of the Naval Institute Press. He believed in this project to preserve part of the history of SEAL Team One. Mark spent many hours with the manuscript, making editing changes and suggestions that helped make this a better book. I am truly in his debt.

I would like to thank my close friends Kirby and Terri Horrell, who stood by me during this ordeal. Terri Juarez Horrell put up with me as I conducted interviews for this book in her home during the time that she and Kirby were preparing to move to an overseas duty station. Terri truly has the patience of a saint. It was Kirby's belief in my ability to tell the story in the right way that opened many doors for me and got me started on this book. I owe him a great deal more than my gratitude.

Finally, I thank my wife, Cris, who supported me in this endeavor and used her free time for the better part of a year to transcribe the taped interviews and make editing changes to the manuscript. I couldn't have done it without her.

Introduction

Navy Underwater Demolition Team (UDT) "frogmen" have held distinguished combat records since World War II, when their primary mission was to swim ashore to reconnoiter—or recon—beaches and blow up manmade and natural obstacles prior to amphibious landings. During his presidency, John F. Kennedy predicted the future of warfare would change. He believed guerrilla warfare would play a large part in the wars of the future. In response to the growing number of wars of liberation, the president directed that each of the armed forces develop units with special-warfare capabilities. A new unit was needed within the Navy to comply with that directive.

On 1 January 1962, in Coronado, California, President Kennedy commissioned SEAL Team One. The task of the ten officers and fifty enlisted men of the Team was to conduct unconventional-warfare operations beyond the UDT boundary of the high-water mark on a beach and into the hinterland.

SEAL Team One's missions would include destroying enemy shipping, harbor facilities, bridges, railway lines, and other facilities in maritime and riverine environments. The Team members would also infiltrate and exfiltrate agents, guerrillas, evaders, and escapees, as well as conduct reconnaissance and surveillance and gather intelligence.

In addition, team members would be asked to accomplish limited counterinsurgency civic-action tasks, which were normally incidental to counterguerrilla operations. These included conducting boat operations and providing boat maintenance, supplying medical aid, and contributing to the basic education of indigenous populations, among other tasks. Finally, they would also be used to train, assist, and advise U.S., allied, and other friendly military or paramilitary forces in the conduct of any of the above.

To accomplish all of this, the officers and men of the new SEAL Team knew that they needed more training. Training had been the key to the success of the UDTs from which they had come. Each of the men, officers and enlisted alike, had endured eighteen weeks of rigorous UDT training. It was this training that instilled teamwork and formed the common bond that would last for the rest of their lives.

The first phase of training conditioned them both mentally and physically, culminating with Hell Week, when they were subjected to continuous physical training evolutions, such as runs in soft sand, tiring swims in the cold waters of the Pacific Ocean, physical training with logs, and long rubber-boat transits along the coast, with only two hours of sleep the entire week.

Those that made it to the second phase—and not many did, as the washout rate for UDT trainees was 60 percent or higher—were introduced to underwater operations. They were taught how to use various types of SCUBA (Self-Contained Underwater Breathing Apparatus) and trained to attack ships in the middle of the night and get away undetected.

In the third phase, the "tadpoles"—as the trainees were referred to by the instructors—learned land-warfare skills. Finishing this final phase of training meant graduating from the course and assignment to an Underwater Demolition Team.

Those selected for a SEAL Team soon realized that UDT

training was not enough and wisely sought out schools conducted by the Army, Navy, Air Force, and Marine Corps that would give them the skills needed to accomplish their expanded missions. These were skills they would soon need. Within a few months, members of SEAL Team One would be deployed to the Republic of South Vietnam. In March 1962 a SEAL Mobile Training Team (MTT) began advising and assisting the South Vietnamese Navy and other military units. The MTT members got the Team's first look at a war in which the SEALs would soon be heavily involved.

In early 1966 the MTTs gave way to direct-action platoons. Operating under Detachment Golf in twelve-to-fourteen-man platoons, or as six- or seven-man squads, SEALs would take the war to the Viet Cong and North Vietnamese Army, using the communist guerrillas' own tactics. Some SEALs, veterans of one or more tours in Vietnam, would be assigned to Detachment Sierra to train and advise the South Vietnamese Navy's *Lien Doi Nguoi Nhai,* or LDNN. Other Team One operators found themselves assigned to Detachment Bravo, advising the Provincial Reconnaissance Units (PRUs). Another group of SEALs from Team One, Detachment Echo, was assigned to the top-secret Studies and Observations Group (SOG) under Military Assistance Command, Vietnam (MACV). Operations conducted by the South Vietnamese Sea Commando Teams, advised by these SEALs, reached far into North Vietnam.

Many of the facts of these operations are preserved in the command histories of SEAL Team One and other official Navy documents. What is missing are the perspectives of the men who conducted the missions, trained and advised our allies, and learned the lessons of combat the hard way.

On 16 October 1970 an insignia was authorized for wear by those personnel who had completed BUD/S (Basic Underwater Demolition/SEAL training) and been assigned to a SEAL Team. It consisted of an eagle with its wings spread, grasping a trident in one claw and a flintlock pistol in the other. The center of the design was a naval anchor. Together, these symbolized the three elements in which the SEALs operated: SEa, Air, and Land. In the Teams, it was simply referred to as ''the Trident.'' Today, the Trident is well known by military personnel and civilians as the symbol of the U.S. Navy SEALs. In the following pages are the personal stories, remembrances, and reflections of the men behind the Trident.

1

Barry Enoch

Mobile Training Team
Danang, Republic of Vietnam,
Deployed March–August 1963

I was in UDT Training Class Twenty-four at the
Naval Amphibious Base at Coronado, California, in 1960. When I finished the course, I received orders to Underwater Demolition Team 12 and
was assigned to First Platoon under Lieutenant Freeman. Several of us were taken from different platoons
and went with Lieutenant Freeman to the Arctic. We
went north of where the ice pack began and did some
demolition work.

When we came back, Team 12 was standing down
in preparation for deployment to WestPac [the Western Pacific] to relieve Underwater Demolition Team
11. We left and first went to Maui, Hawaii, where we
were lifeguards for an amphibious operation. Then we
went to Pearl Harbor, where we went through the one
hundred–foot free-ascent tank to requalify for free as-
cent.

After that we were supposed to go straight to Japan. In those days we home-ported in Yokosuka, Japan; later we home-ported in Subic Bay, Philippines.
Yokosuka was in Tokyo Bay and was the largest Navy

base in Japan. It had been captured by the United States after World War II and had been expanded. That's where we were headed on board an APD [high-speed transport] when we stopped at Okinawa.

About half of us from UDT-12 were given orders sending us to the Airborne Training Course run by the Army's 1st Special Forces Group on the island. The ship went on ahead of us with the rest of our team, and as soon as they got to Japan they deployed to Vietnam to recon some beaches.

It was just before Christmas 1961 before we all linked up in Japan. Of course, we were wearing our jump wings, and they were telling tales of what they had done in the warm waters off Vietnam. At that time we were preparing to recon some beaches in Korea after the first of the year. Doing hydrographic reconnaissance of beaches was a typical mission of UDT. It was good training, but it also kept our charts updated in case we ever had to conduct amphibious landings in the area.

One day I attended a Danny Kaye USO show on the base and was taking a shortcut through some old lighted Japanese tunnels, which ran through some huge rock cliffs, when I ran into some of my teammates going in the opposite direction. They told me that I had better go over to our office, which was in a Quonset hut, because I had a set of orders waiting for me.

I thought they were pulling my leg, but I went over to the office anyway, and there on the wall was a list of people being transferred to SEAL Team One right after the first of the year. I was pretty upset because I didn't know what a SEAL Team was, and nobody else did either. I was happy being a frogman and didn't want to go. Dave Del Giudice, who was the executive officer of UDT-12, told us that he didn't know what a SEAL Team was either, but that only so many men from UDT-12 and UDT-11 were going to make up this new unit and that he was going to be the commanding officer. That shut us up, and we all went back to the States together.

Dave Del Giudice was a great officer, and he commanded respect just by his presence. He was well respected in the Navy and the amphibious community. I had worked with him on some operations, and he was the kind of guy that when he said something, everybody stopped and listened. He was one of the best choices at that time to be the commander of the ten officers and fifty enlisted men of SEAL Team One.

They moved us to a great big gray building over on the amphib [amphibious] base. In those days we were not over with the UDT teams. We were so secret at that time that we wore the same patches that UDT did; we did not want to call attention to ourselves. There was a reason for this, but we didn't know what it was. We were told that everything we did was top secret, on a need-to-know basis. Somewhere along the line we were told that the word SEAL was an acronym for SEa, Air, and Land, which were our methods of insertion.

A week after we were in the States we were broken up into twelve-man platoons. We were trucked up to Camp Pendleton, California, where we underwent basic combat infantry training with a bunch of Seabees [Construction Battalion personnel]. We didn't learn very much and took it upon ourselves to harass the Seabees.

After that we were sent up to Camp Onofre, which was part of Camp Pendleton near San Clemente, where we went through a course that the Marines taught on guerrilla and antiguerrilla warfare. That was where we first started to learn about Vietnam. We ran attacks and learned to evade the Marines who tried to find us.

That was the beginning of our training, and for the rest of 1962 I went to school. In the next year I went to Assault Boat Coxswain school, Marine Corps hand-to-hand combat training, Navy SERE [Survival, Evasion, Resistance, Escape] training, and Army Ranger Training.

We went to Florida for part of the Ranger training and were assigned to training patrols. The Yellow River, which was as crooked as any river in Vietnam, could be crossed maybe two or three times on the same patrol. The Rangers had a special way to do river crossings. First, one of the soldiers would swim a rope across the river and check out the other side. Then he would secure the rope, and everyone would put on their Swiss seat, which was basically a rope tied around the waist to form a harness. They'd snap-link to the rope and go hand-over-hand with their packs and weapons to the other side. Every time we came to a stream or river, the patrol leader would say, "Send that frogman up here," and I'd have to swim across that river.

One real foggy morning I swam across the river, and as I came up to the edge, I saw that the bank was undermined. I looked under there and saw this big cottonmouth lying there. I went down a little farther, and there was another one; so I went down a little farther, and there was another snake. Finally, I swam back and told them that they were going to have to find another place to cross.

At graduation there were over one hundred khaki uniforms out there, and I was the only one in whites, sitting right in the middle of them. During our time at those schools, when someone asked us what we did, we said that we were Navy frogmen. Even the Army guys I was with weren't supposed to know I was a SEAL or what I was doing there. The first thing the Tac officer had me do in training was take the "US NAVY" off of my greens [fatigues] and have "US ARMY" sewn on them. We were all supposed to take the rank and other patches off our uniforms.

Five days after completing Ranger school, I found myself in jungle-warfare training down in Panama. Two things made it great for me. One was that the Panama Canal Zone had terrain that was very close to that in Vietnam. The second thing was that I had just finished Ranger training and knew how to write warning and patrol-leader orders—which none of the other SEALs that went down there with me knew how to do. So I was able to help them out when they were given several blank pieces of paper and told to write out a warning or patrol-leader order.

Toward the end of 1962 we attended Vietnamese language classes at night at the Naval Amphibious Base on Coronado. The language training was conducted by the Berlitz school of language. The class was always taught two or three times a week by the same Vietnamese woman, who never spoke a word of English during the entire course. The first night she came in shaking a pencil and spoke the Vietnamese word for it. Then she would point to one of us and motion for him to say the word. Then she would write the word on the blackboard. After that, she picked up a pen and proceeded to do the same thing. It didn't take us long to figure out that she was teaching us to read, write, and speak Vietnamese. I never was able to pick up a newspaper and read it or write the language, but I was able to speak some of it. Later, when we were overseas, we tried to continue our language training. We always tried to speak to the people in their own language. It was easier than using sign language like the French had done. Those classes and the Ranger training were probably more helpful than anything else we did at the time. In the years to come they gave me a solid base of skills to work from—which followed me all the way through 1971.

In 1963 I also attended the Army Special Forces Foreign Weapons Course and the Special Demolitions School at Fort Bragg, North Carolina. Special Demolitions was also known as "Kitchen Table Demolitions," and it taught us how to take different things that we could buy on the civilian market and make explosives. We learned how to make dust initiators to blow down buildings with a handful of thermite and a handful of TNT. We were also taught how to make an improvised timing device using water, bamboo, and rice. The things I learned at the Special Demolitions School I never used.

The Foreign Weapons Course was excellent. It helped me a lot on my first trip to Vietnam, when I walked into an armory and the only U.S. weapons there were some old Thompson submachine guns. The rest of the weapons were Russian AK-47s, Swedish Ks, British Sten guns, German Schmeissers, Russian PPsH-41s, and a number of others. I was able to disassemble and reassemble those weapons because I had been through the course.

Two guys really helped me in the armory. They were Chinese *nungs,* mercenary bodyguards hired by the U.S. government. They would squat down in the armory around anything that I threw at them and field strip, reassemble, and fire any weapon I gave them from a mortar down to a pistol. Their fathers and their fathers' fathers had been soldiers, and that's where they got their experience with weapons. I understand that we still had those mercenaries in the late 1960s, but I never saw any except for the two I worked with.

Our platoon, which consisted of twelve SEALs, left for Vietnam on 1 March 1963. We landed at Tan Son Nhut Airport and were taken to a holding area, where we were put in tents that had wooden floors. We were briefed and debriefed several times over at MACV in Saigon. All they talked about was security—mostly what not to say.

Then they took us down to Tu Do Street to a certain tailor where we were measured. In five days we had khaki uniforms without our names or any other patches on them. That became what we wore everywhere we went in Vietnam.

In those days we also had to come up with an alias. We only had to pick a first name, and mine was Jerry. That was hard for us because we were used to calling somebody Mac, for instance, and his alias might have been George, so it was tough not to call him Mac. So we had to practice a lot with our alias names.

There was a reason for the fake names. The first detachment from SEAL Team One went over in 1962 and consisted of only two people. They worked with the Agency [Central Intelligence Agency], and some of the people that they trained were captured. Under interrogation they told who their instructors were, and that was broadcast over North Vietnamese Radio. So they decided to get those two guys out of the country and from then on not to use real names.

Once all of this was accomplished, we were taken out to the airport and introduced to Air America, the CIA-run airline, and flown to Danang. In Danang we went through another series of briefings at a place called the "White Elephant," which was the largest building in the city. In the past it had been a headquarters for the French, and it was then the local headquarters for the Agency.

Later, we were taken across a river to a little compound called My Khe, which was nestled in against Monkey Mountain and wasn't very far from the Navy base. That's where our armory and all of our diving gear were. Everything that we could ever hope to need was located there. An old Vietnamese who had cooked for the French cooked for us. My Khe is where I first met the *nungs,* who were the security guards for our little compound.

Our purpose during that tour was to act as a training cadre for indigenous personnel. We were to teach them how to operate in a riverine environment. We taught them some hand-to-hand combat classes and gave them some physical-fitness training. There were also classes on how to shoot and throw grenades.

It was always interesting working with the Vietnamese. The first guys they sent to us had been thoroughly checked out. Something in their background, like a family member being assassinated by the VC [Viet Cong] or North Vietnamese, had made them want to work for, and to be true to, the South. What they failed to check was their physical condition. We received some very sick people—everything from tuberculosis to the plague. We had to put those people back on Air America and ship them back to Saigon. Because of that it took us a while to put together the first training class. Eventually, we must have gotten the message across because the people that showed up were healthier.

Sometimes we would work with small teams of indigenous personnel for a special type of operation. They may have already been trained to insert, using concealment and stealth, to build a cache. Or we worked with a team of indigenous personnel that were operating up North doing something tactical, like blowing up a bridge or destroying a railroad. I would be called on to teach these guys how to use certain types of weapons, such as rockets. I knew what some of the teams I worked with were going to do; others I did not. We would train these guys, then never see them again.

In those days, when you were ready to leave Vietnam, you had another briefing. The briefer told us that what we had seen in Vietnam, what we had heard in Vietnam, and what we had done in Vietnam were not to leave Vietnam. This was at a time when SEAL Team One was taking baby steps, and those restrictions made it hard to train anyone when we returned to the States. It meant that the next platoon would be going over without the benefit of the knowledge gained by the platoon just returning. Later, when the direct-action SEAL platoons began operating in Vietnam, we learned to interview every single operator who came back from overseas. The direct-action platoons weren't advisers; they were the SEAL platoons that conducted missions against the enemy. By interviewing them, we were able to pass their knowledge on to other platoons.

You never get involved in any operation without learning something, even if it is nothing more than how to talk to a man that speaks a different language than you do. You learn about their customs and how they feel about certain things, like their lack of fear of death, in some cases.

In 1963 the SEALs were taking small steps. The SEAL in 1963 woke up in the morning and had no idea what he was going to do that day. He would have to go out and improvise things, like putting a diesel engine in a sea-going junk. We never knew what we would be called on to do next.

The SEAL that went into combat in 1968 had a much better idea of what he was going to do and how to do it. This was because of the knowledge that SEAL Team One had accumulated since the early years. When I went back to Vietnam in 1968 with Alpha Platoon, SEALs were taking giant strides.

2

Bob Henry

Mobile Training Team
Danang, Republic of Vietnam,
Deployed February–August 1964

I was one of the first people to be assigned to SEAL Team One. I was considered a plank owner, which is an old Navy term from back when the first people to serve on one of the old wooden ships were given a plank from that vessel.

On my first trip over in 1964 I knew I was going to be an adviser with a Mobile Training Team. I had completed instructor school a few months before shipping out. I was an E-6 [enlisted rank: first-class petty officer] then and was leading my own platoon. That's really where I got most of my training. Of course, most of it was on-the-job training, which is where a lot can be learned.

There are all kinds of techniques that teachers use, and when I first got to Vietnam, the previous instructor told me the Vietnamese tried to play sick all the time and goof off a lot. He said if they did it to me, just kick them in the ass.

I thought, "What the hell is this guy talking about? That's no way to treat anybody, no matter who they are." I expected them to play sick a lot, so first thing I did was to pick out six guys. I explained to the whole group that the training we were going to do was very important, and if anyone was too sick to get up and walk, then I'd have these six guys carry them out to the training and they could lie in their beds and watch. All of a sudden they weren't sick anymore. They realized I was going to treat them as they should be treated, as equals, and I had no problem whatsoever after that.

That same way of thinking carried over to when I worked with a special group of Vietnamese troops that the U.S. Army Special Forces got together. It was at the end of my first trip, and the Green Berets sent about twenty guys to me. These men were basically the scourge of the earth, from Saigon. Special Forces had been working with them for three years, trying to make something of them. What really helped the situation for me was that my guys met with the new guys. They ended up asking me to stay over an extra month to work with them. As soon as I started working with them, I had no problem at all. They did everything I wanted and did it well. There was nothing wrong with their capabilities. They continued working with other SEALs after I left. I later heard that one day when the Vietnamese troop was flying out on a practice mission, their C-47 [twin-engine troop/cargo aircraft] crashed on Monkey Mountain, and they were all wiped out.

We trained the Vietnamese every day on various skills such as paddling or nighttime sneak attacks. I used to go out and pretend I was a sentry. The Vietnamese we trained were very good at night; they could get you good. The first time we went out, I was walking on a beach with a lot of sand dunes. I was watching for the guys but didn't see a single one. All of a sudden, five of them jumped out of the bushes and hit me. I judo-flipped a couple of them onto the ground. I didn't want to get too carried away with it and eventually let them take me down to the ground. Of course, it was a big joke after that; everybody started laughing.

We did a lot of target practice with the 57-mm recoilless rifle. We would shoot at targets up on Monkey Mountain. One of the problems we initially had was that the Vietnamese didn't understand about the back-blast from the 57s. One guy wanted to stand behind it to see the projectile going forward. Through the interpreter I finally explained to him that the worst place in the world to be was behind the 57. I took an ammo box and set it about ten feet behind the rifle. We fired the recoilless, and the back blast blew the box all to hell. They got the picture, to never stand behind the 57. It was the same way with the 106-mm recoilless rifle.

The Vietnamese team made two or three trips up North with the 57. Tiger Island was a little island just north of the parallel that they would fire on all the time.

I worked with a wide range of Vietnamese personnel. Many of them had some airborne training. I was given one of their green patches that has a tiger and a parachute on it. These men were similar to our Army Ranger groups. I also got an officer's patch and an enlisted patch and put them on a beret. One thing that bothers me now about the Vietnamese is that I didn't take the time to get to know them on a personal level. I did get somewhat close with two or three of them, but as far as their personal life, I really only knew that some of them were married and lived in Danang. They did tell me a story about one night when the airfield was getting mortared, and the VC were right out in their front yards, hitting their houses. The Vietnamese didn't have any weapons, so there wasn't anything they could do about it.

On one mission the guys took two boat teams up into North Vietnam to blow up a major pump house that supplied water to the whole area. That mission was the first and only time my guys were wounded. They went in without any problems, and one boat team formed a security perimeter on the beach to protect the boats. The other team went in with the two 57-mm recoilless rifles and blew the hell out of the pump house. They were on the way back out when some fishermen and farmers ran into the security team on the beach and started beating on them with their rakes and hoes. Some of the North Vietnamese Army arrived, and the team got into a firefight with them. They were able to extract, and the mission was considered a success even though we lost two guys. I later learned that this was one of the first successful missions that the people SEAL Team trained had up in North Vietnam.

They had many successful operations. On one mission during the first tour, the Vietnamese I trained went way up into North Vietnam and blew up two pillars of a cement bridge. It was a major railroad bridge, and destroying it made the op [operation] very successful.

My second tour ran from June through November of 1965. During that tour we used some rocket launchers that the CIA developed. The launcher had three pods—two HE [high-explosive] rockets and one willie peter [white phosphorus]. You could adjust the elevation on them, which made them easier to aim. A timer would be set to fire the rockets after our guys set up the launcher, aimed it, and left. There was an antidisturbance black box on it that had a little trembler switch inside. If anyone walked close enough to it, the vibration would set it off. When that happened, the rockets would blow first, then the launcher would blow up so that there wasn't anything left of it. Those rockets worked well and contributed to the success of our missions.

We did have a problem with the launchers at the beginning. The gunner's mate in charge worked on getting the launchers ready. The first one he had was wired wrong and went off. Unfortunately, it was facing our ammo [ammunition] bunker, where we had a few tons of explosives and ammo stored. The two HE rounds blew a hole in the bunker you could walk through. The willie peter was burning up all over the place.

I ran up there when I heard the blast. I was surprised it didn't blow up everything in the bunker. The gunner's mate was able to put out most of the fire by the time I got there. I started pulling stuff that was smoldering out of the bunker and separated some of the packages of plastic explosive from the burning canvas. We cleaned and salvaged everything we could.

The guy ended up going to the hospital for a couple days to recover. His back was full of shrapnel from the fiberglass and aluminum launcher, and he had a bunch of white phosphorus burns on him too. I guess he talked to whoever the powers-that-be were and got the wiring problem squared away. It was a rough one for him.

On one mission the Vietnamese packed two of the rocket launchers in a boat and went up North. They went to a military camp of some sort and fired the rockets in there.

I went back to Vietnam in 1966 on my third tour as part of a direct-action platoon operating out of Nha Be. Roger Moscone was the acting chief of the detachment and one platoon, and I was the petty officer in charge of the other.

When we first got there, we were living in tents. There were cement buildings in a *U*-shape right out in the middle of a swamp. There were pallets all over, and the tents were built on top of the pallets. The mosquitoes were horrible there.

After a month or so we moved out onto a barge. There were two platoons operating out of Nha Be. There was a screened-in area built on top of the barge for us. It seemed you could see the whole world from up there; it was impressive. There wasn't anything to keep the VC from coming by and using us for target practice any time they wanted. There was nothing to hide us; it was wide open. But the VC never attacked the barge during the time I was there.

My team was not lucky on night ambushes. The VC

stayed clear of where we were, for whatever reason. Another platoon had been pretty successful on their night ambushes. They had gotten a half dozen kills. But we'd go out on a daytime patrol and get all kinds of stuff.

One of our biggest finds was a Viet Cong R&R [rest and recreation] center where we captured the battle plan for the whole Rung Sat Special Zone. One of my good friends—who just recently passed away—Leon Rauch, was with me on this mission and had gone inside one of the hooches.

One trick we used was to spray mosquito repellent on the roof of an enemy structure and light it; the repellent really got them burning. I was outside, lighting the hooch, and said, "Leon, you better get out of there, I just lit the thing on fire."

He said, "Damn it, Henry, I can't, I'm disarming a booby trap."

I said, "Well, you better hurry it up then, buddy!"

The other guys were checking around to see what else they could find. I picked up a radio that the VC had been using. Roger Moscone made a comment that I still remember to this day—he said we were "six men lootin' and three guys shootin'." We were all over everything, getting war souvenirs and all the weapons we could. We ended up collecting a lot from that place, but the battle plan was the best; it impressed the whole world when we brought that back.

That mission was where Billy Machen got his first kill.

On 19 August 1966 we received some intel [intelligence data] that there were some large sampans up one of the tributaries. We were going to look for them, and Roger was the leading petty officer in charge of the op. We went in with Billy on point. Billy was probably one of the best pointmen we had in the Teams at that time.

Billy found the camp. There were some bunkers and a tower, but it was in a cleared area, and he drew fire, basically, to keep us from getting into it. They saw him that quick and fired on him.

I was in the rear end of the patrol. The guys fanned out like we were supposed to do in a situation like this, and I was taking the rear and the left rear perimeter, watching our guys to see where they all were.

I was standing up—which was kind of stupid. I felt bullets going by my ears, and one spanked me on the butt, and I thought, "Henry, you're not very smart!" But I got so engrossed in looking to see where our guys were that I just wasn't worried about it.

I turned around and saw Billy stumbling back toward me; he was all messed up. I pulled him back behind some brush and laid him down. The corpsman, Doc Cline, was on him right away. Billy had received a round down through his neck and into the stomach. Apparently, another round had ricocheted off the hand guard of his AR-15 [automatic rifle] and blown shrapnel all over his face. It wasn't more than half a minute, and he was gone.

We called in air support and started to move out. Roger told me to pick Billy up and carry him out. It was a strange feeling for me as I looked down and started to pick him up. I hesitated for a second. I didn't figure it out until recently when I was talking to Barry Enoch about it. Apparently, it's not an uncommon feeling, but I felt that I didn't want to hurt him. I didn't know how to pick him up without hurting him. Of course, he was already dead, but I hesitated, so Roger picked him up, put him over his shoulder, and carried him all the way out. I don't know how he did it because it was a long way. Air support kept the VC down long enough for us to get back to the boat.

We got back to the LCM [landing craft, mechanized], and we were still taking fire. That was the first time the barrels on the .50-calibers got white-hot, and you could actually see the projectiles going through the barrel. That same thing happened when I was wounded on a later op.

Billy was my good friend. It had been put into our heads for such a long time that you take care of your swim buddy.

For the life of me, I just couldn't see him go back home by himself after all we had been through. They weren't going to send anybody with him, and I got pretty upset about it and voiced it. I believe it was Lt. Maynard Wyers that I was talking to, and he said he understood how I felt, but that this was no way to talk to an officer. I said, "I certainly apologize, but I need you to know how I feel. Somebody has to take him back."

Lo and behold, it ended up being me. I flew all the way back with Billy. We stopped by San Diego, then went right to Gilmer, Texas. Barry Enoch and Paul McNally were at the funeral also. Billy had a nice family. His father was in bed the whole time I was there. I don't know if he had been sick before or if he was just under medication from the trauma of losing his son. He said he had known that something had happened, and he had gone over and stopped the mantel clock. He found out shortly after that Billy had been killed. Apparently, this was a custom in the South; if somebody knew something had happened, they would stop a clock at that time. For some odd reason that stuck with me when he told me. I talked to him for a long time and told him how great Billy was in Vietnam—how everybody loved and respected him.

After that, I went back to the Strand [SEAL Team One area in Coronado] and requested a few items we needed in Vietnam. They filled me up a seabag full of gear. I left the next morning and went back to my platoon at Nha Be.

Shortly after that I got zapped.

Leon Rauch and I always liked to get in on every mission. Either we were out on the op or on the boat—we had to do one of the two.

Leon was something else. He used to sit down in the wheelhouse, and you wouldn't see him for a while, and all of a sudden he'd pop up and have this really off-the-wall camouflage on his face. He'd crack everybody up. It got to be a competition after a while—who could come up with the weirdest camouflage face paint.

On this particular op he was running the boat, an LCM, and I was on the 60-mm mortar. This was to be my final op—I was scheduled to go home the very next day, and I just had to do one more op. That was the one that got me. It was 7 October 1966, the day after my birthday.

The mission's purpose was to take our relieving platoon out for their orientation training on a night ambush. The Vietnamese camp we were in obviously had a Viet Cong in it because the VC knew exactly where we were going. As I understand it, there were about three hundred of them waiting for us.

We pulled off into a little tributary and went in about fifty yards. All of a sudden, we got hit from both sides. I was up on deck by the 60-mm mortar that we had sitting in a sandbox. I fired off one mortar round, but we were so close in—it was maybe forty feet wide at the most—that the enemy were too close for the mortar to be effective. They were well inside the range of the mortar's arc. There was probably about ten feet of water on each side of the boat.

I loaded another round to fire when we got hit by a VC mortar round. It almost knocked me off the boat. I was on the sandbags, off on the side of the boat, and somehow pulled myself back up. That's when I knew my legs were gone—I knew they were paralyzed—I couldn't feel them at all. Somebody helped me up on the deck, and I just laid there on my stomach.

I later worried about the round I left in the chamber but was told they had found it when they got back and dumped it over the side.

Penn had been hit in the back with a lot of shrapnel but was still firing his machine gun. He passed out and fell on top of me. Someone got to him and laid him alongside me.

Dick Pearson, an E-4 [enlisted rank: third-class petty officer] at the time, came up to give me a shot of morphine.

Doc had sent him to help out since he had his hands full with the rest of the wounded. I felt him jabbing me in the arm, and he said, "This thing's not working, Bob. I'll be back in a minute." He had forgotten to pull the ring out of the syringe. That's one of the stories he tells today in his training classes—how in a combat situation, weird things can happen.

Others on the boat were hurt also, including Leon. The commander that ran the missions at Nha Be was injured; he wasn't a SEAL, but he was every bit as good as a SEAL. He took very good care of us and knew the Rung Sat well.

The tributary wasn't wide enough for us to turn around, and we really didn't want to go back into what we had just been through, so we just continued down the canal until we were out of the kill zone.

We saw a bunch of large junks farther down where the canal widened, and I asked somebody to grab my shotgun for me. It was a twelve-gauge cut down to a three-inch barrel, with a pistol grip on it, that I made on my first tour and carried in a custom holster during my three tours. I didn't know it at the time, but shrapnel had hit it and jammed the breech, so I wouldn't have been able to use it anyway.

Someone said, "Just be quiet when we go through these junks, and if they don't do anything, we won't do anything." We got through them OK and got back out onto the main river.

We weren't far from the Vietnamese Regional Force [RF] camp we had started the mission from. Some helicopters were called in, and they medevaced Bill Pechacek, Penn, and myself from the RF camp. We were medevaced to what I believe was called the Third Field Hospital in Saigon. I spent two or three weeks there until I was stable enough to be medevaced to San Diego.

I started my recovery from that point on. I was in San Diego for a month or so, then went to the VA hospital in

Long Beach, California, where I spent about nine months in rehab.

It's been a rough, long road ever since.

You know the old SEAL saying: ''The only easy day was yesterday.''

3

John Fietsch

Automatic–Weaponsman,
1st Squad, Juliett Platoon
Nha Be, Republic of Vietnam,
Deployed March–August 1967

My first trip to Vietnam was with Lt. Ted Grabowsky and Juliett Platoon. Ours was one of three platoons operating out of Nha Be. At that time we were living in a tent on top of a barge. Our operations were set up so one platoon would operate for a week. The second platoon would drive the boats and support the operating platoon during insertion and extraction. The third platoon would stay back at Nha Be and take care of our quarters.

We had a Mike boat, the original "Mighty Mo," with two .50-calibers on the bow, a 60-mm mortar amidships, two .30-caliber machine guns back by the coxswain's cabin, with a 57-mm recoilless rifle on top. Another .50-caliber was mounted on the stern. The well deck was decked over, and below that was where all the ammo was stored. There was so much ammo that the path down the middle was only as wide as my shoulders. The Mike boat and an old LCPL [landing craft, personnel, light] were our insertion boats. The LCPL had one .50-caliber up front and two M-60 machine guns aft. Both of those boats were slow. When the current was running at 6 knots, it was almost impossible to get anywhere because that was about the top speed of the Mike boat.

That old LCPL used to really be a kick when we inserted with it. When it backed off, you could hear the screech of the stern tubes when the screws turned—there was nothing clandestine about it. We would sit on shore and wish that thing would get out of there before it gave away our position.

When we got to Vietnam, there were no rules of engagement. We did have curfews, though, and anything that moved at night was fair game. No one was supposed to move after dark; so if someone was moving, we assumed it was the enemy. There were also free-fire zones, where we could fire on anything that moved anytime. In the areas where we were operating, there were only supposed to be enemy, no friendlies [friendly forces].

The Rung Sat Special Zone was an experience because nobody had really worked in that area very much. One reason was because of the fifteen-to-eighteen-foot tides and the large amounts of mud in the area. The maps of the area were not accurate. The map might show three or four streams in an area, and we would find three times that many. It was a very hard place to work in and navigate in because half the time you didn't know where you were. A lot of times we would ask spotter aircraft for a fix on our position if we were out in the daytime, and at night we didn't go that far.

The Rung Sat was something else—we just couldn't believe it. The tides in the Rung Sat were amazing and made working in that area very difficult. We'd have to walk through the mud, and then set up on a bank or wherever our ambush would be. We'd sit there, the tide would come in, and we'd have to move farther inland. The next thing we knew, our web gear was off and we were hanging it in the bushes above us. We would try to stay above water, but the next thing we knew we were standing up with water right up to our chins. On one op we started out sitting in a dry spot, and the next thing we knew, we were in the middle of a lake.

When we first got to the Rung Sat area, the foliage grew right to the water's edge. By my last trip over there, you had to go three or four hundred yards inland to find any vegetation because everything had been defoliated.

We didn't have much intel on the first ops we ran. Mostly, we just patrolled where we thought there might be targets of opportunity. We would set up on river junctions, where we thought there might be traffic. Our two squads would go out every night for a week, then take a break. We mostly looked for base camps. We'd go on patrol to see what we would run into. We found some base camps but never came across any large forces. It seemed we were always just right behind them. We ran across some river crossings where we got some pretty good hits. We also set up some good ambushes and ended up getting some documents.

One of the best ops we had on the first tour was up North. We went to Vung Tau and practiced the operation for a week. I had taken my Stoner [machine gun] and actually sighted it in so I could hit something with it. A destroyer took us up, and we inserted using boats. We had some intel that a cell of Viet Cong were coming through the area.

When we were on board the ship, our officer told me we needed to bring in prisoners, "So don't you kill 'em."

I said, "No problem, we'll bring 'em out." If we didn't hit them on this operation, we were going to have to hit a sapper school—which I didn't want to do because it was quite a ways inland, and there were only five or six of us on the op.

It was very hard getting in. We drank half our water getting in there. We had to climb these big sand mountains, and it was tough walking. We came down this one hill and went through a village. There were helmets and pieces of wreckage all over the place, and I wondered what we were walking into.

Eventually, we got in and set up. I was in the middle of the line, and there were two people on each flank. We stacked a bunch of stuff up in front of us. We sat there all damn day, and it was hot as a bugger.

An officer and our radioman, Bob Schaedler, sat up on a mountain overlooking the valley. They were our communications support for the destroyer. If we got these VC alive, Schaedler and the officer were going to call in Navy gunfire to make it appear as if these people were just unfortunate and got caught by the gunfire, but we would really have them as prisoners.

I was just sitting there when three VC came walking down the trail. The Vietnamese we had with us yelled for them to surrender, and they started running. I was shooting down my side of the trail, and the other guys were shooting down their side. The woman in the group slipped and fell, and when she did, she got hit by a round that killed her. Our officer up on the hill was thinking, "Fietsch is killing 'em, Fietsch is killing 'em." We don't know who actually hit the woman, but we captured the other two people. It turned out that the woman was the cell leader.

Two helos came in, and we loaded up and went back to the Army base at Vung Tan, then the destroyer put gunfire into the ambush site. The helo pilots asked where the rest of our guys were, and we told them that we were all that went in. They couldn't believe we were in there and there were so few of us. Every time the Army went into that area, they got beat up pretty bad.

The Rung Sat had the worst mosquitoes I have ever seen in my life. We'd put mosquito repellent on, and they'd eat it off in fifteen minutes. Because it was so damn hot and humid, the mosquitoes thrived there. We'd have to wear gloves and scarves around our faces, except for our eyes.

In the Rung Sat we wore Levi jeans with long johns to

help keep us warm while we were in the water. Out of the Rung Sat, we'd get into areas with leeches. Then we'd wear Levis with leotards, which the leeches couldn't bite through. We also wore thermal-underwear tops and our normal camouflage jacket. Sometimes we'd dye the jackets black. The clothes they gave us just didn't last in that kind of environment.

If we went into a village and there were men between the ages of eighteen and fifty-five, we knew they were either draft dodgers or the enemy. When we captured people, we put them in PIC, the Provincial Interrogation Center. That's how we got a lot of our intelligence. We would tell the prisoners they would not be turned over to the ARVNs [soldiers of the Army of the Republic of (South) Vietnam] if they would lead us in on an operation. These guys lived in the villages, so they knew the VCI [Viet Cong infrastructure] cadre members and could tell us where they were. That was the only way we were going to find them. If we didn't operate on good intel or were not flexible and able to operate on short notice, we would miss these operations and not get the VCI.

VC that moved at night had a code. If a guy was sitting in the bow of a sampan, or kneeling or wearing a hat, those actions might be a signal to the enemy on the bank that he was one of them. So if one of us was in a sampan and didn't know these recognition codes, they would open up on us. The VC were organized, and while they didn't have a lot of the facilities we had, they did well operating at night.

When we went out on an op, no one talked, and we didn't make any noise. If something was not conducive to what normally went on in the night, if it was foreign to the area, then the VC knew somebody was out there. In that case, either you were going to get hurt or you weren't going to see anything; the people moving supplies down the rivers by sampan would be gone if there was the slightest suspicious noise.

I think one of the reasons we were so lucky was because they were a little afraid of us. Later, I heard that there were times when the VC could have engaged us, times we didn't even know about, but they avoided us because they knew that even though we were a small group, we had a lot of firepower. I think we got lucky that way.

Things changed when I returned to Vietnam for my second tour. I was with another Juliett Platoon from May to November 1968 and stationed at Vinh Long. On our first operation, we jumped off the bow of the boat and didn't sink up to our chests in the mud. After the op the guys said, "My God, this is going to be okay here." Walking on solid ground meant we could carry an extra one-hundred rounds of ammo. In the Rung Sat we could only carry so much ammo because we were swimming across canals and wading through mud.

When we relieved the East Coast [SEAL Team Two] platoon at Vinh Long, they gave us an idea of what was going on in the area. Then, for the first three weeks to a month, we would go into the villages at night. If we found any males that were of draft age, we would pull them in and take them to the interrogation center. Within twenty-four hours a preliminary report would be ready on the person we captured. Seventy-two hours later another report would cover everything from school until the present day. We also took pictures of them. Some really good intel came from these guys. A lot of our operations were run from this information.

I enjoyed the tour in Vinh Long a lot more because we operated mostly on intel. When we operated on intelligence, we were a lot safer because we had an idea what we were going to run into, and we had something or someone specific to go after. It made a lot more sense all the way around. Sometimes we would use the person we captured to lead us up to the edge of the target and point out the hooch to hit. Sometimes they would go into the hooch with us and point out the person we wanted. Another thing that was good about taking a prisoner with us was that when we moved across the rice paddies and fields, they knew where the booby traps were. We made them walk out in front, so they knew if they tripped one, they would be the one to get it first. We used them well.

I think it was the NILO [naval intelligence liaison officer] that had us implant some sensors, which picked up sounds as the source passed the sensor. They were made to be dropped from aircraft. The electronics were in a three-foot-long tube, about eight inches in diameter, and had rubberlike branches coming off of them. The branches were actually an antenna and blended in fairly well with the foliage. There was a control console, and each one of the sensors had a number. Once the sensors were activated by us, the console operator could query each one of them from the console, which would tell him if the sensor was operational or not. Whether they were on trails or along rivers, we would try to stagger them so that if something went by and number one activated, then number two activated, then number three kicked off, it would give us a direction of travel. Once we knew which direction they were going, we could call in artillery, air strikes, or we could go ambush them ourselves.

The sensors were made so that if anybody messed with them, they would explode. Somebody decided that was inhumane, so they fixed them so that after a certain amount of time the circuits would burn themselves out. When that happened, they wanted us to go back in and get them. When we put them in an area, it was usually a place where there was traffic and people, and we didn't really want to go back in there to get them out. So when I put them in, I was booby trapping them with ADMs [antidisturbance mechanisms]. I told them the sensors were set up so that we couldn't get them back out. It wasn't worth going back and taking a

chance of my people getting hurt while disarming the
sensor.

One sensor we planted was up near Sa Dec. Once it was
in the ground, I rigged it with an ADM and some trip wires.
The trip wires didn't go to anything, but the ADM was
rigged to some C-4 explosive. The idea was to make someone think that if they got past the trip wires, they were home
free. That night that particular sensor was the only one not
working. The next day we took a boat and went past the
spot. The tree we had planted the sensor next to had been
blown down, so we knew it had been tampered with.

Our area of operations went from the Cambodian border
all the way down to the ocean. For a month we were aboard
an APD along with an East Coast squad that had been up at
My Tho. Fred Toothman was with the East Coast group. We
operated in the free-fire zones all along the east coast of
Vietnam. The two squads would alternate nights. At night a
Coast Guard cutter would come alongside the APD and take
us in toward the beach. Then we climbed into an LSSC
[light SEAL-support craft] to go in the rest of the way.

We went on one op that was kind of funny. We got in and
got stuck on a berm and were getting fired at. I called in for
support from a destroyer. They fired a round, and it hit
behind us, bounced over our heads, and went up on the
beach. I called them again and said, "Don't shoot any more
of that shit!" We finally suppressed fire and got in, but I
wasn't too happy with that Navy gunfire. It was kind of
comical.

When we finally got in, the other squad was a little ways
down from us. Some VC came down the beach toward me,
Ray Hollenbeck, and a radioman. I fired and knocked three
of them down. The radioman fired a 40-mike-mike [40-mm
high-explosive round] from his grenade launcher that hit
near one of the VC. One wasn't dead, so we brought him up
and had him sit beside us.

Our radioman had a 40-mike-mike high-explosive round

in the chamber and was going to change it for a canister round. He had a .38-caliber pistol in his hand while he was doing this. I had my back to him, and I heard this *ka-chunk* sound and thought, "Oh, shit! He fired the grenade launcher!" The round hit the Vietnamese in the chest. A 40-mm high-explosive round has to go over three meters before it will arm and explode. The VC was so close to him that it didn't arm. But as soon as I heard that *ka-chunk* sound, I was getting ready to duck! But all it did was knock the guy over onto the ground. It was pretty funny.

After my second tour with Juliett Platoon, Capt. Dave Schaible, the commanding officer of SEAL Team One, wanted me to put together a training course for the LDNNs. Eventually, they sent me, Joe Churchill, and Claude Willis to Cam Ranh Bay. They started recruiting LDNNs out of Saigon in early 1970. LDNNs were operating with platoons prior to this, but they were looking to build up the number of Vietnamese SEALs and start phasing them into our commitments. Basically, they wanted to start moving our people out and give the LDNNs some areas of responsibility—let them do some of the work.

Some LDNNs that had been working with us for years were used as the training cadre. We put together a four- or five-week training course, then took them out in the field. One of us would go along, and we'd introduce them to a SEAL platoon. We would be the go-between between our people and the LDNNs. The first group I took went to Ben Luc. We tried to take some LDNNs to Dung Island, but we had a hard time getting the SEAL Team people there to accept them. I guess the SEALs thought the LDNNs were trying to take their jobs away from them, or maybe the SEALs just didn't trust them.

Cam Ranh Bay was a Korean area of operation, and they had it pretty much under control. The Koreans did a really good job over there, but there were still a few places around there where the enemy was still active.

Churchill and Rich Kuhn, our officer from SEAL Team Two, went on an operation with the LDNNs and some Koreans. One of the Koreans stepped on a mine and blew his legs off. The blast knocked the pack right off Kuhn's back and threw him in the mud. Kuhn and Churchill went to the hospital to see him, and Kuhn said the guy was apologizing for setting off the booby trap. They almost couldn't handle it because this guy had lost both his legs, and he was apologizing to them for screwing up the op!

Some of the LDNNs were real good out in the bush. They had been fighting that war for fifteen years before we even got there. After fighting year in and year out, it was hard to expect those guys to be motivated and go out there every night. But if they thought something good was going on, they were very anxious to get out there.

Later on I was sent up to Ben Luc again with some LDNNs. I was supposed to have twenty to twenty-five people, but on a good day I maybe had ten or twelve. They would always have some excuse not to go out, like they had to go to Saigon or LDNN headquarters. As an adviser, I had no control over them. Some of them were good, and the others would always have to go see their family or something. It was disgusting! So on that last trip I decided that I didn't need it anymore, and that was the end of it for me.

4

Joe DeFloria

Officer in Charge, Alpha Platoon
Nha Be, Republic of Vietnam,
Deployed August 1967–February 1968

I arrived at Nha Be with Alpha Platoon in August of 1967. When we got there, Kilo Platoon, led by Ed Gill, and Foxtrot Platoon, led by Lt. Stan Meston, were already operating. The commander of Detachment Golf, Lt. Bill Salisbury, was also based there at that time. He was responsible for the operational, logistical, and administrative support of all the SEAL Team One direct-action platoons in Vietnam.

As platoons arrived in-country, as was the case when my platoon arrived, the policy was to send them down to Vung Tau where there was a training camp for LDNNs, the Vietnamese SEALs. Ted Kassa, who at that time was a chief petty officer with SEAL Team One, was running the camp. He set up some operations for us. The idea was to get us acclimated to the weather and the environment, although immediately prior to deploying to Vietnam we completed two weeks of jungle-warfare training in the Panama Canal Zone, so we were already somewhat acclimated to the heat and humidity of the jungle. After a week at Vung Tau, we went back up to Nha Be.

We ran one or two ops with one of the platoons that had already been there for a while—which I thought was a pretty good idea. It gave the new platoon a chance to get the feel of things. Of course, these initial operations were not run in the hottest areas of the Rung Sat, but there was still a good chance that we would make contact with Charlie [Victor Charlie, or Viet Cong]. During these early years, SEAL Team ops in the Rung Sat were still pretty basic. The first few ops were fairly easy; they were mostly for acclimatization. There were none of the sophisticated ops that eventually developed with SEAL Teams.

Our first operation on our own was just a couple miles from Nha Be. It was an overnight ambush, which generally was the nature of most of the ops. I don't think it had been too many months prior to that, that SEAL Team One got away from intelligence-gathering operations and changed to engagement operations.

Alpha Platoon's primary mission was to interdict Viet Cong and/or NVA [North Vietnamese Army] traffic in the Rung Sat Special Zone, southeast of Saigon. It was a giant swamp area that had been a pirate haven centuries before. It was very difficult operating in there. It was all mangrove trees, swamps, nipa palms, and the meanest red ants you ever saw. It was primarily SEAL Team One's operating area. Nobody else would go in there. The Army and the Marines wouldn't operate in there. Up until the time we got there, the enemy had pretty much free use of the area. Some South Vietnamese military units operated in the area, but their operations were pretty shabby. We would be going down a river and spot a South Vietnamese ambush five miles away. It appeared as though they didn't really want to make contact with the Viet Cong.

Our job was to interdict enemy traffic and to deny them unchallenged use of the area. The Rung Sat was a staging point for Viet Cong and NVA operations against Saigon and other areas surrounding the swamp. What we did initially was react to intel provided by Det [Detachment] Golf, which was compiled from other platoon operations in the area.

Complete and detailed information from all ops were recorded on "barn dance cards" and indexed to a large topographic map of the Rung Sat. One of the first things a platoon commander would do upon returning to Nha Be from an op was to complete a "barn dance card," file it, and mark the location on the topo [topographic] map. The cards contained the exact coordinates of the operation; tide and weather info [information]; method and time of insertion/extraction; description of contact made, if any; KIAs [killed in action]; WIAs [wounded in action]; direction enemy was heading; captured documents, materials, etc. In other words, any information related to the op was recorded and filed. The topographic map was marked with a pin at the coordinates where the op took place. This system was an excellent source of information to a platoon commander who was planning to operate in that area.

Sometimes we got intel from the NILO, a Marine intelligence officer, who also operated out of Nha Be, but he got most of his intel from Saigon. We seldom ran ops based on this intel because it was usually unreliable and untimely.

Eventually, we built up our own small intelligence net and procedures. After going on several operations, we could also respond to intel we collected in the form of documents or prisoners, if we were lucky enough to get any—which we always tried to do. Even though the primary modus operandi was ambush, if we could capture somebody, we did.

From September 1967 until the time we left in the spring of 1968, 90 percent of our operations were ambushes. We had nothing less than twenty-four-hour ambushes.

Generally, the way an op would go would be to insert either by boat or by helicopter, depending on where the op was. We also had to consider that we didn't want to establish a pattern by always using boats or always using helicopters. We would use boats or helicopters for extraction as well.

Sometimes we used both, going in by boat and coming out by helicopter.

Most of the time we made a predawn insertion, waited until daylight, patrolled to our ambush site, set our ambush, and planned extraction for the morning. Just about all the enemy traffic in the Rung Sat traveled at night. We never patrolled at night because of the difficulty of the terrain. Anyone trying to move through the mangroves, the muck, the "wait-a-minute" grass would have sounded like a herd of water buffalo. Therefore, we always moved in daylight. If the going was slow and it took all day to get to where we were going, that was just fine!

So what we would do, for example, would be to insert by helicopter about two klicks [kilometers] away from where we would want to set up the ambush. At that point, we had already gathered intel and determined that there was Viet Cong or NVA traffic in the area.

We tried to determine patterns: which rivers they moved on, what time they moved, and what they were doing. There were a lot of different-sized rivers in the Rung Sat, and there would be traffic traveling in different directions on them at all times.

Most of the water in the delta was brackish because of it being tidal; there was very little good drinking water. But one area in the Rung Sat had a series of freshwater wells. This particular area in the southern part of the Rung Sat was visited quite often by the Viet Cong to get fresh water. Without overdoing it, we tried to target the well area periodically. I can't remember a single op at the water wells that did not result in success for the platoon.

Once the intel established there was traffic in a certain area, we would line up a helicopter and make an overflight of the area. We ran most of our intelligence reconnaissance from the air. We would just make one pass at the normal helo-transit altitude, so it wouldn't be too obvious that we were up there trying to do a recon of the area. In one pass we tried to collect as much information as we could, including all the river crossings. It turned out a lot of the rivers we ended up crossing were not visible from the air. Those that had potential for good ambush sites were noted and recorded on the "barn dance cards."

We would also try to pick out a good ambush site from the air. Ideally, we wanted a good, dry site so we wouldn't be sitting in water up to our necks for twenty-four hours. There was a very large tidal range in Vietnam, and quite often we found ourselves up to our necks in water about 50 percent of the time we were on an op. The site also had to offer good "fields of fire" that allowed us to get close to the water, even at low tide, while still having plenty of cover.

We would insert far enough away to avoid any detection and also so no one could determine exactly where we were going to wind up. Sometimes it would take us the better part of the day to make two thousand meters or even a thousand meters. We took our time, tried to be quiet. Generally, we operated as a six-man squad, which was just half of a platoon of two officers and ten enlisted. When we got to an ambush site, we had to confirm that it was where we planned to be because there were very few landmarks to navigate by. The lensatic compass and pacing, or counting, our steps were our primary and often our only means of navigation.

We set up fields of fire that gave us the best visibility of the river, but at the same time would keep us from being seen. The way we did our ambush ops was standard operating procedure for most SEAL platoons. We put half the group up on the ambush line during the daytime, and the rest of the guys dropped back a few yards to take a nap or eat. We always had somebody looking out on the river, though, because we did, in fact, at times make contact during the day.

We tried to rest everybody as much as we could during the day of the ambush. Besides the two-thousand-meter hike through the bush—which was very tiring—it was always hot. During the rainy season it rained like hell, and then the sun came out and made it very humid—which took a lot out of you, physically. On the other hand, we often found ourselves shivering for most of the night while standing, sitting, or crouching in the water at the river's edge, waiting for the enemy.

We alternated resting during the day, then just before dark everybody would move up on the ambush line and get settled. We established our fields of fire and had set procedures for initiating the ambush, depending on whether the enemy came from the left or right. Generally, we would initiate the ambush with automatic weapons or claymore mines from the center of our position.

If we were fortunate enough to make contact, our goal was to capture someone if we could. If we couldn't, then we would take them under fire and try to preserve anything that might be in their boats, if it was a river-type ambush.

The usual way we detected the enemy at night was with starlight scopes [night-vision devices]. However, we often heard them coming down the river before we saw them. We'd hear their paddles knocking on the side of the boat. We knew we had done a good job of inserting if we heard them talking on the way down, completely unaware of us. Sometimes there was only one boat, sometimes two or more.

The largest hit I remember was when we ambushed four boats, with two or three guys in each boat. Some of the boats were stacked with rice or supplies. We ambushed a mining detachment once and recovered a bunch of mines and some weapons. On occasion we were fortunate enough to get documents that gave us information on enemy activities in the area and names of local Viet Cong.

We liked to go through the stuff we captured before we sent it up to Saigon. The requirement was to send it to Saigon so the intel weenies could look it over and get their info out of it. But we liked to go through it first and glean what we could in order to run subsequent operations.

Most of that intel usually didn't filter back down, and when it did, it was often too late to react to. Only occasionally did we get good intel from Saigon. Much of the intelligence supplied to us came from the local NILO, and his information was not that good. However, we would look it over and compare it to what we had gathered.

The detachment commander, Lt. "Irish" [Cathal L., later first SEAL admiral] Flynn, who had relieved the original det commander, Lt. Bill Salisbury, came up to me one day and told me that the NILO had some information on an active Viet Cong camp in the Rung Sat. He claimed he had seen large weapons, hooches, and lots of equipment. We went over and talked to him. I was a little skeptical because I had gotten some poor information from this guy before. Lt. Flynn thought we ought to go ahead and run an op on the base camp and said he was going to go with us. The plan was to insert a couple thousand meters west of the camp, patrol over to it, check it out, then keep on going and extract on the river five hundred meters to the east of the camp. It seemed like the simplest thing to do at the time.

It was my entire platoon plus Lt. "Irish" Flynn on the op, as I remember. Tommy Nelson, my assistant platoon commander, had the flu, so he stayed back at Nha Be.

We inserted by helicopter and patrolled over in the direction of the suspected Viet Cong camp. About midday we came upon this old abandoned village. We went through it, checked it out, and decided to take a break there. We set up our security and sat down to have a snack and smoke a couple of cigarettes.

I was sitting with my radioman, taking a good look at the sketch the NILO had drawn. All of a sudden, I started to see things in this abandoned fish camp that looked very similar to what the NILO had drawn as the active Viet Cong camp. I thought, "Jesus," when I realized what looked like a

20-mm cannon on his map was actually an old stove pipe laying in the camp. I told "Irish" I believed we were sitting in the place the NILO had sent us to find.

I wanted to get the NILO down there to make an overflight with a helicopter and verify that we were in the right place. We called back, and within forty-five minutes he flew over and radioed down that we were in the camp he thought was active.

After that, we decided to get the hell out of there. We started out toward the boats that had been waiting on the east side of the area. Up to that point it had been a high and dry op. As we moved out, it started to get a little muddy. We found ourselves having to walk on these monkey bridges, which were nothing more than six-inch-diameter logs suspended on stakes so you could walk above the mud instead of through it.

The op wasn't a total waste, though. On the way out we spotted a little factory where the VC made hand grenades. There was no one there at the time, and it didn't look like it had been used in recent weeks. But there was enough equipment lying around to determine that the VC had made hand grenades there. We also ran into a small rice cache that we destroyed along with the grenade factory. The area was booby trapped, so we knew it was still active.

As we went toward the river, it kept getting muddier. We ran out of monkey bridges and were up to our armpits in mud. It really turned into a goddamn nightmare. We still had to go a couple of hundred yards to the river, and I knew there was no way we were going to make it. I even weighed the idea of going back toward the camp for a helo extraction, but I never liked to backtrack because of the possibility of having been followed.

I decided that since we had done a lot of training with McGuire Rigs, we could use them to get us out of there. Part of our standard operating gear that each man carried was a length of rope and a snap link called a Swiss seat. Using the radio, I called back and requested a couple of helicopters rigged up for McGuire Rig extraction.

It was fortunate that Tommy Nelson had stayed back at Nha Be, because no one else there knew how to rig the McGuire Rigs to the helos. Tommy got himself out of his sickbed and rigged up a couple of slicks [troop-carrying helicopters]. In fact, he even accompanied the slicks down to where we were.

An hour and a half later the helicopters arrived. The jungle canopy was fifty to sixty feet above us and fairly thick. The hovering helos dropped their lines down with sandbags attached to the ends, to get them down through the canopy. By that time we were all hanging on to tree roots to keep from sinking in the mud and disappearing from the face of the earth.

To use the McGuire Rig, we had to sling a big loop around the shoulders and under the arms. Another loop hung down with a clip that the snap link attached to. It ended up with a three-point suspension: the snap link down by the crotch, and the two under each armpit. It was imperative that the helicopters went straight up in the air because the lines were fixed and hanging off either side of the helicopter.

The bird went straight up, lifting two people at a time up through the canopy. They climbed to about six or seven thousand feet so we would be out of sniper-fire range. It was a six- to eight-mile run down to the nearest friendly village, where they sat us down. It was a great ride on the way to the village, though. As far as I know, that was the only McGuire Rig extraction that the SEALs did in Vietnam.

On another op we made a hit on three boats. We set up a double ambush. I had my squad set up on one river, and Tommy's squad set up on another river, each of us one hundred yards from the junction of the two. That way, we could pick up traffic that was going in either direction. The idea was, if it looked like the Viet Cong were going to pass by us and move into Tommy's kill zone, then we would let them go by because on the river the Viet Cong ran pointmen, or pointboats. So they might have one or two boats out in front, then a larger force not far behind. We would let the first boats go by for the other squad to ambush, and we would still be in place in case more boats were coming.

Late that night we heard, then saw, three boats coming down the river. It was clear to me, from the side of the river they were on, that they would not be turning in front of the other squad. So we went ahead and initiated the ambush on them, using the M-60 machine gun and everything else we had to inflict as much damage as we could.

The idea of an ambush is to gain fire superiority as quickly and as relentlessly as you can without giving the enemy a chance. No matter how overwhelming the odds may be that you have over them, you just don't want to give them any chance at all. I think that was one of the reasons why the SEAL Team casualties in Vietnam were so low.

I had six guys spread out, six feet in between, and we had a tug line [a piece of rope] between us for signaling. By the time the tug line went off, we could all hear them coming anyway.

Philip L. "Moki" Martin was right next to me with his Stoner; Ronald Ostrander with his M-60 was on the other side. Walter Gouveiau was one up with his M-79 grenade launcher, and James M. Cignarella had his M-16. Our pointman, Richard "Indian Willy" Williams, used an M-16. He was an American Indian from Montana; he was great as pointman. I had my CAR-15, a carbine model of the M-16.

We initiated the ambush when the boats were right in front of us and completely overwhelmed them.

Every time we initiated an ambush, I would pop some illumination flares. I'd be sure to get it behind the enemy, so it would illuminate them but not us.

When the flares went off, we could see a couple bodies in the water. We didn't see them long because once a body went into the river it was gone. It would either be washed away or sink. The three boats were out in the river, floating around.

Prior to the ambush, I had arranged for a couple of PBRs [patrol boats, river] to stand off a few thousand meters to support us with their weapons in case we got into trouble or to help us recover any boats that we ambushed. I radioed to the PBRs that we had made the hit, and they replied they would arrive in three to five minutes.

The VC boats were slowly drifting away. Inevitably, during an ambush you hit the boats, and they started to take on water and began to sink. We could tell these boats were pretty heavily loaded, and we just knew there was all kinds of good intelligence and weapons on them. There was nothing we wanted more than to get those boats. Sometimes I would put people in the water to recover the boats, but in this area the river was wide and the current so swift that I didn't want to take the chance. Because of the very large tidal range, the water was always moving in one direction or the other. There was slack water for only a very brief period. On all ops we designated a couple guys ahead of time for boat recovery, just like we designated POW [prisoner of war] handlers beforehand to carry ropes, handcuffs, and blindfolds with them.

We started to lose sight of the boats, so I called the PBRs again. They advised that they were on the way. They should have been racing in at thirty knots and have been there already, but we couldn't even hear them yet.

An Army helicopter, called a Firefly, was flying by and heard our radio conversation. He had a big searchlight and said he could see the three enemy boats and would keep an eye on them until the PBRs got there. A couple of minutes later he said he lost sight of one of the boats in the bush. He could still see the other two, but one of them looked like it was about to sink.

I got back on the radio and asked where the PBRs were. Tommy Nelson came up on the radio and said he saw the PBRs coming by him, and they looked to be doing one or two knots, like they were out on a search-and-destroy op. By the time the PBRs finally got to where we were, the three boats were gone, either sunk or lost in one of the little tributaries off the river. We never did find any of them.

It was that sort of thing that made Vietnam frustrating at times. Fortunately, though, most of the time we were able to recover the boats. But we always wondered what we would have found on those three.

On every op we had Seawolf helos [Navy gunship helicopters] standing by for air support. After a hit we called in the Seawolves for cover because we never knew what was coming down the river or what enemy was in the area that might come over to see what was going on, so we always had the Seawolves out there. We'd mark our position, and the Seawolves would identify the color of our flare or whatever it was we had arranged with them.

Before every op we had a warning order. As soon as I knew we were going on an operation and got an idea of what it was about, I issued the warning order. I got all the guys together that were going and briefly outlined the op and determined what each was going to carry.

Everyone who carried an M-16 took two hundred rounds of 5.56-mm ammunition in ten twenty-round magazines. That's all we had in the early days. I didn't see a thirty-round banana clip [curved magazine] until close to the end of our tour, and then we managed to get only a few. The M-79 [grenade launcher] man carried twenty to twenty-five rounds of 40-mm ammo in bandoleers. Sometimes we would take shotguns along with fifty rounds, if we thought we were going to have a close encounter. We had duck-bill shot diverters for the shotguns that spread the shot pattern out horizontally to cover a wider area. The duck-bills were experimental at the time, but we managed to get them from the Naval Weapons Center at China Lake.

We got a lot of equipment from China Lake to use on an experimental basis. One of the things that comes to mind besides the duck-bill was a sheet of plastic explosive that contained BBs. It could wrap around a tree and have 360-degree coverage; or you could just put it on one side, and it would be directional, just like a claymore mine.

The equipment we used varied from mission to mission. We had the M-60 machine gun, which was always my favorite because it was so reliable and had such great knockdown power. The M-60 would always fire; very seldom did we have a problem with it. The M-60 guy carried a couple hundred rounds. I liked the M-60 better than the Stoner because the Stoner had some problems at the time. It had to be kept meticulously clean, or it would jam. But there wasn't a better Stoner man than "Moki" Martin. He cleaned that Stoner like his own teeth. His was always in nice shape and performed well. We had M-16s, M-79 grenade launchers, Stoners, M-60s, and sometimes the Ithaca Model 37 shotgun.

I carried the CAR-15, the shortened version of the M-16, with the ten-inch barrel, triangular hand guards, and a telescoping stock. It was an outstanding little weapon. It didn't have quite the range that a full-barreled M-16 had, but it was close enough for the type of ops we did. As platoon commander, I liked using it because I could sling it over my shoulder while looking at maps or while I was on the radio. I also carried flares and liked to have maybe five or six white illuminating flares and a few foot-long, cylinder pop-up flares. All I had to do with those was take the cap off, put it on the bottom, hit it, and they would pop up and ignite. I also carried red and green flares. The colors had different purposes, and during our mission briefing we defined what each of the colors meant. One color might indicate loss of radio communications; another could be to show our location or request emergency extraction. Those were all part of the standard load.

Alpha Platoon left Vietnam in the spring of 1968 with an excellent success record, with no one seriously wounded in action.

I transferred from SEAL Team One to the Experimental Diving Unit in June of 1968 for a two-year tour. They were developing a closed-circuit, mixed-gas SCUBA rig designed for long-duration, shallow/deep diving profiles. Having been a former deep-sea diver, I had a lot of experience in closed-circuit mixed-gas diving, so I was selected for the job.

Even though the work was interesting and challenging, I couldn't wait to get back to SEAL Team One.

5

Philip L. "Moki" Martin

Automatic–Weaponsman,
1st Squad, Alpha Platoon
Nha Be, Republic of Vietnam,
Deployed August 1967–February 1968

I did six tours in Vietnam, including two short tours with Underwater Demolition Team 12.

My platoon came to SEAL Team One, en masse, from UDT-12, with the same officers. We had already deployed to Vietnam several times with UDT-12. We went through SEAL cadre training and predeployment training together, then deployed together. It was important that we train together and that everybody in our platoon had already been to Vietnam. Later on, in 1968 or 1969, we got people who went right from boot camp into BUD/S and directly to SEAL Team. As the platoons began losing people in Vietnam, either through normal attrition, such as people getting out, getting burned out, or being killed, we started getting more inexperienced guys in the platoons. The policy was to always have three to six experienced SEALs in a platoon. Team One kept that policy going for survival.

Gen. William C. Westmoreland [Commander, MACV] determined a need for more than a thousand SEALs, so they cranked up BUD/S and got a lot more

classes going through. All of a sudden there were a lot of
SEALs and not enough deployments. It wasn't unusual to
have guys come out of my platoon, change their war bag,
and immediately try to get in the next platoon going back
over. Some guys just wanted to go back as quickly as they
could.

I was in 1st Squad of Alpha Platoon as the automatic-
weaponsman. Joe DeFloria was our platoon leader and
squad leader. After I carried the M-60 a few times, I started
to appreciate the Stoner because of its lighter weight. Ninety
percent of the time I carried the Stoner 63 light machine gun
in its original configuration. The Stoner was originally designed with a left-hand feed and a 150-round drum. For
extra ammo, I carried five or six 100-round or 150-round
plastic boxes.

Using the 150-round drum, I only had to reload the
Stoner a half dozen times in seventy-five operations. The
drum would flip forward and up against the forestock with
the feed cover up, then a plastic ammo box could be attached to the feed tray. A lot of SEALs would break off and
use one of the belts they wore across their chests. You've
probably seen a hundred pictures of guys carrying their belts
crisscrossed over their chests. A couple of times I tried
carrying it across my chest, but I didn't like it like that and
never wore it that way. One problem was that the Stoner
links wouldn't disintegrate if there was any mud on them.
Another reason was that at night you could see that brassy X
reflecting across the chest and back.

Carrying ammo crossed that way may have been the
cause of one of the deaths in SEAL Team. We were water
oriented, and if we went in over our heads, we had to be able
to dump our gear and come up to the surface to survive. One
guy didn't. The belts of ammo he was carrying across his
chest may have prevented him from being able to surface.

I carried my ammo inside the boxes, which I put inside
the standard universal green pouches that were designed to

carry four M-16 magazines. I preferred 100-round boxes; I felt the 150-round boxes were only good for training because they stuck out a little bit more and were heavier on the weapon. Because it stuck out more where it clamped onto the feed tray, if you bumped it against something, the plastic box fell off.

The Stoner was a very close tolerance weapon. Because of an adjustable gas port, you could fire it at 700, 850, or 1,000 rounds per minute. The men that carried the Stoner had to take very good care of them. In the field they made sure mud and water didn't get in them, and they kept the belts clear of debris. For all its superiority in firing, the Stoner was a poor weapon for going through mud and water.

The operations we ran out of Nha Be in 1967–68 during my first tour were mostly ambushes. Other operations included body snatches and search-and-clear missions. We also changed the name of one of our key missions from "body snatch" to "the abduction of key enemy personnel." It was a time when the war and the SEAL role in it were becoming a bit more definitive.

We were at the Nha Be Naval Base on the tip of land between two rivers, the Long Tau and the Soi Rap, that led to Saigon from the South China Sea. The base was right at the top of the Rung Sat Special Zone, which meant "Forest of the Assassins." This area was made up of a lot of small rivers, which were patrolled by PBRs. The SEALs and the PRU teams did a lot of work in that area. The Australian SAS [Special Air Service] did their missions on the southeastern end, and the U.S. Army was running long-range patrols in the western areas. We had the middle of the Rung Sat that the Long Tau River ran through.

Our mission was interdicting the Viet Cong; the most effective tactic was the ambush. It got to where the VC would not move because they feared running across any of the three SEAL platoons in that area. The three platoons were from SEAL Team One based in Coronado, California.

In addition to Alpha Platoon, there was Foxtrot, with OIC [officer in charge] Lt. Stan Meston, and Bravo, led by Lt.(jg) Bruce Van Heertum. Each platoon was composed of two fire teams, so we could go on six different operations if we wanted to.

When SEAL Team One first deployed direct-action platoons to Vietnam in 1966, they lived on a barge that they moved around to different locations in the Rung Sat Special Zone. The barge anchored at Nha Be in early 1967 while the base was being built. The SEALs moved off of the floating base and into the barracks when the base was completed.

We ran most of our operations out of Nha Be. A few special operations were run north, south, and west of there. Those ops were primarily done using helicopters for insertion and extraction, although some extractions were by boat. We also had an MST [Mobile Support Team] detachment from BSU [Boat Support Unit] 1, comprised of eighteen to twenty sailors that ran the ''Mighty Mo,'' a landing craft converted for SEAL operations, and ''Black Power,'' an LCPL. The MST crews provided fire support for most of the operations, as well as the primary and secondary means of insertion and extraction for the SEALs based at Nha Be. They didn't have enough people to support everybody all the time, so they supported the three platoons as best they could. We also used PBRs to insert or extract, and helicopters as well.

Most of our operations were night ambushes. On occasion we ran ops that lasted as long as three days, but typically they were just overnight. We didn't run many of the three-day operations because it was an awful waste of time.

On some of the three-day missions we'd set up at the junction of two canals and later move to set up in another area that night. By the third night, we moved again so that we would be in a different location. We rarely moved at night, and we always moved in the water. When you take into account the six-to-eight-foot tidal change and the six-knot current, moving in the water was not an easy or pleasant task.

Our first few operations were with the full platoon of twelve men. We found out that a full platoon was harder to control, so we split up into two fire teams of six men each. Later in the war the fire teams were called squads. We were able to conduct more operations this way. Sometimes we met up in the field, which was very rare because it took so much coordination.

Each platoon had its own Vietnamese LDNN. Eventually, we got another LDNN, so we had one for each fire team.

The more we operated in the Rung Sat Special Zone, the more intel we developed—which enabled us to begin to target the VCI. We began hitting tax collectors, proselytizing cadre, and members of COSVN [Central Office of South Vietnam: headquarters for the Viet Cong]. The more we talked with the SEALs running the PRUs, the more we understood the infrastructure side of the Viet Cong and realized that was who we should be targeting. We always tried to target the highest level of the VCI and capture them if possible.

This was a complete change from when we first arrived. In the beginning it was important for us to have a good "body count" because we were caught up in the Westmoreland idea of a high body count being most important. As a group, we found that we could be more effective by capturing these people. So we went out and captured the woodcutters, farmers, and fishermen who once a week took out their old, rusty, bolt-action rifles and fired a round or two at a PBR and then went about their business. It wasn't really important to try to ambush those people. It was more important to capture them in the field and find out who gave them their orders. Or we would find out where the proselytizing cadre was that had won them over to the Viet Cong side. We also questioned them about any American prisoners they might have seen being moved through the area. It was more important to get that kind of information in the field and be able to react to it, than run up a high body count.

Eventually, the word came down that our body count was not high enough, and we responded by showing them the number of people we had captured. It wasn't always important for us to kill.

When our UNODIR [unless otherwise directed] went out, it stated we would conduct SEAL operations at these grid coordinates, at these times, unless we were directed to do otherwise by a higher authority. After it was sent through our chain of command for clearance, the UNODIR went through the Vietnamese complex for clearance. We only gave them as much information as we had to in order to clear an area for ops. We knew the Vietnamese side was not all that pure. I have to give credit to people like Joe DeFloria and his assistant, Tom Nelson, because they were very vague when giving our area-of-operations information to other people. At the same time, they were very specific in telling us what we were to do during the operation. We had to coordinate with our boss, who went through his Vietnamese counterpart, so that it went through the Vietnamese complex of people to clear a grid square in the area of operations. Because of this process, the chance of being compromised was tremendous. As Bruce Van Heertum will tell you, there are only so many times you can reschedule an operation and keep the same insertion/extraction plan. He got hit real bad because of that and lost two people and had several others wounded.

We gave them an eight-grid-square area of operations. Anybody could look at it and say, "OK, the SEALs are in this area, but we don't know exactly where." They knew we would be in there from 0800 in the morning until 2400 the following night; we gave them that kind of general time frame to protect our insertion and extraction point and time. It was very critical to keep this information secure.

We didn't always do combat operations; sometimes we went in on recon missions. We'd go in, look around, check things out, and confirm or deny intelligence we had gotten from the SEAL PRU adviser and others. We did quite a bit of that. We'd go in to take pictures, and we also did BDA [bomb-damage assessment]. So we got to do a variety of things, but always there was the ambush, and the ambush always had very basic goals: to deny the Viet Cong the use of the trails or rivers, and to make it safer to travel on the two rivers up to Saigon. The ambush was psychologically effective. That's why the VC had good proselytizing chiefs; they always had to recruit new guys to go down those trails or rivers because experienced VC, those that were lucky to be alive, knew not to go down there.

I led a couple of ops against the Viet Cong infrastructure. We were able to generate our own intel for the areas we wanted to operate in by going to different intelligence-collection points, such as the NILO or G-2–level intelligence. While we were at Nha Be, our most important source for intel was the SEAL PRU adviser, who I believe was Howard Paulson. He was able to tell us that if we went into a particular area, we might find anything from a tax collector to the remnants of an enemy battalion. With this information we would generate our own operations and run them from start to finish.

On one mission I planned, we inserted and set up on the junction of a river and a canal that we knew a tax-collecting team had to travel on to get to their destination. They didn't show up that day, but several Viet Cong walked through our ambush site, and we opened up on them, killing two.

Because of the careful planning of our officers, we were able to run some outstanding operations. We collected a lot of intelligence. We never took any unnecessary chances and really only exchanged fire with the VC on a few occasions. I don't mean we didn't get any hits, because we got quite a few when the VC never had a chance to return fire. The platoon's enemy body count was up around fifty by the end of our tour.

We got very good at initiating ambushes. Everybody opened fire together, and we stopped firing at the same time. We fired only as much as needed. It was that clean. We knew what we were doing; we did it efficiently and then got out. We didn't attract attention, we followed our SOPs—our standard operating procedures—and we established a few more of our own.

We didn't forget what we originally learned in predeployment training. It is important for today's SEALs and future SEALs to understand this. We took what we were taught and added to it from the lessons we learned in combat. If they don't use what we did in Vietnam, fine, but they still have to understand why we did it. It's these lessons that we pass on to the next generation of SEALs. It's most important for SEALs today to understand that the SOPs were developed as a result of a SEAL fire team, as a result of a SEAL platoon, in a variety of combat situations against a specific enemy in a specific environment.

I think the whole philosophy of history is important. You have to learn from the past. The SEAL today has a bigger bag of tricks to start off with—many more than when I went to Vietnam. SEALs back then weren't as high-tech. A lot of emphasis was put on physical training. When I got to SEAL Team One I could draw only on the very limited experience of SEALs in Vietnam. I knew very little about jungle warfare. By the time I became an officer, the technology had changed, and warfare had changed. I tried to make the young guys aware that they could still use the same bag of tricks we had learned in Vietnam and that we could not afford to forget the lessons of the past.

They really need to understand that they don't need to do everything the way that we did it—that's not important. It is important for them to remember what we did so that they can carry on and further the operational skills and traditions of the Teams.

6

John Ware

Pointman, 2d Squad, Alpha Platoon
Sa Dec, YRBM-18, USS Weiss,
Republic of Vietnam,
Deployed August 1968–February 1969

I was with Alpha Platoon when it went over to Vietnam in August 1968 and came back in February 1969. I was in Scott Lyon's 2d Squad. Lt. Rip Bliss had the other squad.

My job was pointman—which to me was the absolute safest place to be. During my tour I had an opportunity to be a radioman one time, and rear security once, but rear security scared me to death. I felt the safest at point because I knew that all my guys were behind me. I was supported by six other SEALs. If you knew the six people I'm talking about, then you'd know why I felt safe.

Traditionally, the pointman is the eyes and ears of the squad. I walked point when in Scott's squad, and he directed me. I was first, then the LDNN—if there was one with us—then Scott along with Steve Frisk, the radioman. Don Crawford was the M-60 guy, and Harlin Funkhouser had a Stoner. Frisk carried a CAR-15 with an XM-148 under it. Doc Hubbard was also in the squad.

We changed off a lot. The first five days I was in-country I went out every night—I volunteered to go out with the other squad as well. Everybody was doing it; we were all going back and forth.

First we had a break-in op. Jess Tollison was left to break us in, and I remember the first time he took us out. You know when it's time to do it for real. We had trained for twelve months before we went overseas. I thought I was prepared for the experience, but I did have some anxiety.

For this first op, we were on the YRBM-18 [repair, berthing, and messing barge]. The very first thing I did when we came out of the lighted compartment into the darkness of the night was bump into the railing. I thought, "Great, I'm two feet out into the dark and I've already stumbled into something." Then you took a boat ride down to the first insertion that you ever made.

That first op went pretty smoothly getting in; we walked into an area that was relatively safe, just to become familiar with the terrain and how to set up on beaches. I remember Jess Tollison and I went directly into an area where there was a hooch. I walked within five or six feet of the hooch, and I stopped the squad and turned around.

Jess was looking at me like *What is wrong with you?*

I said, "There's a hooch!"

He kind of slapped me in the back of the head and said, "We could see that from the river, stupid."

After you were there for a while you understood the terrain better. At first you didn't really see the obvious things. You really did get to see things differently after a while.

We didn't get into a firefight on the first op out, but it was a great learning experience. Jess was an old salt—I don't know how many tours he did—but he was a great operator. He had a lot of fun with me, and I think that actually helped take away some of my anxiety. It was serious business with some undertones of humor—similar to my personality.

By the time we left Vietnam, we were a well-oiled machine. We knew what to expect from the Vietnamese people, and we knew what the enemy was going to do.

Scott Lyon taught us with repetition. It seemed goofy when they had us practice the *V*-formation, oblique movements, and other patrolling techniques in Niland, California. We practiced so that every time you stepped with your left foot, you fired. You picked out a target and fired as you walked. Scott told us that if we all did it together as a team, even if it's wrong, we had a chance of getting out. From UDT training, to SEAL cadre, to my experience overseas, we learned that the essence of SEAL Team was the team. You were not an individual. Team members were as dependent upon you as you were upon them to get through.

We walked into an ambush once and got out. We were on Phu Quoc Island operating as a full platoon—nine of us—during the day—which we didn't normally do. Steve Frisk had the radio. Bliss and Lyon were there. We had taken two LSSCs down a river, and we were looking for inland trails. When we saw a trail, we inserted and checked it out. We were trying to find someone to take as a prisoner.

We made contact with some people, and there was a brief firefight. One VC was killed. Bud Gardner and I checked his body out to see if he had any documents on him. A big piece of his head was missing.

After Scott Lyon got on the scene, we looked around and saw some people moving. Scott asked where Bliss was, where the radio was. We didn't know if it was some of our guys we saw moving or somebody else. Scott grabbed me and said, "Get us out of here." We left the body and started walking back toward the river.

We had left the LSSC we came in on on the bank. A couple guys were in the other LSSC on the other bank and had set up an ambush in case anybody came at us from the rear. We headed for the LSSC straight across an open clearing through waist-high elephant grass, straight for the tree line where the river was.

I got within fifty yards when all of a sudden I heard this *CRACK!* The elephant grass just started laying down. I heard the crack by my feet, then heard it go off over in the trees. They told us that the instant this happens you were to get down and take up your field of fire.

Well, I was up front, walking in a straight line, so I was blocking everybody's field of fire. I turned around and looked—I was the only guy standing. Everybody had already gotten down in alternating positions and taken up their fields of fire. I realized I didn't need to be standing up, so I hit the ground. I was standing there like an idiot for what seemed like a long time but was actually just a few seconds.

When I got to the ground, it seemed like the whole world was erupting around me. There was so much fire coming in. I had my Stoner out in front of me, trying to hide behind it. At that time I was so skinny that I could almost do it! I was able to turn the weapon and put out two or three bursts.

The guys in the platoon started coming up on line as I backed up toward them. We fell back to where the river wound around behind us and were able to get to a berm. We climbed over the berm and behind some trees and vines. There was a little lull in the firing as we moved back. Just as I started going over the berm and through the vines, I got caught in one. Then all the firing opened up again.

This time there was some major fire coming our way. I thought, "If I get killed here because of some stupid vine that I can't get through . . ."—but I was able to fight through the vine and get back behind the trees and below the berm line.

Our dilemma was that we were cut off from our boat, and Mr. Bliss and Steve Frisk, who had the radio, were missing. We couldn't even communicate with the boat. All this firing was going on, we didn't know if the guys in the boat had been hit, and they didn't know our situation. I remember

looking at Paul Bourne, and he asked if I had any red flares
we could put up to let the LSSC know to come and get us.
But we were operating during the day and weren't carrying
any flares.

I was about ten feet away from where Scott Lyon was
back behind a tree. Zin, our LDNN, was separated by about
the same distance. The firing started again, and I remember
Zin's face in the Y of this tree, and he kept saying, "Mr.
Lyon, Mr. Lyon, I can't get over there." There was a little
lull, and Zin moved his head just as a big burst of fire came
at him. He looked back where his head had just been, and all
the bark was gone off the tree. The next thing I knew, he
flew right over next to Mr. Lyon.

I was so scared, I didn't know what we were going to do.
I think everybody else was as scared as I was when we first
started taking fire. I got next to Scott, and he said something
like, "Well, it looks like they know where we're at"—
which I thought was the understatement of all times. But he
was so calm and collected that everybody calmed down after
he said a couple of things.

First he said, "Let's figure out how we're going to get
out of here." Another understatement. We looked around
and saw that we had to move about fifty yards to get to a tree
line. We would actually be going right toward the ambush. I
think what happened was the enemy initiated the ambush
early because we were walking right into them. Maybe it
was just a few guys in a tree line, and as we started moving
toward them, one of them got scared and cranked off a
round too early, and it started.

Then Scott said, "OK, we're going to duck-walk out of
here." At first I thought he was kidding, but the way he said
it I knew he was serious. We waited for the next lull, and we
duck-walked straight at those guys through grass about
waist deep. We just skirted the area we had just come out of
and duck-walked right to the tree line and then on to the
boat.

Bliss and Frisk had made contact with the boat and said they were okay, but they didn't know what our situation was. They told Bliss and Frisk to just hang in there. Scott was able to contact Bliss and told him to move to the river so we could pick them up on the way out, back toward the Gulf of Siam. He asked Bliss, "Are you closer to the Gulf of Siam, or are you deeper in." I was praying that he would say they were out by the sea, and he did. He said come toward the Gulf of Siam.

There were still a lot of guys shooting a lot of rounds at us. There were a couple of places on the way out where the bank was higher than the river, and it would be easy to shoot down into the LSSCs.

As we started out in the boats, Bliss and Frisk came on the radio and said we were getting weaker. So we had to turn around and go back in, past where we had been in the firefight, going in deeper. Bliss and Frisk worked their way to the river, and we picked them up and hauled ass back out toward the Gulf of Siam.

Once we got out there, Scott decided that everybody was a little shaken from the whole experience, but that we had to get back into it. So immediately we went into another area and started doing the same thing.

We had just gotten off the LSSC and walked in—maybe thirty or forty feet—and heard some guys coming. We set up a quick ambush, and two guys walked out of an area right in front of me, walked right up next to me. I had my Stoner pointed away from them, but I was in a position where I couldn't move.

When they were right up on top of me, I swung my Stoner around and fired about three or four rounds. These guys just hauled ass, and everybody opened up.

But they opened up in a different direction than I was, and I didn't know what was going on. I was confused but still fired at these two guys running. Pretty soon I got some help, and everyone fired at my two guys. I don't know whether we hit them or not, but they ran completely across an open field into a tree line.

Guys were coming out, and Zin started hollering at me because I had initiated the ambush too quickly. But he had seen different guys, some that had come from the left flank. The two that almost stepped on me came from the right flank.

We got up, and while we were discussing it, the guys that ran across the field started popping rounds at us. We decided we better get in our boats and go.

We kept a log of our ops, and when we approached one hundred ops, it became a goal to get over one hundred. I wrote about that in a letter to my girlfriend, Jimmie, who is now my wife. The letters I wrote were a kind of release.

Mike Beanan, who was the pointman for the other squad, was an artistic type, and I've always been that way too. He was dating a girl at the time and writing her letters. We drew cartoons of the ambushes or whatever was in our letters. We tried to outdo each other. He would put a cartoon on his letter, and I would put one on mine, and we would compare the two. Whatever experience we had been through that day or week we would try to do as a cartoon to send back. Sometimes I'd draw a cartoon for his girlfriend, and he would draw one for Jimmie.

A sense of humor is something that you need in a situation like that. You've got to have some kind of release. We'd joke about things relating to the ops. Fortunately, no one in my platoon was killed. Guys were wounded, but we didn't lose anybody. Other platoons did lose people, and we'd say they went to hillbilly heaven or couldn't hack the program, stuff like that. Although it was sad, we'd find some humor in that; but it was just a way of handling it. It didn't take away from the great respect we had for the guy and the real remorse and sadness we felt over losing somebody.

. . .

I was a radioman on one op later on in our deployment. The
enlisted guys were taking patrols out, and this was Doc
Hubbard's patrol. You could be anything you wanted to be.
Whoever was running the op would come to you and say,
"This is my op; where do you want to be?" I said I'd never
been a radioman, so they let me be one on this op.

We had good intel that there was movement in the area
called Football Island, where three rivers came together. We
came in just after dark and inserted on one side of the island.
After the LCPL crew dropped us off, they went down the
river, pulled into the bank, and set up a boat ambush. If
anything happened to us, they could get there in a hurry. I
had the handset in my right hand; and every fifteen minutes I
clicked it, and they clicked back, so we knew everybody was
OK. The radio procedure and all that was new to me, so I
was having fun with everything that was going on.

There was a full moon out that night; it was incredible
how light it was. We waded through a trench-type canal to
the side where the moon was behind us and sat down in the
shadows that went out three or four feet from the bank. I was
sitting on the bank with an M-16 across my legs, which were
dangling in the water. To my left was Don Crawford with his
M-60 behind a lot of foliage, the barrel of the M-60 in the
middle of it. To Don's left, Richard White was looking
around on a flank with a starlight scope. To my right was
Doc Hubbard with his Stoner, and Garry Abrahamson was
rear security. Others in the squad were off to the right.

We got settled in and had been there for a little while
when I heard White say something on the left flank. Word
got passed down that a sampan had come across from the
opposite bank about one hundred yards down. It had crossed
over and was in the shadows on our side, hugging the bank,
headed our way.

First I heard that it was one sampan, then two, then it was

three sampans that were coming. The word was passed from White to Crawford to me, then I passed it on.

I wanted to know where these things were. Hubbard asked me, ''Where's he at, where's he at?'' I turned around, and there was one guy in the lead boat. He had a camouflage poncho on his knees with a weapon slung and was paddling the boat. There were two guys in the next one and three guys in the third one. Hubbard had just asked me where they were, and all of a sudden they came right out of the shrub where Crawford was. I mean this guy could have reached out and hit Crawford.

I went to put down the handset, and when I did I hit the hollow stock of the M-16. It probably didn't make that much noise, but to me it sounded like a drum going off.

I dropped the handset, grabbed the pistol grip of the M-16, and stuck the barrel a fraction of an inch from the lead guy's temple. I squeezed the trigger and immediately realized it was on safe. But luckily, at almost the same instant that I squeezed the trigger, Doc Hubbard hit the guy with a burst of about five rounds from his Stoner.

Normally, you could blow on a sampan and turn it over. But when this guy got hit with those Stoner rounds, it blew him straight out of that sampan, and it didn't even wobble. It just kept going right on down the river.

At almost the same instant Doc hit him with that burst, Crawford stuck his M-60 straight out into the face of the guys in the second boat and just cut them down. He just opened up.

By this time I was hollering on the radio to tell the boat we made contact. I was looking out at the firefight. I had put my weapon back down in my lap, and I was hollering in the handset for the boat to come and get us.

The third boat flipped over, and all you could see were tracers going into it.

We started firing in the direction the sampans had come from.

The LCPL and the LSSC came in and picked us up. We started putting fire on the opposite bank. We fired the LCPL's minigun [machine gun with six revolving barrels and a high rate of fire] on the bank and got a secondary explosion that went 150 feet in the air. I mean it was a huge explosion.

In the light of the explosion we saw other sampans on the bank. We were firing at the bank, everywhere.

Abrahamson was rear security, and I guarantee he never left his field of fire to the rear. Knowing "Abe," he may have joined in the ambush by firing a few rounds toward the opposite bank, but it was his responsibility to make sure no one came in from the rear.

I was concerned during the firefight that we were going to be flanked from the left side, but White was watching the left flank. Everybody had a field of fire, which overlapped, so there was no chance someone could get in.

We scrambled the Seawolves and left the area. By the time the Seawolves got over the area, a large volume of automatic-weapons fire came up at them. They shot holes in the helos; they made major contact. We found out later it had been a battalion crossing, and we caught just the very point of it. But we had hit them and hit them hard, then got out none too soon.

Once we went on a daylight op to find a medical cache. We were in the barracks down in Sa Dec, and Scott came through and said to get ready. A *hoi chanh* [enemy soldier who had surrendered] had come in the night before with information about the cache.

Normally, we met for our warning order, which told us who was going out, what the line of march was going to be, and what everyone needed to take. Then we had the patrol order, which explained the specifics: what we were going after, what we were going to encounter, and all the details of the op. On this mission we got all that on the run. We grabbed our stuff and headed out.

It was the middle of the day when the PBRs came in and got us and—*boom*—we were gone. We inserted by PBRs, we had the Seawolves overhead, and the *hoi chanh* led us in.

I was in the lead boat, and we started receiving small-arms fire out of a hooch. The PBRs made a couple of passes with the .50s going, and the Seawolves made some gun runs on them and fired rockets, just to prep the whole area. It was a beautiful sight.

We inserted, and Mike Beanan and I were walking point together. We patrolled down a wide dike that went straight in the direction that the *hoi chanh* indicated. He led us right to the place. We were taking small-arms fire the whole way in, but the Seawolves were right over us, putting fire everywhere.

The intel was that the cache had just been buried in the ground the night before. We set up a perimeter and uncovered a few inches of dirt. We pulled back some log boards, and the whole cache was right there. It was all in ammo cans or wrapped in plastic. There were amputating tools, pharmaceuticals, just everything. It was quite a deal.

We were right on this dike, and there was a canal next to it, so the helicopter had to land on the other side of the canal. We had to ford the canal to load the cache on the helicopter.

We also captured a communist flag with the hammer and sickle on it. After we got back to the base we lined all the stuff up with the flag in the background and took some photos. It was a great op all around.

I actually got to lead a couple of ops, but we didn't make any contact on those. We went out and set up ambushes, but nothing happened. The ops weren't exciting, but it was exciting for me because I was in charge. It was a little different after being the pointman for so long, then actually running the op and coordinating everything and everybody. It was a great experience, and I thought it was good that everybody in the platoon had an opportunity to do that. It was like playing baseball as a kid: if you always make practice but always end up sitting on the bench and never get in the game, you never really get the experience that you need. I think it was great that they let enlisted guys lead.

A lot of guys in my platoon went on to be officers in SEAL Team; Don Crawford and Steve Frisk are still in the Teams today. As enlisted men in Vietnam, they also got to run some ops. Although we always had the greatest respect for Scott Lyon, sometimes I think we didn't realize what real leadership Scott brought to our platoon. Allowing us to run some of the ops made us all realize what Scott had to go through on each mission. Here was a guy that had been an enlisted man and had tours in Vietnam prior to coming to SEAL Team One. He was an East Coast SEAL and had transferred to the West Coast. As a warrant officer he brought some real experience to a pretty green platoon.

Barry Enoch is also one of my real heroes. He was the salt of the earth, and he was the guy that made sure all of us were squared away, had the right equipment, and knew how to use it. That was his job as petty officer, and he did it as well as it could be done.

Enoch had been our UDT instructor. A lot of the guys in my platoon came directly out of UDT training, went through SEAL cadre training, and then were sent overseas as part of a platoon. We thought it was kind of an honor that Enoch would want to go overseas with us because he could pick and choose who he wanted to go with. First of all, he was part of the process that got us to SEAL Team out of UDT training. I was flattered that he thought enough of us to put us directly into SEAL Team. The fact that I got to go to

Vietnam in the same platoon made me feel like I must have done something right during training.

Our lieutenant, Rip Bliss, had just gone through UDT and SEAL cadre training, and had just come to SEAL Team. Though he didn't have any more experience than I did, he was going to be our officer in charge. One thing I can say for Rip Bliss is that he was fearless—fearless to a fault sometimes. But Bliss recognized what Scott brought to our platoon, and when Scott told him something, he would listen.

Scott would never send me anywhere that he wouldn't have gone himself. I was absolutely sure of that because I walked point for him.

In fact, there was a situation on Phu Quoc Island—where we patrolled a river toward a beach on the Gulf of Siam and we got to a mangrove swamp. Everybody stopped to rest. We could see the beach about twenty yards in front of us. We were just relaxing, then Scott said, "Come on, Ware, let's check this out."

I had my *H*-harness and my Stoner, Scott had his CAR-15, and Zin had his M-16. We walked out to the beach area, still in the tree line, and could see these big bunkers. They didn't look like they had been used in a while.

We heard noises in the jungle from our right. There was a group of huge monkeys swinging in the trees. We walked parallel to the beach, down the tree line, and we were just watching the monkeys.

We probably got farther away from the rest of the guys than we should have. We were about 150 yards away but had lost visual contact with them. All of a sudden, the whole world opened up. There was solid firing for a couple minutes nonstop, then it all stopped.

Don Crawford was our automatic-weaponsman, and normally you could hear his M-60 over everything else. Scott's first reaction was to take off in a real quick walk back toward the firing. I was right behind him, and Zin was behind me. I grabbed Scott and said, "I didn't hear the M-60. Man,

Crawford never misses a chance to pull the trigger on that thing.''

He looked at me and said, ''If that was our guys firing, we're OK, but if that wasn't our guys, we're in a world of shit.'' He said to get us over to where we left them, so I led the way back.

We got to the area where the bunkers were and were looking around, just fixing to go back around the corner to where we had left the others. Scott grabbed me and said to give him my Stoner. I handed it to him, and he handed me his CAR-15. He said to wait with Zin while he went around, and if we heard any firing we should not even look back, just haul ass out, swim through the surf zone, and stay out there until the Swift boat came by to pick us up.

I said, ''OK, sure.''

He started walking, and I was right behind him.

He turned around and said, ''I told you to stay there.'' Scott wasn't about to send me around the bunker; he was going himself.

I said, ''I'm not staying there; I'm going where you're going.''

He ended up saying, ''OK,'' and as we came around I saw Lenny Horst and all our guys standing around a dead guy. They said they had seen two enemy, and they opened fire on them. I guess I just didn't hear Crawford's M-60. They had already called in the helicopter to pick us up.

As we headed out over the ocean an argument was going on. Crawford said he got the second guy, and everyone else said he missed him and that they saw him run off. Crawford said they were wrong and asked the helicopter pilot to please make one turn back down the river.

The pilot swerved around, and as we got to a little curve in the river, there was a guy floating face down. I remember Don Crawford had a big smile on his face as he said, ''See, I did get him.''

. . .

We went on a POW op once. We got intel from a Vietnamese lady that her husband was being held as a POW on an island. We went in with a bunch of PRUs, and she led us in to the island. We patrolled in at night and set up all around the POW camp.

One of the PRUs brought out a bullhorn and told them we were there and that we were coming in. He was screaming all kinds of commands at them, but about that same time, someone started firing. I think only one of the guards was actually close enough to fire on us.

One or two of the guards were killed, and the rest of them threw up their hands to surrender. The PRU kept screaming on the bullhorn to try to tell the prisoners what was going on so that they wouldn't be afraid of what was happening.

It was one of the most rewarding ops I ever went on. These people were so appreciative that we were there and had gotten them out of their situation. I think it was a labor camp. They had little shacks, like cells, but the men didn't appear to have been tortured or anything like that.

I wasn't around for the interrogation of the guards later on. I know they were turned over to the NILO but didn't hear anything else about it.

The prisoners were all smiling at first, and we started to round them up to get a photograph. When they saw that they were being rounded up, they got all scared. I guess they thought we were going to execute them or something. But we did get a couple of pictures, then got out.

We brought in a junk boat and an LCPL, and there were people hanging all over them. People were crying, they were so glad to be out of that camp. The lady was ecstatic; she got her husband back.

It was early in the morning; I can remember how the sun was just coming up. It was just a very rewarding experience. You had to feel real compassion for these people. It was the first op that I was on where the Vietnamese people really appreciated the fact that we came in and were there to help

them escape. We released twenty-six prisoners from the island. Some had been held there for over a year.

I felt this op was the reason we were really there in
Vietnam. We were there to help the Vietnamese people, and
I felt like that day I had done my job.

7

Darryl "Willy" Wilson

Automatic–Weaponsman,
1st Squad, Hotel Platoon
Mobile Support Base II and Qui Nhon,
Republic of Vietnam
Deployed July 1968–January 1969

My first tour of duty in Vietnam was on board the USS *Towhee* (AGS 28) in 1966 and 1967. We surveyed the Danang approach, generating a map of the ocean floor.

My second tour was with Hotel Platoon, Det Golf, SEAL Team One. I carried the Stoner, which I just loved. The Stoner never let me down; I felt invincible with it. I could open up and fire sixteen rounds a second. Every fifth round in the belt was a tracer, which meant there were three tracers a second coming out of it. It would light the place up like day. It was a hell of a great weapon!

Gary Parrott, our platoon officer, has said that the only problem he had with me over in Vietnam was trying to get me to stop shooting after a firefight. I guess I've always believed in a little overkill. I was the automatic-weaponsman, and when we got into a firefight, it was my job to spray down the whole area to keep the enemy's heads down.

Certain people in the squad were supposed to shoot on single shot, really take aim and concentrate on hitting the target. Every other person was supposed to shoot bursts of automatic. We also had a grenadier who used an M-79 to lob in high-explosive shells.

We were primarily based on Mobile Support Base II [MSB II]. The base was a group of barges anchored on the upper Mekong River about eleven miles from the Cambodian border. We operated along the Cambodian border in the area of the Mekong and Bassac Rivers, and along the Vinh Te canal that paralleled the Cambodian border and led to the Gulf of Thailand. We also went up to II Corp and operated in the Qui Nhon area twice during this deployment.

WO [warrant officer] Eugene Tinnin worked with our platoon for a week or so just after we got in-country to indoctrinate the platoon.

We received hostile fire on the very first operation that I went on in Vietnam, one week to the day after getting in-country. Parrott, Tinnin, Dan Bratland, our radioman, and Eric Arumae, who carried the M-79, and I loaded in the Boston Whaler and headed upstream in the Mekong from Mobile Support Base II. I was driving the whaler, which was powered by a 105-horsepower Chrysler. The plan that night was to get up near the Cambodian border, shut the engine off, and float down the Mekong to see if we'd detect any movement on the river after curfew.

We floated downstream, and when we were about a mile below MSB II, someone opened up on us from the shoreline of an island in the Mekong. We could hear the supersonic crack of the bullets going by us and see the tracers that were right over our heads.

I started the boat and opened it wide open at the same time! We accelerated so fast that all four of the SEALs on board slid all the way to the back of the boat on the floor, and at the same time were throwing everything they could back at the shoreline.

We went back to MSB II, went into the galley, had a cup of coffee, and laughed about what had just happened and how damn lucky we were that no one had been hit. In SEAL cadre training, we were taught that when firing a gun at night when you can't see the sights, everyone has the tendency to shoot high. The "shooter" that night would have been right on target if he'd known that little trick!

After we finished our coffee, we loaded back into the whaler and went back out on the Mekong for another "float trip," without making any contact that time.

On 20 August 1968 Tinnin was killed near Vinh Long when his fire team split up at night, and the group he was with apparently became disoriented and ended up walking back through the kill zone of the rest of the squad. They opened up on them, and he was killed.

One of the first ops we ran was northeast of the Mobile Support Base, along a canal right on the Cambodian border. We patrolled back in there that night on the way to a small village near the border. I believe the CIA had targeted a tax collector, and they wanted us to break into his hooch, do a prisoner snatch, and bring him back for interrogation. We inserted that night on the Mekong and patrolled all the way to the canal and set up on it for a while.

There were several large junks anchored out in the canal. They were large enough that I think families lived on them. We could see candles burning in them and noticed signaling taking place between several of the junks. It appeared to be Morse code, but we weren't 100 percent sure. Eric Arumae had gone to Vietnamese language school, and we had some people in the patrol with us that could read Morse code. One of the guys said he thought he could make out the word *camouflage*. We didn't know if that meant they knew we were in the area or what, but it made us pretty damn nervous.

We stuck around for a couple hours, but nothing seemed

to be going on, so we patrolled southeast along the canal and went into the village after the tax collector.

The standard procedure was for the seven of us to patrol in to the front of the hooch. It was my job as the automatic-weaponsman to go to the outside left rear corner of the hooch and cover the back side of it in case anybody came running out. Gary Parrott, our platoon leader, and John Billiot, our pointman, busted into the hooch, grabbed the guy the CIA wanted, taped his mouth, and handcuffed him. They came back out of the hooch and with the rest of the squad patrolled out of the area; I was still in the village.

This whole prisoner snatch took thirty to forty-five seconds. The VC's wife and kids were screaming, lights were coming on in the village, dogs were barking, and I could hear people moving around. It wasn't long before I realized the squad had patrolled out of there and left me behind. I was on my own there for a while.

Our plan had been to get this tax collector, go west from his hooch out of the village, then cut across a fairly large open area to get back to the Mekong to extract. There were a lot of trees around the village before the open field.

When I got to the edge of the village, to the tree line, I looked out into the field and saw the SEALs, my fire team, out there all lined up facing back at the tree line I was coming out of. It was pretty damn scary because I was looking down the barrel of all my teammates' guns. I hollered so that they knew who I was. I was worried as hell about walking out of the tree line and getting blown away by our own guys.

So we had the VC the CIA wanted, and we got out of there, which made it turn out to be a fairly good op, and our first prisoner snatch. We turned him over to NILO or the CIA, and I never really heard what they ended up getting from him, if anything.

·   ·   ·

There was a skinny island on the Mekong River, part of it in Cambodia and part of it in Vietnam. We inserted on the lower end of the island and patrolled north up to where we got close to some hooches. John Billiot, our pointman, crawled out in front of us and set up a couple of claymore mines. We were in there for two or three hours. Then, for some reason, the geese and ducks around the hooches started making a lot of noise, quacking and honking. About midnight, a Vietnamese came out of one of the hooches and started looking around.

This was another case where we thought the operation had been compromised, so we decided to just get the hell out of there. We were right on the Cambodian border and weren't 100 percent sure that we weren't actually in Cambodia. We called in the LSSCs to extract us, and the geese and ducks kept making more and more noise. Billiot was the last one out of there, and rather than going out and picking up the claymores, he just cranked them off as we were leaving. I don't know if he killed any of the geese, but it scared the hell out of them. A lot of Vietnamese used geese as warning devices, like a watchdog.

Just down the river from this island on the east side of the Mekong River was an abandoned church. We got word from the PBR crews that every time they went past the area of the church, they were fired on by VC using a 57-mm recoilless rifle. We planned an op to go in and search the area and blow up the church if necessary. We inserted by Boston Whalers about four o'clock on Sunday morning. We had PBRs standing by out in the river and Seawolf gunships in the air fairly close by to back us up.

As we inserted, a Vietnamese heard us and came out of his hooch. We grabbed and gagged him and called the Boston Whaler back in to extract us right away because we felt we had been compromised.

We took the guy back out into the river with us and joined up with the PBRs. The Vietnamese was scared to death; he told us his wife was in the hooch, and he wanted to get her out. We loaded from the Whaler onto the PBR and went back into the riverbank and then to the hooch to get her. We took him along with us so he could communicate with her.

When we got the both of them back out into the river, he admitted that there was VC activity in the area. We then put a helicopter rocket strike into the area to neutralize it in preparation for a third insertion. The very first damn rocket hit this guy's hooch, and he just went ape-shit. He was really upset with us.

Our fire team inserted a third time and patrolled down the shore of the Mekong to the church and set up a perimeter around it. After searching the church, we loaded it full of explosives on a time fuse, then extracted to watch it go off. We were back out in the river on the PBRs again when she blew. It was a beautiful sight, sunup on a Sunday morning, and we were looking toward the east. We could see all these sheets of tin from the roof going up and up, like Frisbees flying in the air.

We went back in and patrolled around the area again. We found several bunkers and tunnels all along the bank but didn't have any enemy contact. We called it a day and headed back to MSB II.

Another night op that we ran was downstream from the MSB II. We took a Boston Whaler and decided that everyone would stay in the boat. We pulled into the lower end of this island and sat there for several hours to just watch the river and see if anyone was moving.

There were some damn water buffalo on the shore close to where we were. They kept moving around in the water— which kept our hearts pumping. We didn't know what the hell the noises were at first, if it was people walking around or what. We finally realized it was water buffalo.

From where we were on the island, we heard dogs barking for several hours along the west bank of the Mekong. We found out the next day that a hell of a large contingent of Viet Cong carrying supplies had moved single file down the west bank of the river that night, and we didn't even know it. That was unfortunate because we could have gotten a helicopter strike in there and really done some major damage.

In the upper Mekong area, in upper IV Corps, we worked along the Vinh Te canal. This canal paralleled the Cambodian border between the Bassac and the ocean to the southwest. The PBRs were getting shot all to hell along this canal. The commander in charge of the PBRs talked to Gary Parrott one day about this brilliant idea he had. He wanted us SEALs to ride on the PBRs until they were ambushed, then they would pull the PBRs right into the bank where the ambush was, and we SEALs were supposed to jump off and charge the enemy and wipe them out! Parrott was so upset about this plan that he took our whole platoon downriver to Can Tho to talk to this commander's superior and explain to him how insane the idea was. We hooked up with Alpha Platoon while down there and had a hell of a party, which really made the trip worthwhile.

We did operate for about a month out on the Vinh Te canal. We spent a couple weeks in the Tinh Binh area just north of the Three Sisters Mountains and then went to another little place called Vinh Gia just west of the Three Sisters.

It was pretty scary operating out of there. The only action we saw was on an operation with about sixty LDNNs. They were swimming, joking around, smoking cigarettes, etc. We didn't think there was a chance in the world that any VC would happen by.

All of a sudden, about 11:00 P.M. they all got quiet, and all hell broke loose. Two VC were coming from Cambodia into Vietnam in a sampan. When the Vietnamese opened up on them, they shot back on full automatic with AKs. Our fire team was lying on a dirt knoll on the bank of the canal, and the incoming rounds were hitting so close to us we had dirt in our eyes.

When the smoke cleared, there was one dead VC and no other casualties.

We'd be riding the PBRs right before sundown, and the Vietnamese would be running along the bank on the Vietnam side of the canal, hollering, "VC, VC!" and pointing to the west, over in Cambodia. We could look over into Cambodia about a mile away and see armed patrols of Viet Cong looking back at us. They had weapons and were all bunched up, getting ready to cross over into Vietnam after it got dark. So we knew they were in the area and that they were going to come across the border, but we weren't really sure where they would cross.

We pulled one night op down there out of Vinh Gia, where we were expecting to lock horns with the enemy. We carried extra Stoners and extra ammo and actually dug fox-holes on the north bank of the canal and wore helmets. There must have been a million mosquitoes in that foxhole with me that night. I usually carried about eight hundred to nine hundred rounds on an operation. On one operation down in the Vinh Te canal I carried way over a thousand rounds. There is a picture of us from that night, with all the bandoleers crisscrossed on us. But normally, I had eight hundred rounds with me. It wasn't overly heavy, and it didn't bother me.

I never carried water with me. I'd take a hell of a big drink right before the op; rather than carry the weight in water, I carried it in ammo.

We sat there all night long, and the next morning a South Vietnamese patrol came along and compromised the whole mission. We had planned to stay in there at least twenty-four hours, longer than just an overnight op. But the mission was compromised about nine o'clock the next morning, so we ended up pulling out. I was damn glad to get away from those flying teeth.

I'll never forget one op up toward the Tinh Binh area. The PBR sailors were really jumpy. They had been getting shot up a lot, and some had been killed, so they were really trigger happy.

We were set up on a canal ambush one night. We could hear the PBRs coming from a long way off; you could hear the low drone of their engines. They kept getting closer as they patrolled down the canal, and Gary Parrott leaned over to me and said that he was going to throw a rock at one of the PBRs when they came by. I started pleading quietly with him not to, because I figured they'd open up on us and kill us all, just for throwing a rock. I could see Parrott's teeth shining in the darkness and realized he was just jerking my chain, but the thought of it scared the hell out of me.

Another night we worked out of Chau Doc in sampans. We had one SEAL and two Vietnamese LDNNs in each sampan. We had to sit perfectly still because there was only about an inch of leeway. If you leaned one way or the other, the boat started taking on water. The Vietnamese paddled the sampans, and each SEAL bailed water to keep the boat afloat. We paddled upstream from Chau Doc toward the Cambodian border, to a little village called Ap Vin. It was during the rainy season, and you could paddle right across the banks of the rivers and into the rice paddies.

We came to the backside of this village, and Parrott got out with some of the Vietnamese. They went up to a hooch, and one of the Vietnamese with us spoke to the people inside. A lady came to the door. She misunderstood the Vietnamese with us to be a VC friend of her husband's who was with some Viet Cong that were immediately up the river, right across the border in Cambodia.

We waited there a while, but the VC never showed up. It

ended up to be a hair-raising night. Some of us were left guarding the boats, and others were out walking through the village. When we finally left the village in the sampans, we had to paddle all the way back to Chau Doc.

Twice during our six-month deployment we were sent up to Qui Nhon, and it seemed like we were always getting into it with the North Vietnamese Army up there. That was where our platoon saw most of its action and where most of our people were wounded.

Almost all of our ops were patrolling and ambushes at the north end of Qui Nhon Bay. It was a long bay that extended six or eight miles north of the city of Qui Nhon. At the north end of the bay was a whole bunch of islands, and along the north shore was a mountain range. The NVA lived in caves in those mountains and would come down into the north end of the bay at night to fish. They used fish traps and grenades to get fish to feed their troops. When we flew over that area in the daylight, we could see a trail they used to get down to the bay, and we nicknamed it "Broadway." We would go up in there a lot and set ambushes along that trail.

On one op in Qui Nhon, five of us had gone up to the north end of the bay and set up an ambush on an island. Three NVA were paddling around in a sampan, fishing with grenades that night. The one in the front and the one in the back were paddling; the NVA in the middle was naked and would jump into the water to gather up the fish. We could hear them joking and laughing. They would get relatively close to us, then paddle farther away north, even up around the north end of the island to where we could hardly hear them. Then they'd come back down toward us. This went on for two or three hours.

We finally decided if they weren't going to come to us, we would go to them. By that time the tide had come in, so we patrolled in waist- to chest-deep water up the east side of the island. We went around the north end of the island and saw their silhouettes out on the water at least forty or fifty yards away from us. Parrott initiated the ambush, and everyone's tracers went right through that damn sampan. I can still see them, ricocheting off the sampan and up into the sky. It was amazing how concentrated everyone's fire was on that sampan.

On an op like that one, we'd always ride a Swift boat from Qui Nhon, and when it got too shallow to go any farther, we'd get in a Boston Whaler and ride it until it ran aground, then we'd get out and patrol or wade the rest of the way into the island or wherever we were operating. On this night, because the tide had come in while we were on the op, we were able to call the LSSC to come in and extract us, since there was quite a bit more water.

After we blew the hell out of the sampan, John Benanti radioed the LSSC to come in and get us. We went out to the sampan in the LSSC and put a spotlight on it. We knew these people had grenades, so we had our guns trained on the sampan as we went up to it. Somebody said they thought they saw one of them move, so everyone opened up on the sampan again. It looked like the closing scene from *Bonnie and Clyde,* the three bodies were just flopping and rolling around inside. We shot the sampan so full of holes that it started to sink.

We pulled up alongside the sampan and tied it up to the LSSC to keep it from sinking. We took it back to the NILO, and they took the bodies and searched them. We also got some weapons and grenades from the sampan that night.

On 14 September we went up in that area and set up a night ambush on one of the islands. A lot of the islands around there were real skinny. They weren't very wide east and west but real long north and south. The island we inserted on that night had a thin channel that ran from east to west. We set up an ambush on the south side of the channel. I remember real well getting in there that night. We sat down, and it was relatively dry, sandy, a little muddy soil; but then the tide started coming in, and after a while we had to hold our guns in our laps. Then we had to lay them on our shoulders. Before we initiated the ambush that night, I was holding the gun on top of my head to keep it out of the salt water.

We heard a lot of talking going on over on the island to the east of us.

We had a Vietnamese with us that night, one of the two that were assigned to us when we first got in-country. This guy kept whispering, "VC, VC!"

We kept telling him to shut up because voices traveled well over the water, and we didn't want these people to know we were there. The meeting was between some high-level VC. They were putting together a battle plan to attack Qui Nhon a month or two later.

The meeting went on for two or three hours. We could hear voices rising at times.

Their meeting finally broke up, and three of them got into a sampan and came down the east side of the island where we were. Our Vietnamese later told us that right before they got to the channel we were set up on, one of the VC in the sampan said they'd better watch out, this was a good place for an ambush. They were so close, it seemed like we could reach out and touch them. They were only fifteen to twenty-five feet away at the most. We opened up on them, and the tracers lit the place up like day.

The ambush didn't last very long at all. Our radioman got some parachute flares in the air. I shot a 150-round belt with the Stoner and reloaded it.

Then I noticed some movement out of the corner of my eye. One of the NVA had swum underwater to our right. I took a couple steps out in front of our firing line and fired at a ninety-degree angle to everybody else at this guy. I think this was another one of those cases where Parrott was probably having a little trouble getting me to stop shooting.

We rounded up the three bodies to search them and gathered up all the information we could. We got five kilos of documents that night—which included the battle plan for a major attack on Qui Nhon. I think during the whole year, SEAL Team got twenty kilos of documents. So on that one night we got one-fourth of the documents that SEAL Team One captured during the entire year. As far as intelligence gathering and damage inflicted on the VC go, that was our best op.

We found out the next day through the Vietnamese that was with us that the higher-ups in the meeting had guards set up around them. One of the guards had complained about having to stand sentry duty because they were safe; nobody was around there. And here we were, right next door, on the next island over from them.

Probably the most memorable operation while in Qui Nhon—and really, during our whole tour—was when Don Hyslop was wounded. On this operation, we traveled by Swift boat up into the bay north of Qui Nhon and inserted at about 4:00 A.M. The plan was to patrol to the east from the insertion point for about a mile, then spread out in a long line and sweep a valley in a southerly direction to the ocean, where we would extract at the friendly village of Mui Yen. We had arranged for three wooden Vietnamese junks to pick us up at this village.

This was to be a daylight operation with the whole platoon, plus Mike Bailey from SEAL Team Two and his German shepherd scout dog. We also had a group of Vietnamese with us—I don't recall how many.

The purpose of the operation was to look for signs of enemy movement, equipment and supply caches, caves, etc., in this valley that paralleled the coast. The line of SEALs and Vietnamese ran from about halfway up the mountainside on one side of the valley, down through the valley, and about halfway up the opposite mountainside.

It was a warm, sunny, peaceful day; the only noise we

heard during the sweep was birds singing. We didn't encounter any evidence or sign of any activity during the patrol that day. We all were relaxed when we exited the valley at the village of Mui Yen.

This was a beautiful little village that sat on a quiet, small bay that was protected from the open ocean by a coral reef about an eighth of a mile offshore, and several islands beyond that. The beach was clean white sand, and the water in the bay crystal clear. A lot of the villagers were on the beach, watching us, and children were playing, chasing each other and swimming in the bay. Everyone thought that the threat of any trouble was over, and that all we had to do was stroll down the beach to the junks, load up, and cruise back into Qui Nhon.

When we were about halfway past the village, one old Vietnamese yelled something in their language that we didn't understand. The children started running, the women were screaming, and in a matter of seconds everyone on the beach had disappeared.

We all started looking at each other and began pulling our guns down off our shoulders and getting ready to defend ourselves. We picked up the pace to get to the junks so we could get the hell out of there.

I was one of the first there. I climbed up on the junk, laid my Stoner down, and was helping others aboard by either taking their weapons or helping pull them up to the high bow.

About the same time we got loaded, we looked up into the village and saw about ten armed Vietnamese running toward us. In unison, they seemed to drop into a trench or foxholes and opened up on us. There was probably forty to fifty yards separating us, and we felt like we were sitting ducks in that wooden boat with nothing to hide behind.

I couldn't believe this was happening, and I was never so scared in my life. I remember falling to the deck and curling up in the fetal position, knowing that I was going to get hit, and wondering where. My mind actually went blank from fear for the time it took the junk to back off the beach and turn around. Bullets were going straight through the boat, and splinters were flying everywhere.

The next thing I remember is standing at the left front corner of the small cabin on the junk, firing that Stoner like never before. This was a fierce firefight, with all of us fifteen SEALs throwing everything we could back at that village to try to suppress their fire until we got out of the kill zone.

The Vietnamese pilot of the junk made a run straight for the open ocean, and forgot that he had had to skirt the reef when he had come into the village earlier that morning. The junk ran up on the reef and stopped dead in the water momentarily, until our wake seemed to pick the back of the boat up and push us on over to the other side.

We continued to head out to sea, still exchanging an unbelievable amount of gunfire. We were beginning to receive mortar rounds from the village that were going off in the water around us.

Gary Parrott was standing behind Don Hyslop when he spotted a mortar round as it cleared the tree line around the village. At the same time Hyslop took a round in the neck that paralyzed him instantly. As he fell overboard the sling of his Stoner wrapped around his neck. Parrott and Bill Doyle, our senior NCO [noncommissioned officer], grabbed Hyslop's legs as he fell. The Stoner was dragging through the water, pulling Hyslop's head under, but somehow the two of them managed to get him back on board.

The mortar round that Parrott had spotted as it left the village found its mark. It hit the cockpit in the back of our junk, killing one of the three-man Vietnamese crew immediately and disabling the steering in the boat.

The second crewman crawled along the deck, up the outside of the cabin to my feet. He was covered with blood, was moaning something in Vietnamese to me, then died at my feet.

The third Vietnamese crewman was seriously wounded and lost one of his arms below the elbow. The German shepherd scout dog was also wounded from the mortar round. All of us SEALs were in the bow of the boat and were protected from the mortar blast by the cabin on the junk.

By this time the firing had ceased. We were very fortunate because the Vietnamese crew were all either dead or wounded, the steering and throttle didn't work, and we were helplessly bobbing around in the ocean.

Tom Lawson had called in a helo strike on the village during the firefight. The helos managed to make one pass and dump some rockets before they were called off by the NILO in Qui Nhon. The NILO was pretty damn upset with us for putting a strike in on a "friendly village."

A couple of Swift boats came to our rescue that morning right after the firing ceased. We loaded Hyslop, the wounded Vietnamese, and a few others on one of the Swifts and rushed them to Qui Nhon. The rest of us boarded the second Swift and towed the junk back to the naval base.

It was questionable for several days whether Don Hyslop was going to pull through. He did eventually become stable enough to be transferred back to the States.

Shortly after this operation, our whole platoon was called into Saigon for interrogation. They took us, one at a time, into a room full of brass and tape recorders and questioned us about what had happened that day at Mui Yen. It was almost as if we were being accused of attacking innocent people in a friendly village. We were told later that the village had a beef with the Vietnamese Navy that picked us up that day in the three junks. No one ever explained why they only fired at the junk with Americans on board.

Another op we did was along the trail we called "Broadway." That night we decided to take the whole platoon, all fourteen of us. We had Mike Bailey from SEAL Team Two and his German shepherd scout dog, Prince, along with us.

We inserted on the east end of the bay, then patrolled north up the peninsula to the trail. We got fairly close to "Broadway," then we split up. We had Tom Lawson's fire team go down by the bay where we knew the VC had sampans hidden. Our fire team was going to go north of the ridge, where we could overlook the trail. Our pointman, John Billiot, had Prince up front with him.

As we started moving to the north, the dog stood broadside right in front of Billiot and stopped him. Billiot tried to walk around the dog, but Prince would just run around in front of him again. Bailey was right behind the pointman and immediately recognized that Prince was trying to tell him there was somebody up in front of us.

At the same time, some NVA were in a little brushy draw just north of us, and we saw one of them light up a cigarette. We swung around into a firing line and started backing down the ridge.

About that time, the NVA spotted Lawson's fire team down in a little clearing, and they opened up on them.

We were up on the ridge and wanted to try to hold our position to provide fire support. We were in a key point on that ridge, but the problem we had was that we weren't exactly certain where Lawson was down there, so we couldn't do any shooting to support them. There was a lot of radio traffic going on between Lawson and the helicopters to try to get some helo strikes in there.

We were using Army helicopters in Qui Nhon for support. I have to hand it to those guys, they did a great job. They came in and put some strikes in right where the NVA were. Lawson and his men were down from the steep ridge we were on, shining their red flashlight. The helos were guiding in on Lawson's light. The helicopters came in very close to where we were, going down in after Lawson and all his wounded people.

One helicopter actually hit the ridge we were on and bounced off the ground. The pilot kind of lost control, came back around, and glanced off the ridge again before he got control of the helicopter. He started to receive fire and had to leave the area. They put in some more helicopter-gunship strikes, then he came back in.

There were seven SEALs and one Vietnamese in Lawson's fire team. Six of the eight of them were wounded that night. Only Doc Brown and Dave Wilkenson were not wounded. The two most seriously wounded were Fletcher "Bill" Wright, who had one of his eyes shot out, and Al Yutz, who got hit real bad with shrapnel. Both Wright and Yutz had to be shipped back to the States.

In the helicopter was the pilot, copilot, and two door gunners. They went down in there and picked up all eight of those guys. The helo was way overloaded with twelve people on board and all their guns and ammo. I'll never forget the sound of that helicopter that night. While they were loading the guys on, the pilot had the engine wound up tight. He revved that thing up and changed the pitch in the blades and just shot off the ground, gaining all the altitude he could. He had to fly six to eight miles back across Qui Nhon Bay to get to the airstrip and was losing altitude the whole way. The pilot thought he was going to have to touch down somewhere and have Dave Wilkenson and Doc Brown get out of the helicopter and throw out some guns to lighten the load. They managed to make it to the end of the runway before touching down.

They were met with ambulances and fire trucks, but the pilot didn't shut the helicopter down there. He actually dragged it on its skids part way down the runway to get to the medevac hospital at the other end of the airstrip.

In the meantime, we were still up on the ridge. There was so much radio traffic going on, and we weren't 100 percent sure they had gotten all of Lawson's people out. When we found out that they were all out, we started working our way back down the ridge to the south, being shot at the whole

time. We got quite a way south while the helicopters continued to put in more strikes.

One slick came in and got everybody out except for Dan
Bratland, our radioman, Parrott, and me. Then a second
chopper came in and got the three of us.

It was a hell of a hairy night: a real scary op. John
Benanti, Tom Lawson, Frank "Hopper" Mihatsch, Al Yutz,
and Fletcher "Bill" Wright, and the Vietnamese had all
been wounded. We were lucky someone wasn't killed on
that op, with all the lead that had been flying around.

We also operated off the USS *Weiss* with Alpha Platoon on
Phu Quoc Island. On the southern tip of the island was a
POW camp where the VC and NVA prisoners were kept.
The rest of the island was a free-fire zone—which meant we
could shoot anybody at anytime out there. It was some of the
easiest action that we had seen. I think the Viet Cong on the
island had no idea that any U.S. troops were going to be
there. We really caught them by surprise.

We were on the *Weiss,* anchored about fifteen miles offshore. We would wait until it got dark and get on an LSSC
and ride it into the beach. It was different from working up
on the Mekong River or in Qui Nhon because the *Weiss* was
in the open ocean. Inserting was also different because we
had to take the LSSC in through swells and the surf zone or
insert by helo. Operating down there was a little easier. It
was in mountainous country, so we didn't have to wade
through rice paddies, swamps, and canals. Usually when we
inserted, we were on dry land—which was a nice change.

On one operation we inserted by helicopter just before
dark along a well-traveled trail in the central part of the
island. We jumped out of the chopper and ran into a tree line
that paralleled the trail. We had no more than got set up in
the trees when a Viet Cong came walking down the trail,

carrying a rifle over his shoulder. Gary Parrott shot this VC. Billiot and Parrott searched him and took the weapon.

We sat there for three to four hours, in ambush, waiting to see if any other VC might come to pick up the body so we could waste them. No one did, so we patrolled on inland and had no more contact that night.

We found out the next day that the guy Parrott shot was the top VC on the island. He was missing one of his arms from the elbow down and had been carrying, of all weapons, a Chicom [Chinese communist] carbine. We've always wondered how he could have operated a bolt-action rifle with only one arm.

On another op on Phu Quoc Island our target was a two-story structure way up in the mountains. We had a hell of a time getting up to it that night. We ended up having to go through some dark jungle, the darkest jungle we had ever seen. It was so dark that we had to hold hands while we patrolled through it, because you couldn't see the guy in front of or behind you.

After patrolling until two o'clock in the morning, we realized that we were not going to make it to the target.

We came across a lighted hooch and decided to go in there and snatch a prisoner. We wanted someone to interrogate to find out about any enemy activity in the area. We surrounded the hooch, and Parrott and our pointman, John Billiot, went into the place and grabbed this guy out of bed. He had two kids and a wife, and they were all screaming as we handcuffed him, gagged him, and took him off into the darkness.

We took him down the trail about a half mile and interrogated him. He told us that there was a trail not too far from his hooch that the Viet Cong would use every morning when they came down off the mountain. He took us up there, and we set up an ambush on this trail. We didn't realize that he had positioned us on the inside of a hairpin curve in the trail.

It just started to get light out, and I could see that there wasn't anything but tall grass between us and the trail. Our original plan was to shoot and wound anybody that came down the trail so that we could capture a prisoner for interrogation. I was concerned that if we wounded somebody here, they could fall on the ground in the grass and shoot back at us. There were eight of us on the op, our seven-man fire team plus Stan Meston, the officer in charge of Detachment Golf.

Just after daylight I saw a VC come down the trail carrying an M-1 carbine. I raised my Stoner and trained it on him. I was following the guy with my sights when Parrott saw him and fired one round with his M-16. It was a tracer round, and I saw it go through the VC's legs in the area of his knees. When that happened, I leaned into my Stoner and opened up.

My rounds hit him around the waist, and the bullets went up through his chest and head. The impact picked him up off the trail so that it looked like he was running through the air. The rounds blew his brains out and totally gutted the guy. He landed in a ditch about ten feet from the trail.

We ended up stripping the guy naked and left a grenade under him. The weight of his body would hold the spoon on it. We hoped that anyone coming after his body would get injured or killed when the grenade went off.

Before we left on this op, we had prearranged a time for extraction by helo. When the shooting started, the helos that were supporting us were several miles away at the POW compound. The pilots and crews were just coming out of the chow hall after eating breakfast and heard the shooting as they were walking to their helicopters. They were in the helos and on the way to help us before we even radioed for help.

First, a couple of Cobras [attack helicopters] came in and started receiving fire from the hillside just above us. They put some rockets in on the hillside—which I didn't know was going to happen. We were laying low and trying to shoot back at the VC, and all of a sudden these rockets came in right over our heads. It scared the hell out of us when they started blowing up in front of us on the side of that mountain.

They got one slick in there and got everybody out except for Dan Bratland, who was our radioman, Gary Parrott, and myself. It was normal for the three of us to stay behind and wait for the second helicopter because I was an AW [automatic-weapons] man, Bratland had the radio, and Parrott was the squad leader.

The second slick tried to come in to get us but received so much fire from the mountainside that they had to pull out. The Cobras came back in and blew the hell out of the hillside again. After that the slick came back in, picked up the three of us, and got us out of there and back out to the *Weiss*.

Those two ops were the most memorable for me while we were operating on Phu Quoc Island. In the two weeks or so that we were operating on the island we really terrorized the enemy. The VC were running scared because Alpha Platoon and our platoon were getting some real good hits. We wasted a lot of the enemy, and no SEALs were wounded.

I spent two years in the fleet before I got into the Teams. I think the two years that I spent in SEAL Team One were some of the best years of my life. I was in SEAL Team from '67 to '69, then got out of the Navy. Four years later I reenlisted and went back in for two more years. But those years with SEAL Team One during the Vietnam War—I'm glad that I did that; I'm proud of that. I met some of the best people on the face of the earth. I come from a large family and have five brothers and a sister. I'm as close to my old SEAL Team One buddies as I am with my own family.

8

Paul Lee Pittman

Radioman, 2d Squad, Charlie Platoon
My Tho, Vinh Long, and Rach Gia
Republic of Vietnam
Deployed November 1968–May 1969

During the course of any operation, whether it was an ambush or you're out there just trying to catch the higher-echelon guys, I usually had some kind of a system set up so that at least on every hour I would give two clicks [keying the mike without talking] on my radio. Just so that I would know, and the MST guys would know, that we were OK and that we actually had radio communications. We didn't want to talk; so as long as I could get that click back, I knew we had comm [communications].

If you got in a firefight, and you were pinned down, or it was a little more brutal than you thought, the radioman would come in pretty handy, calling for an extraction if the boats were close, or calling for air support.

When we set an ambush, I was rear security. My job was to face to the rear of the ambush position and make sure nobody came up behind us. Even when the VC were approaching the kill zone, I couldn't turn around. I was dying to see what was happening or how many guys were coming, but I couldn't move because I didn't want to give myself, or the other SEALs, away. So everything was getting ready to take place, and I was looking 180 degrees out. It was really a heck of a feeling— waiting for the ambush to initiate—knowing it was going to initiate and you were not part of it.

When you were rear security and you knew the VC were coming, it seemed like an eternity: waiting for the ambush, waiting for these guys to get into the kill zone. You didn't want to move—you didn't even want to blink—and you could almost hear your heart beating. You couldn't see anything, then all of a sudden the firing started, and you knew it was over for those guys.

Our platoon was still pretty green at the time we ran this op. We inserted at night and walked quite a bit and the next day came across a village. We captured a number of people we suspected were VC. Each of us carried Smith and Wesson handcuffs to secure the prisoners.

At this point, we realized we were lost. Everybody was looking at the map, trying to figure out how to get to a place where the boats could pick us up. We weren't sure where we were, but we guessed that we would run into a river and get the boats to come in.

Shortly after leaving the village, we saw eight or nine guys running into a tree line. We weren't sure they saw us, but we were sneaking and peeking on these guys. As it turned out, they had seen us.

We were in elephant grass up to our waists, and all of a sudden it just started lying down. I mean, you couldn't hear any shots, but all of a sudden you would see a streak of elephant grass just lie down. And I said, "Hey, guys, take a look at that. What the hell do you think this is. I've never seen anything like it."

Finally one of the guys said, "Hey, we're getting shot at."

I had this prisoner with me, and when we realized we

were taking fire, I grabbed the prisoner and started running toward a ditch. I ran through the branches of this tree, which unbeknown to me was covered with red ants. By the time I landed down in the ditch, these guys had already started to eat me. The prisoner was covered too. He was in handcuffs, and I was trying to get the ants off him and trying to get them off of me—it was quite a sight.

I wanted to call in a Seawolf. I said, "Come on, let's call in the helicopters."

The patrol leader said we weren't going to do that. So we had a little firefight. We couldn't see them, they couldn't see us, and we shot for a little bit and then broke contact.

We arrived at another village, and we were going to rent a sampan from these people to get us out to the main river. I didn't even have any radio comm; I couldn't even get the boats—that's how far in we were.

The people in the village told us that all our prisoners were out of a tuberculosis village. All of them had TB, and we were feeling pretty sorry at this time. So we said OK, the best thing we can do right now is unhandcuff these guys and let them all go; but nobody had a key. So we had to take them with us; we didn't want to leave them handcuffed. The handcuffs were supposed to be stainless steel, but after about two times out they rusted right up, and that was the end of that.

So we rented sampans from these people. I say rented: I don't know if we paid them or not. We had to get in these sampans, one or two at a time, with people that we didn't know. They took us down to the main river, which was like a fifteen-to-twenty-minute ride. And you know, it was kind of spooky. You were in the sampan, which only drew about an inch of freeboard, with people you didn't know. We were lost, tired, and we were with this guy that had TB, and he had our handcuffs on, and there was no way to get them off.

· · ·

We relieved John Fietsch's platoon in Vinh Long; they had some intel in this area that they turned over to us. There was an Army outpost on the main river close to a canal that went inland. The intel was that it was not feasible to go up the canal; it was bad news.

Dave "Willy" Wilson was a first class [petty officer]. It came down to a point where everybody else was gone, or doing something, and Willy ran the op. It was a daytime op, which is something we normally didn't do. Willy was an M-79 grenade man; he carried a sawed-off grenade launcher, which he was very good with. He had a vest that could carry a ton of those 40-mike-mike grenades.

We went out in a small boat and were going to go down this canal to a village that was supposedly fortified with a lot of bad guys. We had a guide with us who was going to take us to this hooch where there were supposed to be seven high-echelon VC.

Usually, when we went into hooches, it was at night, and I would go in after our squad leader—that was the way we worked it. But Willy was going in, and I asked him, "You want me to go in with you, Willy?"

He said, "No, I'm going in by myself."

I couldn't believe it. "Now, Willy, let me get this straight. You're going in with your M-79 grenade launcher—against seven bad guys, and the rest of us are just going to hang out front?"

And he said, "That's right. I suggest you guys just lay low."

So that's what we were going to deal with, if and when we got there. That's what was supposed to happen.

Once we passed the Army outpost and turned into the canal, the VC had *tu dia* [danger] signs up on both sides. The river was heavily fortified with booby traps, I mean, and they had plenty of these warning signs up.

As we started around a little bend in the river, a sampan came up with three people in it. Our guide went crazy. He knew these guys and said, "Hey, these are three of the VC right here!" So we kind of had a standoff with them, for what seemed to be thirty or forty seconds. They were watching us, and we were watching them. Finally we *lai dai*-ed them, told them to "come here" in Vietnamese, but they just weren't moving.

Being the radioman, I was very seldom in a position to shoot. But in this case I was on the boat, an LSSC, and I was in a position to shoot. We kept trying to convince these guys to come to us. We were probably thirty or forty feet from each other. There were no weapons that we could see, but they'd made up their minds that they weren't coming.

Suddenly, there was some movement on their part, so another SEAL and I opened up with our Stoners.

When it was said and done, the sampan was gone, two of the VC were gone, and one guy was struggling. He got to the riverbank about the same time we beached the boat. We had pretty much forgotten about all the booby traps, from the excitement.

Three or four guys jumped off the boat to capture the VC who had struggled to the bank. Willy and I jumped off at the same time. Unfortunately for him, he landed on a booby trap, which I believe was later determined to be a 105-mm howitzer round.

I didn't hear a blast; the sound was like somebody hitting an anvil with a ball-peen hammer—that's the only way I can describe it. When I woke up I was on the bottom of the canal, but I managed to get to the surface. Somebody grabbed me and pulled me up into the boat.

The others were in the process of retrieving Willy, who had been blown approximately thirty feet into the air. In the explosion he lost one leg at the thigh, and I think one arm.

The boat was covered with mud from the explosion, which left a tremendous hole in the bank. The mud probably saved most of us, because a 105 has a killing radius, I think, of thirty-five meters under normal explosive conditions.

I wasn't sure what had really happened—the whole world just kind of went off. During the explosion I was hit by a lot of mud and some small pieces of shrapnel. One piece went into my eye, and I lost vision in that eye. Another piece of shrapnel went through the side of my mouth and into my tongue, which started to swell, and I had a little difficulty breathing. I had a lot of little "nickel and dime" abrasions up and down my body—a couple to my groin area—which, you know, I was kind of concerned with.

At this point all we could think of was to get on the boat and get the heck outta there—which is basically what we did. When we got to the Army base, the Army personnel were kind of irate that we had gone down the canal. When they saw what had happened to us, they said, "We told you guys not to go down that canal."

A helicopter came and medevaced Willy and me. The medevac already had seven guys on it. Of course, Willy was deceased. There was some kid lying below me that was constantly kicking. We were on cot-type stretchers, and this kid kept kicking me; he had been shot numerous times with an AK-47.

We flew to a base nearby, but a mortar barrage started as we were coming in, and we couldn't land there. We pulled off and flew from wherever the heck we were to Long Binh, right outside of Saigon. I was put in a ward where all the patients had injuries from the neck up. I was probably the luckiest guy in that ward because everyone else was messed up big time.

Three days later I got my vision back. I was in good shape then. After a week, I was going to be medevaced back to the States. That's when two other SEALs came to the hospital and told them I had escaped from a Navy brig, somehow been wounded in the process, and they were there to take me back to jail. And so I left Long Binh in a pair of medical pajamas. We went to Saigon and partied for about three days, and then I went back to my outfit.

The day that Willy got killed was the same day he made chief—pretty ironic.

The platoon was split up: seven went to work out of the Green Beret camp at Ha Tien, and they were living pretty good. The other seven of us were in a tiny Vietnamese village called Vinh Gia, which was on the Vinh Te canal. On the other side of this canal was Cambodia. We could see these huge aluminum buildings on the Cambodian side, and every day at approximately one o'clock we'd watch the NVA come out and play soccer.

We would go out and work the border. We had a little handheld radar that I think was invented at China Lake. The VC and NVA would cross in battalions; they had an eleven-man point element. We would work in threes—three guys against an eleven-man point element. It was during the dry season, and it was flat out there. It looked like Nebraska in the wintertime—you know, there was no place to hide. In the canal itself, the water was so low that when we traveled in the PBRs, they couldn't get their twin .50-cal. [caliber] machine guns up high enough to shoot over the top of the bank.

We were there for five or six weeks, but it wasn't long before the VC realized we were there. We got messages that the VC were going to come over and kick our ass. There wasn't much to stop 'em—there was really nothing there. Nobody had ever really interfered with these guys because the good guys were outnumbered, and this was just a little Vietnamese village—you know, you don't bother me, and I won't bother you.

They flew in a battery of 105-mm howitzers so we would have some artillery support. I think they had three or four guns. The gun crews were pretty dismayed about being there because living conditions were zero. We had C-rats [C-rations] and had some cots flown in, but we didn't have any mattresses, so we'd take the cardboard off the C-rat boxes for padding.

Mosquito nets became extremely important; the mosquitoes were so thick up there you couldn't breathe. Plus, there were a lot of rats in this village, this little compound, and that's basically what you kept your mosquito net for, to keep the rats out of your bunk at night.

We would go out at night and set up this little radar on the Cambodian side and watch the NVA cross. We couldn't actually see them, but we could hear them.

We had what was called a "Blackhawk flight" that flew up and down the border. They had infrared sensors and could pick up the NVA, or anything that had a heartbeat. They could distinguish between man and animal. They usually flew around with a couple of F-4 Phantoms.

One night the Blackhawk was by himself, and he picked us up with infrared. He radioed the 105 battery guys and gave them our coordinates. The 105s didn't want to fire because they had to actually fire over the base, and they were a little worried about the radio waves from the base radio antenna possibly setting off the artillery rounds. So they didn't—which was good, because it would have been right on top of us.

A mountain close by on the Vietnamese side was called Million Dollar Knoll. I think it got its reputation because the Air Force was dropping a million dollars' worth of bombs on it every day.

One night seven of us went in there. It was triple canopy, and we entered a heavily booby trapped area. We got into the enemy's trenches and were so close we could actually hear them talking, and we stopped. As the sun came up, they were moving out, and we were moving in; we were right behind them. We found all kinds of bunkers. We found a claymore that weighed 55 kilos. In one of these trenches we left a claymore in the bunker, one of those kind that you set the trembler switch—which meant that the mine would detonate if it was picked up.

As we extracted, we got out of the tree line, and they started shooting at us. We were way out, with no place to hide. It seemed like they were taking shots at me; I guess because I had the radio, they assumed I was the most important guy.

We called in the helo and got on the slick and then flew back over that area, firing into the foliage and dropping grenades. Some intelligence we got shortly after that indicated that eight or nine VC ran in that bunker for cover. Obviously, they picked up our claymore: everyone in the bunker was killed.

9

Dwight Dee Daigle

Pointman, 1st Squad, Delta Platoon
Nam Can, Republic of Vietnam,
Deployed January–July 1969

I made three trips to Vietnam. My first deployment was with Underwater Demolition Team 11 to the Danang area, Camp Tien Sha. We had a short stay in the Philippines, where we did some submarine operations. We did river recon and riverine work out of Danang.

After my first deployment, it was back to the Strand in Coronado for SEAL cadre training, then deployment with SEAL Team One to Nha Be in the Rung Sat Special Zone. I stayed overseas for the duration of that tour, then came back to the Strand for more Stateside training in various tactics, then made my third and final deployment to Vietnam with SEAL Team One, Delta Platoon, to the IV Corps area and the Nam Can Forest.

Other men in my platoon were Frank Willis, Phil Martin, Pat Omera, Mike Ambrose, Gerhardt Klann, Rick Solano, Jim Gore, Doc Schrier, Bill Tucker, Gene Peterson, Rick Knepper.

We divided our fourteen-man platoon into two squads, or fire teams, led by Lt. Timothy Wettack and

Lt. Joseph "Bob" Kerrey [Medal of Honor winner, Nebraska governor, and U.S. senator]. Ours was led by Lieutenant Wettack, the OIC of that detachment. Initially, the two squads were in the Cam Ranh Bay area. We ran a couple of operations jointly for a brief period, then we separated. Lieutenant Kerrey's team went up the coast, and our team stayed down in the IV Corps area around the Nam Can Forest.

Our ops in the Nam Can were river ambushes. We inserted on the South China Sea shore from support craft like Coast Guard cutters or LSTs [landing ships, tank] that had a company of Swifts and river boats in tow behind them. We would patrol from an insertion point to a predetermined target. Sometimes we would do a recon, just observe, then get extracted from a predetermined extraction point, on the South China Sea or a river. We made several body snatches, bringing out known Viet Cong and NVA.

We received good but perishable information from *hoi chanhs*. The success of those operations depended on our quick response to the information before everything we heard became old business.

The operations weren't always successful. On one of the unsuccessful body-snatch operations, we made multiple attempts to catch this guy named Bay Tho, who was an NVA training and organizing forces in the U Minh Forest in the Nam Can area. We had good information on him several times, and we were always so close to capturing him. One time we got to a hooch, and his hammock was still swinging. One thing or another always allowed him to get away.

Chickens and ducks were always very vocal when they heard any strange noises or when people came around that they weren't familiar with. The VC didn't have to drag these chickens or ducks around with them; every person in every one of those nipa-palm-hooch villages had a gaggle of fowl with them to live off of. It wasn't anything for Vietnamese people or children to walk among them; they wouldn't ruffle a feather. But any new smell or noise, like a SEAL squad coming through the area, and they'd squawk and scream. It was difficult to patrol in those areas. I think the VC sentries were attuned to listening to the animals—which also made patrolling difficult. The best way to patrol was to catch a bad night of weather. If we patrolled in a lot of rain, we could make the noise we needed to make just to slither through the jungle and get very close to the target without anyone or anything hearing us.

We were on one op where we had information about a weapons cache. We set up our typical hooch-busting perimeter on this one hooch, went in, and got a man and his wife at the supper table. We took them along through VC territory to look for the cache. We didn't get to our objective because we drew enemy fire from a tree line that we had to respond to—which compromised our position. I think it would have been one of our more successful missions had we been able to get to the cache with this guy. He was a hot guy; he knew some stuff. We took him back to let the NILO and Vietnamese work with him. Whatever happened with that information, I don't know. They may have run some Army ops on the info.

I was pointman in our squad. The pointman was basically half of the forward element of the patrol. The pointman and the fire-team officer would be the advance eyes, ears, and nose of a patrolling body of men. The pointman's job was to be a few yards or, depending on the terrain, several hundred yards ahead of the rest of the squad to recon particular danger points—river crossings, open roads, and rice paddies that had open fields of fire. As pointman, I just had to take my time, make judgments on past experiences as a field person, then go back and give the information to the officer to make command decisions on whether to advance, set up perimeters, fall back, initiate fire, or call in artillery.

The safety of the patrol required having everything from rear security to automatic-weaponsmen and radiomen. Everybody couldn't know everything at the same time, out there stomping in the bush. Everything the rest of the patrol needed to know was relayed back down through the line by hand signals, whispers, and body language. Information was everything on a patrol. We relied on our past experiences patrolling, our confidence in our weapons and training, the knowledge of the terrain we received through warning orders and operation briefings, and information from the pointman and officer.

The pointman's weapon was very seldom anything larger than a rifle or a Stoner light machine gun. He also carried a couple of fragmentation grenades, smoke grenades, an illumination flare for nighttime use, a small medical kit, and the basic navigation gear: a compass. We were always on water ops, so we always wore our personal flotation, which was a UDT combat-swimmer chest vest. Most carried Ka-Bar knives. Some people opted for something smaller, but the old basic Ka-Bar were plentiful, free, and they always did the job.

As pointman, I was very intense and focused. Just the fact that I was out there with an automatic weapon and was backed up by experienced people with a like mind-set—I didn't consider myself so much a predator as an analyst and a domineering presence. I was just out there sniffing and smelling and looking and thinking about the terrain, the weather conditions, the enemy, and what information we had about the enemy in the area, and what surprises we might run into.

We were in their backyard; they knew all the tricks. We learned in the early '60s and through early teamwork in Vietnam what the VC were doing to small units. Sometimes we learned the hard way, but using those bits and pieces of information, we trained and learned enough to be able to combat those people in their own backyard, under their rules, and we often came out quite a bit ahead.

I think we succeeded by never taking the easy route in or the easy route back. We were not expected to do certain things or go in certain areas, so that's the way we went—whatever was not the normal route, or the logical, easy approach. Sometimes it was the more time consuming and more vulnerable routes that we took to get in and out. It could be by villages, waterways, known travel routes, or areas where we were outnumbered, areas where we would go in knowing that any contact at all would compromise our chances of getting out. We would go in there just to call in an air strike or to observe enemy movement, and not to make contact with the enemy.

Sometimes we would just sit there on a riverbank during an air strike. They'd be swimming across the river, coming at us in almost total darkness. We'd hear hundreds of people around us, and we were just there because they needed an air strike called in with good coordinates. We certainly didn't want to initiate any kind of action on those ops, because even though we could neutralize several of the enemy in an immediate firefight, it would have been one fight we would not have come back from. It would have been pointless to fight. Sometimes it was better to just check the situation out and come back to that area later.

On a patrol, the ideal situation was for the pointman to encounter the enemy first. That point element was out there, if not to encounter and engage, then to guess where the enemy might be and make some determination as to how to keep the patrol from confronting and finding the enemy where you didn't have any advantage. My experience as a pointman in hearing, seeing, and smelling the enemy first was a great advantage for the firepower and the objective of the mission that was lined up behind me. I felt a great freedom, being out there—where even if what I saw was not that good and didn't have any hope of doing good, at least I saw it first. That seemed to make point a better place than rear security, who just had to act on everything that was happening to him. I liked it out front, I guess because it was special and because pointmen got intense training to keep their skills up. It made me feel confident.

Apparently, it was recognized that good pointmen needed to be constantly operating. That's why we had so many ops in such a short period, and I tried to go on all of them. There were a few I missed because I was out doing something else, like on R&R somewhere. But getting back and going to work always made me feel better.

I grew up in the saltwater marshes and cypress swamps outside of New Orleans—which is a natural waterborne environment. Enjoying it as much as I did when I was a kid helped me understand what to do over in Vietnam, in that primitive, jungle environment. I liked it; it seemed like I wasn't really that far from home. The feeling and empathy I had with my surroundings caused me to enjoy the jungle. To this day, I think I am happiest being in a jungle where the basic needs for living and comfort are all around you for the gathering—and it ain't cold.

We were trained for sentry removal, using a knife. All of the SEAL cadre gave good demonstrations and background information. It was part of the job, just like patrolling properly. I guess you would call it tactical response, or some kind of martial silencing. Call it any kind of thing, but they taught us how to take out the enemy using a knife.

I had occasions to use that training during my first tour in Vietnam with SEAL Team One. One spot report we sent back to the command in Coronado reported four VC killed in action, no rounds expended. It was an operation run jointly with SEAL Team Two in the Nam Can area. We ran it off a large ship, either an LSD [landing ship, dock] or an LST. We were acting on information from a *hoi chanh* about a large weapons cache in a battalion-sized area. A Viet Cong battalion was supposedly massing weapons and explosives for a major offensive. This information came in right at the last moment, that either that same night or the next night, depending on the moon and the weather, the weapons in the cache were going to be moved from a fake well bottom out to their troops.

We went out to get the cache and found out after a patrol that the area this well was in was surrounded by sentries. We quietly took out four sentries and located the well and the weapons. The four people taken out quietly were the ones in the spot report.

My biggest recurring thought about this mission was that even the most fragile, smallest-framed person, once adrenaline is thrust through their veins and pops out of the brain, was capable of great strength and a lot of noise. I found that to be true. The hardest part of the kill was trying to squelch the noise of the thrashing. And it didn't happen fast, not like you might have imagined or how you may have seen it in dramatizations of a knife kill. It took quite a bit of physical overpowering, and then, like a raptor, you had to just sit there until things quieted down. The old story of "go in low and come out high and run to the next one" didn't apply, from my experience.

In training, they taught you to put your thumb up underneath the enemy's jaw to help get the head back, which was fine, but then you'd find out that their jaw was awful close to their teeth, and that was where your thumb would end up most of the time, getting chewed off. The most effective and probably the fastest way was to go for the lungs. Going down through the clavicle area into the chest worked best, unless you could grab and hold them. You also had to hold any kind of area that air could come out of, because that air would be a scream of some kind. Of course, in training, I never had to actually stab through the chest of anybody, so I didn't know exactly how to gauge what velocity and how much thrust to use. In training, we practiced the movement a lot, but they didn't exactly give us somebody to do this to.

So, I was a new guy at all this. Not knowing that the enemy didn't have the beef and mass of a few-hundred-pound GI, I guess I just stabbed a little too hard. The knife went right through the Viet Cong, out his back, and stuck the OIC of my platoon, Lieutenant Freedley, in the knee.

Lieutenant Freedley did not say a word because we were trying to be quiet. He didn't let on that he had about a quarter of a Ka-Bar stuck down in his knee until later on when he told me I shouldn't go around stabbing officers!

I said, "In whose Navy?"

We got some of the weapons out and loaded up the boat. There were just too many to bring out, so we blew up the rest in place. We encountered some ground fire on the way out because the blast had alerted other sentries guarding the area. After all that noise, of course, they were going to move on us, and we were in the midst of extracting.

In our platoons, we weren't really involved with what each other was like as a person as much as what everybody was doing at the moment as far as their preparation for ops, equipment, and job readiness. As long as no one ran amuck and caused personnel or logistical problems, everyone was just fine and didn't give a regard to the pluses or minuses of what they were like.

My recollection of Lieutenant Kerrey was that he was very efficient, very thoughtful, quick-witted, humorous, and a dedicated person toward his men. If he had anything to do about it, he wanted to know that everything, as dangerous as it was, would go as well as it could.

While in Vietnam, some of us became kind of deadened to a lot of immediate, personal emotion. When Kerrey's squad got hit, we all wondered how bad they got whacked, who was still alive, and why it happened—so we didn't do the same thing. It was a very dry reaction. We were grieved by the fact that one of our blood brothers was wounded and in bad shape, but it was sort of, like, you just had to carry on as quickly and as hard and as fast as you could. Of course, we thought about it, we slept with it, ate with it. But it was one of those things—we figured there would be a replacement on the plane in a few days, and we would have to do something about training him.

Good men going down was never something that anyone liked to see, especially us. We'd hear about hundreds of Marines killed at Khe Sanh and think, "Oh shit, that's terrible." But when one SEAL went down, or any Navy man, we took that real personally. I thought about putting it out of my mind until I had the time to worry about it, and that wouldn't be until I got back. It didn't affect our operations at the moment; no one shut down and went into slow mode or anything like that. We were burning up the radio net and the telephone lines to find out just what went on, and we got what information we could. There was anger and frustration about it all.

Kerrey's squad was on an op on Hon Toi Island, a big island in the bay of Nha Trang. Everybody thought just birds roosted on the thing and it was of no real logistical or strategic importance for the North or the South. Since it was just a big rock out in the ocean, it wasn't paid much attention to by anybody—which made it a great meeting place for the NVA and the Viet Cong. They didn't use it often, apparently, because it was still secret. Anytime a place got traveled to too many times, our people would know about it.

From what I understand, the VC massed a group of very important high-level NVA and Viet Cong people on this island. Some word got out about the meeting, and the SEALs took the back door in—which was a very dangerous climb up a tall rock cliff on the ocean side. It was made more difficult because of the pitch-black night, and they were trying to be quiet while climbing with all their ammunition and weapons. When they got up the cliff, they got right to the core of the matter, right into the enemy base camp.

With all the sneaking, peeking around, crawling under people sleeping in hammocks, one thing led to another and someone bumped something, and of course the whole base came to. Illumination went up, and point-blank gunfire was exchanged. Grenades were thrown in the dark, in no particular direction, and were rolling around among everybody. Lieutenant Kerrey was standing too close to one, unknown to him. When it cranked off, it took part of his leg.

The documents and the information and the identification on the Viet Cong and NVA killed in action on that op led the intelligence officers of the U.S. Navy, Army, and the South Vietnamese to believe that this was a real high-powered meeting. It was interrupted that night for sure. I think the next day they went in with a sweep and got some good info. It was typical procedure for a sweeping element to go in and see what had been going on after an operation like this.

One memorable situation during my first tour with SEAL Team occurred on an insertion in the Rung Sat Special Zone. We knew it was a heavily occupied area. We were operating out of Nha Be. One of the best support groups any special-warfare agent could have were the boat groups or the riverine forces, the PBR crews and the Swift boat crews. These guys were totally dedicated and very good at what they did.

We went in on a PBR. The plan required that the boat nose up to the beach—which could be done during high tide. It couldn't be done during low tide because the mud flats kept it off the beach. We were going to sneak right on in.

Equipped on the PBRs for dockside safety was a siren hooked up to the bilge pump. This siren would warn the crew if the boat took on water. Through some oversight, the siren wasn't turned off. As we nosed up to the beach, the bow of the boat pushed up on the mud flats just enough so that the bilge water that was left in the boat rolled back to the sensor on the siren. So there we were, sneaking over the bow, and this siren went off! All of a sudden we heard warning shots, illumination flares went up, and all kinds of hell broke loose.

There was nothing like going out there and saying, "Hey! We're here!" It had nothing to do with the sneaking and peeking of SEAL ops, other than the fact that, holy shit! it was totally unexpected. Something like that could catch you at the most dangerous time of a patrol, which was the insertion, when you were unloading all your people in one place. Then to get compromised so completely and so quickly right there, it was as if they'd had a news crew catch us when we came up on the beach. It was quite a surprise.

I remember a lot of other situations that had to do with engaging the enemy, communicating with my officer and the people in the patrol, the weather and surf conditions on different ops. All of those things are memorable, but that one insertion stuck in my mind as being a real "Aw, shit!"

During our tour in the Nam Can we operated out of a small Vietnamese village at the foot of a waterway system that led into what used to be French colonial farmland. There was a dilapidated iron bridge that was impassable, but we used it as an observation post and a .50-caliber post for the defense of the village. We based some support craft there—the Boston Whalers and some small utility river boats that were armed with machine guns, miniguns, and M-79 grenade launchers. We kept some fuel bladders floating in the river so they'd be low profile and away from any kind of attack. We ran operations out of the village. Sometimes helicopters came in and picked us up, or we'd go up and down the rivers in small boats. On some ops we'd get taken out to the South

China Sea by Swift boats. That was kind of dangerous, though, because the Swift boats had to come upriver to get us, then turn around and go right back down the same river. Of course, every time they did that, we'd get rocketed—which was no big surprise. The VC had B-40s [rockets], and they had homemade water mines that they would drag out in the water and try to crank off. When they saw the boats go in, they knew they had to come back out; the boats weren't going in there to be decommissioned!

Some ops we called administrative, or admin, ops. We loaded up some boats with demolition charges. The area around there was pretty secure during the daytime, so we'd just go right out on the river, sort of like taking a walk in the woods, and plant some charges and blow up a river barricade. The VC placed barricades to slow down river traffic so they could set up ambushes. It was a sort of speed bump. Several nights later, the Viet Cong would swim out there and build up the barricade again. A few days later, we'd go back out and blow it up again.

The hairiest operations were during my first SEAL deployment in the T-10 area, running around the Rung Sat Special Zone. We were definitely outnumbered in there. On one op we were going to observe enemy movement while an Army operation scared up some enemy and got them moving. We had predetermined grid coordinates for the artillery and Navy gunfire. When the VC were in the area, we would initiate the air strikes. A lot of times that backfired on us. We could hear hundreds of people around us. They'd be coming across rivers at us, running away from the Army operation. This happened to several platoons, not just Delta, and in different areas. We would go in to aid large-scale operations and wind up having it all turn around, and the bees would come running back out of the hive at us. We just sank down in the mud and got as low as we could, for as long as we could, and just hoped we weren't seen because we would have to get out of there sooner or later.

. . .

The reason I joined the Navy was for the SEAL program. I had met some of these people in the Gulf of Mexico as professional divers prior to my military enlistment. I was a youngster, and I was tending divers then. I realized that I was facing the military draft in the near future, and I certainly had no intentions of going into the Army, as I had always been a maritime-type person. I was very interested in the program from the stories and the reminiscing the fellows had done, and I thought I'd like to try it. So I joined the Navy.

Back in those days you couldn't just go to a training class by putting in a request; you had to come from the fleet. I served on the *Pritchett* (DD-561), a destroyer. That ship was so old it was the name of a whole class of destroyers, the *Pritchett* class. After putting in as many requests as I could, I got into an Underwater Demolition Team training class. The XO [executive officer] of the destroyer said, "You're no good here; you don't want to be here; go do what you joined the Navy for." He sent me off to the training unit, where I started Class 39.

I knew I wasn't a military career–type person, but I did want this program for what it had to offer me and what I could do for it. The only thing I knew was that I wanted it a lot. I had no guarantee that I would hold up through the training, or that I would not be injured, or that I would not be administratively thrown out by the training department. But I did want to go try it to see what I could do. I made it through the training one day at a time and managed to graduate in Class 39. From there I made overseas deployment with the Teams.

I consider the time in Vietnam very intense, very focused, and very fulfilling at the same time. I enjoyed it; I was afraid of it; it was an exhilarating time, and it was a frustrating time. They didn't really know what to do with us; they were still trying to define our role and our type of operations. We were trying to stay out of trouble when they were actually putting us into trouble. Because we were best in trouble, we worked best in troubled areas. We were elitists; we were in very great shape, very motivated, and sometimes lackadaisical toward the overall military establishment: we were unusual. And I enjoyed being unusual in that kind of way.

I did that for as long as I thought I was a benefit. Then I decided I had been in the military long enough; I couldn't see staying there much longer, running those kinds of risks for my young life, and I wanted to do something else. So after my enlistment was up, I got out. I came back to work in the oil fields, where I had first met these people, working diving operations in the Gulf of Mexico and overseas in the North Sea.

During my years in the Navy, I answered a lot of questions about myself that some young men don't get a chance to do. They might envision what they would do—"would I," "could I," or "if I had the chance." I'm sure not everything I did in the military or in the Teams was totally admirable or commendable in some people's eyes, but there were some basic questions I asked myself that were answered to my satisfaction. I met some of the most dedicated, interesting, and genuine people that I've ever run with in my life—and some of the biggest sons-of-bitches I've ever known too.

I was asked once, what was the worst thing I ever did in Vietnam? I said, "Get there." Then I was asked what was the best thing you ever did in Vietnam? And I said, "Leave."

I got to thinking about it and thought maybe that was reversed. Because I went there first to find out what the story was from the ground up. I went back the second time to try to change it. I went back the third time just to get out; the war just was not working. I wanted to get out one way or another. To get out of the Teams as a full-fledged experienced combatant: work hard and do it right, take my chances. Or go over there and maybe be the odd card out and get killed, which happened a lot in those days.

You didn't know; there was no guarantee. I just wanted to do as many ops as I could. If I was lucky enough, I'd come back and say, "Gee, that was one hell of a deal; I was a lucky guy." And to this day, I am a lucky guy.

10

Louis McIntosh

Grenadier, 1st Squad, Echo Platoon
Sa Dec and Moc Hoa,
Republic of Vietnam,
Deployed February–August 1969

I never really felt I was ready to go to Vietnam, although we did lots of training out in the desert and up in Vallejo in the swamps. We had six months of workup, but I felt there was something missing in my training; I just didn't feel sharp enough. I've often thought about it since then, and I think that if you are going in on a specific mission, you train for that one mission and know every move you will make. That's what I think was missing with our training at the time: we didn't have the specifics of what we were going to do. We just did general training—like, here's how you set up a claymore, here's how you set up an ambush. I guess I wanted more specific training before we left. Don't get me wrong on this: it was excellent training overall.

On our first patrol at Sa Dec, we went out with some members of Alpha Platoon. We were bright eyed and bushy tailed; we were on edge—hair-trigger. But we were in a pacified area, and the patrol was just to help take the edge off.

Our platoon was at Sa Dec/Vinh Long and the Moc

Hoa area before being sent down to Cat Lo, which was near the river access to Saigon. The VC were hitting the merchant ships that came up the river, so we were sent to curtail that activity.

Once the VC knew the SEALs were in a particular area, and we had a couple of kills in that area, the VC were smart enough not to go in that area again. The VC knew that if the SEALs were around, they were going to get their asses handed to them. They would go clear around our area, like they were thinking, "The Men with Green Faces, we can't deal with them. They're sneakier than we are. They could be anywhere." Every time our boats came up the river, the VC knew the SEALs were out there somewhere, so they wouldn't move. We had to start making fake insertions so the VC didn't know if we were really there or not.

We had an LSSC, which was very fast. It was designed specifically for SEAL missions and was perfect for the types of operations we ran. Get into trouble fast, get out of trouble fast. You could only take nine people in it; it wouldn't get up on step if you took one body more.

Not far from Cat Lo was Vung Tao, which was the R&R port for everybody in Vietnam, including the VC. The VC didn't bomb or mortar Vung Tao very much. Everybody was just there to have a good time, the enemy along with the good guys. We roamed the beaches and through the streets, and the VC had opportunities to kick ass, but they didn't.

The regular Aussies and New Zealanders had a low-lying camp just up the road from us at Nui Dat. The Australian 3d SAS Squadron was up on a hill overlooking everything. The whole base had a fence around it, and the grass was cut back from the perimeter—giving them a clear field of fire.

They never let any Vietnamese into their camp; it didn't matter if it was the South Vietnamese president himself. They didn't have Vietnamese scouts; they didn't have Vietnamese interpreters; not even Vietnamese maids. The Aussies were smart that way. Unlike American base camps, where there were Vietnamese everywhere, the Aussies' SAS rarely got hit from the outside. Due to the fact that the VC had no insiders in the SAS camp, their operations never got compromised.

Eventually, the Australian SAS extended an invitation for us to come up and work with them. Our pointman, Mike Emerson, was the first to go up and patrol with them. We had just gotten the Stoner light machine gun with the short barrel, and he took his with him. The Aussies loved that weapon because of its light weight and the firepower it could deliver.

The Aussies were real big on separating the enlisted men from the NCOs. So we sort of lied to them about our rank; we told them we were E-4 or E-5 NCOs [third- and second-class petty officers, respectively]. That way, we didn't have to stay with the "blokes"; we could stay with the sergeants, who had better quarters.

The Aussies had odd-numbered patrols, usually nine men. They patrolled real slow and quiet, and they always stopped for tea. At ten o'clock in the morning and at two o'clock in the afternoon, teatime! Whether or not they needed it, they stopped and took out their little stove and canteen cups. Of course, they had to have big backpacks because they stayed out for nine or ten days at a time. They also all carried a Syrette of morphine on their dog tags, and each of the Aussies carried a claymore mine. All they did on their patrols was gather intel and send it back by Morse code. They practiced Morse code every day.

During a patrol, they would observe the hardcore North Vietnam regulars as they came down the trails. They'd watch their movements, direction, and note which days they moved. Then they would know, for instance, that a particular guy always traveled a certain trail on a certain day. At the end of a nine-day patrol they would pick their target of opportunity. And when they blasted somebody, they really blasted them.

One day the SAS set up their claymores and waited for one guy they targeted to come down a trail. When they initiated the ambush, the force of the explosion from the mines slammed the guy's AK-47 rifle into his chest. They had to literally pull it out of him. They loved that American claymore.

The Aussies were excellent as far as their discipline, quietness on patrol, and professionalism. I think we learned a lot from them in that regard.

There was a time when we weren't getting any kills or fresh intel, so we decided to try something new. We went down the Mekong River to a Vietnamese base camp and conducted a daylight sweep with the Vietnamese Army. They didn't want any Americans killed on their watch: it looked bad, you know—the Asians are into saving face—so they put us in the middle of their big *V*-formation.

We patrolled all day with them through the rice paddies. We searched a hole that a VC was supposedly in and found a grenade and a belt. It was getting dark, and the Vietnamese officer seemed nervous because he knew VC were in the area. He said their mission was complete and intended to head back to their base. We said we would have our boat extract us from where we were.

We stayed in the area and set up around this one hooch. However, we committed a tactical error—Rocky, Black Mac, and I crossed a stream. Now we were separated: we were on one side of the stream, and the main group was on the other.

Our squad was setting up for a late lunch of C-rats when we heard a burst of machine-gun fire. Rocky was eating with his Stoner lying across his lap.

All of a sudden this VC came up the trail, right smack dead in front of Rocky. The guy was armed with an old M-1 carbine. Rocky dropped his can of C-rats, grabbed his

Stoner, took it off safe, and zipped the guy up from the right hip to his left shoulder. He fell over the bank of the river next to where Rocky was.

Another VC had been a little farther behind the first one. Rocky shot at him, and he fell behind a tree.

We knew we had one confirmed kill, our first, and another possible kill. We took a gun and a belt with some American grenades off the dead VC.

Not long after, another VC came up from behind us, across a rice paddy. He had his carbine on his shoulder, and we watched as he walked right up on us. We yelled, "Stop" in Vietnamese, but he reached for his gun.

Rocky zipped him across the chest with his Stoner, which then jammed on a tracer round. Rocky yelled, "I've got a jam!"

The VC went down but got back up and started running through the banana trees. I immediately jumped up out of the hole with my M-16/XM-148, and that's when my quick-kill training came in. I shot the running VC in the right shoulder with the M-16, and he fell down in between some banana trees. I put two 40-mm grenades from the XM-148 over in the area to make sure he was dead. So that was a second kill for us.

Since we had our claymores set up, we just stayed there next to the stream. I was sitting in a little mud-hole area where sampans could be pulled out of the stream so they wouldn't float away in the main current.

Night came upon us, and sure as shit, here they come creeping up on us. Rocky threw a grenade, but it was a dud and didn't go off.

Black Mac said, "Give me one of your grenades." He threw that one out, which went off OK, but the second one he threw hit a tree and bounced back in our hole.

I looked back at Black Mac, and he was out of there—he was gone.

It was all slushy mud where we were, and all I had time

to do was just fall down, away from the area where the grenade landed. I just lay there; it was the longest five seconds of my life.

The grenade went off, and the blast threw mud up in the air. The mud was falling down through the trees as Black Mac came running back to see if I was hit. I told him I was fine—it was just the mud falling, not me!

Eventually, we shot up the area with the M-60, lit off the claymores, and extracted by boat.

On one op we inserted during the day to set up a night ambush. When we were part of the way to the ambush site, we stopped and ate lunch. We started to set up the perimeter under some bamboo, and I looked up and saw a deadly bamboo viper. Black Mac didn't like snakes, so we moved and set up a perimeter near the canal. We had claymores on the side where Rocky Cochlin was. He was sitting near one of the places where the local people pulled their sampans in.

Pretty soon, here came two VC in a sampan; they pulled right in there next to us. We were sitting there looking at them, but they had no idea we were there. I was up on the other side of the perimeter. The way they pulled up, so nonchalantly, not even realizing we were there, it looked like they were supposed to be with us.

Cochlin whispered, "Are these guys with us?"

We said, "No! Shoot 'em!"

We started shooting at the two VC as they ran through the jungle. You know which direction we were shooting? Right toward the main river. We didn't know it, but just as we were shooting, a Navy boat was cruising by. Of course, they thought they were being ambushed by VC and opened fire toward the shoreline.

We didn't know what happened; it seemed like the world just opened up on us. We thought we must have been on the edge of a VC base camp. Fifty-caliber bullets were coming in everywhere, buzzing by our heads. Big tree limbs were falling all around us. Black Mac figured out what was going on, radioed the boat to cease fire, and had us cease fire.

The Navy boat had swept from the left flank to the right flank, firing about two hundred rounds of .50-caliber ammo. Those bullets from our own boats almost tore us up. That was one of those situations you could never train for; it just happened.

The LDNN that was with us shot holes in the bottom of the sampan. By shooting in one spot he created a big hole in it. If you shot a bunch of little holes all over the boat, they would just swell and close up, and that sampan could be used again.

In the end it turned out we had killed one VC and wounded the other. We got a whole backpack full of intel from the one dead VC. It had a lot of propaganda leaflets and a set of American dog tags in it. We gave it to the NILO, and he was in high heaven. Of course, we never really got any intel back from him, except that the guy we killed was a high-ranking VC cadre instructor.

The worst thing that ever happened to me was when I was crossing a river. The tide was out, and I was down in the mud, carrying the M-60, and I sank in up to my waist. I could not lift my leg up for anything. The pointman and radioman had already made it across. The rest of the patrol was behind me, and they wanted the machine gun up toward the front. I whispered, "I'm stuck! I'm stuck! I can't get out."

Guess what they replied? "We got movement up here!"

I was thinking, "Great. I'm going to be shot here like a damn sitting duck."

But whoever was out in front of us must not have seen us because they finally left, and my teammates came and got me out of the mud.

• • •

I think the SEAL experience in Vietnam was significant. We were the only ones fighting the war the way it should have been fought: guerrilla warfare against guerrilla warfare. The units sweeping across rice paddies were just moving targets. If we could have trained enough people quickly, and sent them out to operate in small groups the way we did, we could have really played havoc on the VC and NVA. That's how they were doing it to us. We had the big-ass Army, we had the mobility, and they were kicking ass on us.

The SEALs figured that if the enemy wanted to play that way, then we could play that way too. We went out there and put the fear of God into them. We were out in the jungle at midnight, just seven Americans. The VC could never believe there were Americans out in the jungle at night. They knew Americans liked to travel in large groups. They figured, "We'll hear them coming; we'll tear them up." But we realized, as long as you kept your mouth shut, they didn't know who was out there.

We set up an ambush one night and could hear the VC a mile upriver. They were coming down, making all kinds of noise. The myth was that the VC moved like the shadows of the night. That was pure bullshit. They sounded like a bunch of turkeys gobbling.

Vietnam is where SEAL Team made its name. The SEAL Teams of today are being trained on the guerrilla warfare experiences from Vietnam. They are losing it as fast as they lose us, the Vietnam vets.

They have a saying, "Vietnam is over; it's dead."

And I say, "Yeah? Well, you're living on the reputations of dead men."

You never know where in the world guerrilla warfare will pop up. We learned a lot of lessons in Vietnam—lessons we paid for in blood.

11

Garry "Abe" Abrahamson

Provincial Reconnaissance Unit Adviser
Bac Lieu, Republic of Vietnam,
Deployed Summer 1969–February 1970

My first deployment to Vietnam in 1968 was with Alpha Platoon. We were initially stationed aboard the *YRBM-18*, anchored where the Ham Luong River and the Mekong River fork. Our platoon was extremely fortunate to have Barry Enoch as its lead petty officer. Barry was one of the original SEALs selected in 1962, when SEAL Team One was first organized. At this time Barry Enoch was already an unsung hero in the SEAL Team for his early accomplishments in Vietnam. Once again, he was in Vietnam with eleven green SEALs, who were fresh out of training and had not yet experienced combat. His job was to mold us young SEALs into a combat-ready team that could handle all the challenges that would confront us.

The city of Ben Tre was located east of us. A SEAL Team One operator, Frank Bomar, was the adviser of the PRU at Ben Tre. The PRUs he advised respected him, and he earned their loyalty. Frank was responsible for my first experience with PRU operations. He used Alpha Platoon on several operations against high-echelon Viet Cong infrastructure cadre. He was a very keen and shrewd PRU adviser, and while operating with him, we all gained knowledge on tactics and maneuvers.

I remember one particular operation. Bomar had contacted Barry Enoch from Ben Tre. We were aboard the *YRBM-18,* and he advised Enoch that he needed "X" number of players for a baseball game [codeword for an operation]. Enoch asked for volunteers to assist Bomar with his operation and received a sufficient number of SEALs for the op. I happened to be one of the volunteers.

We left the *YRBM-18* for Ben Tre around 9:00 P.M. that evening aboard the "Old Blacksheep." She was an old diesel-burning, slow boat that chugged down the river, but she was reliable. It was a long, straight road from the river to the city of Ben Tre, where the PRU compound was located. A jeep driven by Bomar picked up Enoch. The rest of the SEALs loaded up in a pickup and proceeded behind the jeep.

We had no more than left the pier and were traveling down a dimly lit road, when we heard a click; but nothing happened. We proceeded on into the compound.

Once in the compound, we began our operational briefing, and Bomar brought up the fact that he had heard a click during our ride from the pier to the PRU compound. After some discussion, he and Enoch thought that it might have been a command-detonated claymore, and the click was the detonating device. Evidently, the detonating device was defective and failed to trigger the explosive. Upon conclusion of our briefing, we left the compound on foot.

We crossed over the main canal that ran north and south by Ben Tre and proceeded eastward. There were nine SEALs and perhaps fifteen or twenty PRUs in Bomar's group. Our target was a VC village chief and a VC tax collector. The tax collector would come to this large market area and meet with the village chief to collect taxes from the marketers. We patrolled along the canal to the target area and crossed over a little monkey bridge (this reference comes from how the Vietnamese would wrap their bare feet, resembling monkey's feet, around a thin bamboo pole that had been placed as a means for crossing a narrow canal) and then proceeded into the village, where we set up an L-shaped ambush.

The market area consisted of a concrete slab and was covered by a thatched roof. All the villagers would buy and sell their vegetables, livestock, poultry, and other wares there. Bomar and the rest of the PRUs set up a position along the northern edge in an empty hooch. The rest of us SEALs strung out along the western side of the open-air-market square, inside a livestock-stall area. We were concealed behind thatched walls and made little peepholes through the thatch in order to see the market area and routes to and from it. From the western side of the market square we could see the hooch where Bomar was located.

We had an ID [identification] on the targeted VC individuals, and they were supposed to be accompanied by several armed guards. The force with them were supposed to be carrying AK-47s, plus various other weaponry, so it wasn't going to be difficult to identify the targets once they entered the village. We knew our targets and were ready for the opportunity to pay our taxes and give our best wishes for a prosperous day.

It was predawn when the Vietnamese people began gathering in the marketplace, as was their daily routine. By daybreak there were numerous Vietnamese preparing their goods, socializing with one another, and wandering around.

Bomar's empty hooch location was quite popular with the villagers. The people were going into the hooch, but not coming out. As the people entered the hooch they were being detained. The PRUs were tying them up and gagging them. They were then made to sit in the back of the hooch for their safety. The activity at the hooch continued for quite some time. It was later determined that this particular hooch was some type of store. By 0730 hours the hooch was filling up, and Bomar had too many villagers to handle.

Bomar made the decision to break ambush and return to Ben Tre. He walked out of the hooch, towering at six foot four inches tall, a massive body taking up 240 pounds of space, with a darkened face, wearing tiger stripes and followed by several smaller Vietnamese dressed in black pajamas carrying M-16 rifles, M-79 grenade launchers, and radios. The villagers were focused on what was happening around the hooch, watching in amazement.

Bomar signaled to us to break ambush. From behind the thatched walls emerged nine Navy SEALs, collapsing the wall and resembling "demons from hell." We wore camouflaged clothing, with black and green painted faces, carried Stoner machine guns, M-60 machine guns, and M-16 rifles with XM-148 grenade launchers.

Startled by this sight, the villagers appeared to be frail, fearful, and confused at such an unusual occurrence. I do believe, at that point in time, that if anyone had a serious health condition among the villagers, there would have been several KIAs without a shot being fired.

As a protective measure, the much shorter PRUs started encircling Bomar, attempting to enclose the space this "bear of a man" occupied, and on his signal moved out of the village in a manner much like a fine-tuned SEAL platoon. They were followed by us nine "demons from hell."

Barry Enoch and I took up rear security and were going to leapfrog back to protect the rear. We no more than crossed a monkey bridge when we began receiving some small-arms fire. I don't think they knew where we were or the direction in which we were going, so they were reconning by fire. There were several sharp cracks around us, and Enoch and I dropped to the ground. Our mission was to protect the main body of men, so we moved off the trail and waited to see if anyone would follow.

Well, unbeknownst to us, the main body had broken into a run and had gone several hundred yards down the canal. Enoch and I finally moved out, leapfrogging back to the main group. After regrouping, we patrolled out of the target area and continued back to the PRU compound. We debriefed and later that day returned to the *YRBM-18*.

During my deployment with Alpha Platoon, the PRU adviser in Can Tho was wounded. One of my officers received a message to send up a couple of individuals to take over the PRU program there. So Harlin Funkhouser, nicknamed "Funk," and I were selected and sent as temporary advisers, to keep the program functioning. A lot of the PRUs were converted VC.

Harlin and I worked with the PRUs in Can Tho on numerous occasions and used several different means to deploy an operation. On the majority of the ops we mainly deployed by truck. Once we got as far as we could by vehicle, we off-loaded and proceeded on foot to the target area. On other occasions we would use what was called Ka-Bar packages—which involved helicopters: slicks, gunships, and a communications helicopter.

During my time with the PRUs, ther was another adviser. We would split up on a Ka-Bar operation and take two teams in. The other adviser would take in a team of about fourteen as a blocking force, and I would have a team of about the same size that would sweep through the target area, depending on what the target consisted of. We were trying to drive the enemy into the blocking force.

A lot of times on Ka-Bar packs we were operating during the day, and we were faced with a hot LZ [landing zone under fire]. We would send the gunships in first to lay down a base of fire that would get everybody in the bunkers; keeping their heads down was the idea. Right behind the gunships, depending on how many sweeps they made and

Barry Enoch with Vietnamese child in Hai Yen.
Courtesy of Chip Maury

Bob Henry wearing his short shotgun in a custom-made holster during his first tour in Vietnam.

John Fietsch *(front row, right)* with members of Juliett Platoon in front of a situation map.

Joe DeFloria in Ben Tre during 1970.

Philip L. "Moki" Martin with his Stoner outside the SEAL barracks in Nha Be.

Steve Frisk and John Ware *(right)* ready to go out on an op.

Mike Beanan
and Garry "Abe"
Abrahamson of
Alpha Platoon,
with Darryl
"Willy" Wilson
on board the USS
Weiss.

Paul Lee Pittman
in Vinh Gia.

Dwight Dee Daigle as a pointman in Vietnam.

Louis McIntosh sitting in the door of a Huey. A Stoner machine gun is leaning against a crate in the foreground.

Garry "Abe" Abrahamson in Rach Gia, 1970.

Skip Crane *(second from left)* with members of Kilo Platoon.

Hal Kuykendall *(left),* Mike Thornton, and Mike Lacaze in Long Phu.

Jim La Vore, Tom Leonard *(center),* and "Kit Carson" scout clean captured AK-47s in Rach Soi.
Courtesy of Jim La Vore

Kirby "Danny" Horrell *(lower left)* with members of Foxtrot Platoon.

Jim Day in Sa Dec with his Stoner in 1970.

Paul Lee Pittman on board a YRBM during his first deployment to Vietnam.

Echo Platoon, 1969. *Top row:* Rocky Cochlin, Gilbert "Espi" Espinoza, John Marsh, and Bill Noyce. *Bottom row:* LDNN An Lac, Lou Hyatt, and LDNN Nguyen.

Courtesy of Lou Hyatt

Dodd Coutts turns to engage VC running out of the tree line.

Lt. Cdr. Joe DeFloria
(left) talking with
members of SEAL
Team Two at Ben Tre.

Jim Berta as an LDNN
adviser in Long Phu.

Eddie Farmer and Bill Hill *(right)* in Hoi An.

what kind of hostile fire they received, the slicks with the PRUs would come in, and the operation would begin.

Sometimes on a sweep operation we were after enemy documents. Those were much larger operations. There were more than one hundred PRUs working in Can Tho. One hundred forty pops into my mind, but I couldn't say for sure. Usually, a PRU group would vary from eighty to over one hundred men. So this was a relatively large group of PRUs in Can Tho.

When we operated by truck we usually had a specific target, possibly a member of the VC infrastructure. Most PRUs had converted from VC guerrillas so they could have their families in the camps with them and wouldn't have to worry about their families being hurt or molested by the VC. They also didn't have to worry about constantly hiding from the Americans or whoever. So it was a good program for them, and they received some training and political indoctrination. They had to meet certain qualifications before they were even entered into the program.

The rumor at the time was that the PRUs were run by the CIA. There are things that you read today, and some of the scuttlebutt in-country at the time referred to us as "plumbers"—which basically meant we worked for the CIA. But we were military people, not CIA.

In fact, on one Ka-Bar operation, the slicks had picked us up near Can Tho. "Funk" took one team, approximately twenty-one PRUs, in three slicks. I took another team of PRUs of the same strength. The targets of the operation were a VC village chief and a small group of VC guards.

The gunships, spotter ship, and communications choppers lifted off and got airborne about ten minutes ahead of us. The gunships pulled in over the target village, which was a known VC village, laying down suppression fire and receiving small-arms fire in return. Funkhouser's team went in to the target area, off to my team's right. All six choppers went in at the same time, dispersing all the ground forces.

The two forces were separated by approximately 150 meters. Both forces formed into skirmish lines and moved toward the village through high elephant grass and water. I had a radioman and interpreter with me. We moved a few feet when the PRUs around me opened fire into the high grass and began yelling commands. A few moments later a VC stood up, bleeding from his forehead and bottom lip. This person had been grazed by gunfire. He was taken prisoner, tied, and handed over to the prisoner handlers.

We continued into the village and began our sweep and search of the hooches from left to right. We were to move toward "Funk's" team, link up with him, clean up all activities, and prepare to move to an extraction point. However, upon reaching the village, we began receiving small-arms fire from the opposite side of the canal. Fire support from the helicopter gunships was called for. Smoke was popped, the color identified by the pilots, and the gunships rolled in. The small-arms fire was suppressed, and the PRUs continued with their search for VCI, documents, and booby traps. Needless to say, all three were found, mostly booby traps. The VC had booby trapped the monkey bridges, boxes of documents, and even some of the food caches.

The captured prisoners were field interrogated without success. Both teams linked up, and we extracted by helicopter.

Aboard the slick I was sitting next to a young Army door gunner. I had all these indigenous troops with me, and he said to me, "What does it take to be a mercenary?" I couldn't have been more than two or three years older than him, and he thought I was a trained mercenary, doing this for a living.

He didn't know I was a SEAL because we didn't wear any insignia that designated our rank or service. On occasion we'd get scruffy with a beard and all, but the best thing to do in-country was to stay clean shaven, blend in with the rest of the troops. If they saw a hairy face out there, they'd know there was something going on. So we tried to be pretty clean shaven when we were working with indigenous troops.

"Funk" and I worked with the Can Tho PRUs for a month to six weeks, until SEAL Team Two brought in another adviser to relieve us. Once an adviser arrived, we returned to Alpha Platoon, which had been assigned to a small complex in Sa Dec, to finish out our deployment.

When Alpha Platoon's tour was over in January 1969, we returned to the States. After a short deployment to Taiwan, I reported for formal special-operations cadre training. The Special Operations Training course consisted of studying foreign and domestic weaponry, a portion of the Vietnamese language, and intelligence operations: how to gain intelligence and how to set up intelligence networks, and who to employ and deploy for intelligence gathering. We learned about various military facilities where we could gain access to maps and to corroborate our intelligence to make sure it was good information, to make sure we weren't getting false information from our field intel workers. If they came back and told us something, we would corroborate it, verify it, then work on it or forget about it.

PRUs targeted nonmilitary targets. Their targets concerned the VCI. PRU operations or missions were supposed to be assigned by Vietnamese authorities, but things happened—simply meaning, SEALs used their resources, imaginations, and expertise when developing targets. I remember one of the first things we were told as SEALs was that "the key to ingenuity is flexibility." Therefore, as a PRU adviser, all aspects of our training were put to the test. Believe me, it worked!

We learned about the VC infrastructure, how the government within the VCI was set up, who knew who, who didn't know who. If we were going to interrogate someone from a lower echelon, we knew he would only be able to take us up to a certain level because of the compartments within the structure. So the higher ranked prisoner you could capture, the better it was because he could take us either upward or downward to a point. Again, we were then cut off because of the different pockets or cells within the structure.

VCI were grouped into three categories: A-members in command, B-members not in command but could take command, and C-volunteers, or nonvolunteers, not in command.

The time frame for turning the various classifications of VCI over to the proper authorities varied. All district-level VCI and NVA prisoners had to be taken to the Province Officer in Charge [POIC]. Levels A and B had to be turned over within twenty-four hours. C-level would be held by the PRUs for forty-eight hours. All VCI could be interrogated by the PRUs during this period. PRU advisers assigned to a PRU unit had to make a statement in front of the PRU chief, all the PRU team leaders, and at least one American, that no force would be used during an interrogation. PRU advisers had many rules to follow; however, "the key to ingenuity is flexibility."

Harlin and I deployed again shortly after training to Bac Lieu, in the southeastern part of Vietnam on the southeastern seaboard. We went there in the summer of '69 and took over the PRU program from another Navy SEAL Team One operator, Clarence Betts. Clarence had operated with the PRUs in Bac Lieu for the past several months; he was familiar with the operational area, personnel, and all the important information necessary to get "Funk" and me off on the right foot. Clarence remained in Bac Lieu to familiarize "Funk" and me in the operational procedures as related to the Vinh Loi district, Bac Lieu Province.

The PRU program was basically set up as a paramilitary unit. Clarence introduced us to the PRU chief, team leaders, and the other PRUs. We inventoried all records, supplies, and inspected the PRU compound. We examined the fortification of both the PRU compound and the Province House.

The Province House was an individual compound that housed the Province senior adviser, his staff, and the PRU advisers. The Province House had its own security force, many of which were from different backgrounds and cultures. The PRU advisers were responsible for the security of both compounds and their personnel. It was extremely important to maintain proper security and develop an effective intelligence network.

Another responsibility the PRU advisers inherited was the smooth operation of the Province House. We would take over anything that needed to be done, whether it had to do with entertainment, security of the compound, or making sure there was plenty of food.

PRU advisers wore civilian clothing the majority of the time and were believed to be civilians by many military personnel.

On occasion, we would schedule an Air America helicopter for transportation to and from various locations. Sometimes I would schedule a chopper and fly south to Seafloat to visit the SEAL Team One members there. Seafloat was a group of U.S. Navy barges that floated in the middle of the Cua Lon River, west of Nam Can, in An Xuyen Province. I dressed in civilian clothing and carried a briefcase full of various types of liquor; the preferred "flavor" was gin. No, this shipment was not for the purpose of partying with my fellow SEAL brothers, but to replenish the kitchen pantry of the Province House. I also carried two or three mail sacks in order to smuggle my soon-to-be-obtained goods aboard the Air America chopper for the return flight to Bac Lieu.

I traded with the Seafloat company cooks—my liquor for several gallon cans of fruits and vegetables, plus at least a case of steaks; occasionally, the cooks would throw in a case of lobster tails. The Air America flights were always prosperous.

·   ·   ·

We spent a lot of time with the PRUs, sometimes spending long hours and several days. It was just "Funk" and me with a large group of Vietnamese, and to a certain extent our welfare depended on them. Earlier on in the PRU program it was probably pretty scary being the only Americans. The advisers at that time probably didn't really know what they were getting into. The PRU program was pretty much fine-tuned by the time I got involved. Of course, we had people killed and had to go out and recruit new people to take their places. We had to make sure that we stayed up to strength, but at the same time we could pretty much trust the men in the field.

Even though we didn't have a common language, we still communicated quite well. We used pidgin English, a little mixture of everything. An interpreter was available, but not on every mission. We tried to take one on most missions just in case something really bad happened and we had to communicate; or in case I got hit, I needed someone else to call in the medevac or gunships, someone to take my place for the support part of the mission. Basically, that was really what our function was, to ensure the safety of the PRUs. They knew that we had to be there for their well-being, and so it was kind of a trade-off. If something happened to us and they got in a world of trouble, then they were dead meat too. So they wanted us there, and they protected us pretty well. Especially if it was necessary for us to call in gunships or artillery fire.

Before we'd go out on an operation, the commanders and squad leader would decide what the target would be, how big a force we needed—all the regular military things. As advisers to the PRUs, we'd all sit down to plan everything out. They might have a way of wanting to do something, and we would say, "No, this other way would be better." So we had our input, but we just had to do it diplomatically, and it usually wasn't in front of the subordinates, just the higher echelon.

In Bac Lieu we specifically targeted the VC infrastructure. The PRUs had been used to carrying out intel operations on foot, by boat, or by any other means of transportation necessary to get the job done. "Funk" managed to procure nine brand-new Honda 90 motor scooters. We instantly put these scooters into operation. In fact, we had an influx of volunteers to run intel ops.

Our intel people would leave and remain gone for several days. "Funk" and I were curious why these individuals were taking so long to gather intel that could not be corroborated. We found that our intel workers were volunteering for these missions simply to visit family members in other provinces. In reality, all they were doing was getting a paid vacation.

We began weeding out the volunteers. When someone volunteered to go into a certain area, we started checking around the camp to find out if the person had family in that area. We kept dossiers on each individual: what his status was, where he came from, was he previously an NVA officer or Viet Cong regular, or perhaps a member of the VC infrastructure.

We started receiving information that there were three U.S. POWs being held in an area along the seacoast, north of Bac Lieu. Harlin had already gone back to the U.S. by this time, which left me all by myself with the PRUs. I started coordinating the info I was gathering with the info available through the other intel agencies, and it looked like we were getting some pretty hot stuff. The information looked reliable. Apparently, these POWs had been there for a long time. We talked it over with the senior adviser, told him what we had, and that we were really interested in going in to see if we could liberate these three POWs.

We didn't exactly know what branch of the service they were in. We assumed they were Army, but we weren't sure.

They could have been Navy guys, from some PBR boats, or even Australians. But when a Vietnamese saw individuals with round eyes, immediately they were Americans. So the intel we had said they were Americans.

We made arrangements with the Navy for support and requested PBR boats; what we got were Swift boats. A new Swift-boat skipper in-country received the assignment. I think he saw it as an opportunity to make a name for himself. Then again, I don't think he really knew exactly what the operation was all about. It was kept so quiet, so hush-hush, that he might not have even known what kind of op we were going on.

We loaded up two Swifts and started downriver. We inserted and got no more than seventy-five yards inland when all hell broke loose. Two of the PRUs were killed and eight wounded in a matter of seconds.

What got us was the trails had water puddles on them, and the VC had put trip devices under the water on the trails. Our point element got hit immediately, and we could not suppress the enemy fire. It seemed to me we probably had fifty PRUs on that operation, and we still could not suppress fire. We couldn't even see where they were shooting at us from. We medevaced the casualties out and cleared out of the area.

We ran intel back into that area for several months and never received anything, so our assumption was that they had moved the POWs north out of the area. I don't know if the operation had been compromised or not. I never received information that it was. But, obviously, something or someone had to have been there. I had been on so many operations with PRUs, with really good intel, and I never had hit a security force of that strength before. When I was with a SEAL platoon, we hit battalions that didn't have a security group set up like these people had.

You have to remember that at the time Vietnam was going through the Vietnamization program. The U.S. was starting to turn all the programs over to the Vietnamese. Even the PRU commander at Bac Lieu was a regular Vietnamese Army officer—which was very unusual. Usually, a PRU commander was an individual that had clout or status as a Viet Cong in the past. He had that leadership ability to know how to control his men. All the PRUs still worked in that VC guerrilla operational-type mode in their patrolling and with their habits. They were a military unit, but they didn't have the same discipline and the same training as a regular military unit. Seeing these tactics was another interesting aspect to being an adviser with them.

The PRU was basically an intelligence-gathering group. We gathered intel and then executed missions based on the intel gathered. On several occasions we turned over some of the information we gathered—for instance, on a target area—to a regular Army agency. They would react on the intel we gathered and send U.S. troops or whoever to the particular target that we had developed.

We worked with the Phoenix program [CIA/MACV-run operation to neutralize VCI]. MACV kept the intelligence in a central location and tracked the advisers within the country, within the Mekong Delta, or within the IV Corps, which consisted of sixteen provinces. There were perhaps two advisers in each province, so thirty-two advisers was a pretty large advisory group. MACV had other SEALs that worked as civilians to assist the adviser in the field with logistic needs. Whatever kind of support we needed, such as air transportation to and from a location, MACV could schedule a flight, and they took care of the necessary paperwork.

We went on operations to capture targeted individuals. On Ka-Bar packages, we'd go in and get known VC as prisoners and get their documents. With those people, we'd do a short interrogation in the field. If the individual would not cooperate with our people in the field, then we would take him back and turn him over to the proper authorities, and they would possibly send him back to MACV for further interrogation. But if we could get any additional information from them in the field interrogation, like possibly another target of opportunity within a two-klick area that we could walk to, we would patrol in and hit that target. If the guy had intel, we could run with it.

The PRUs would do the interrogation, not me, and turn the intel over to me. It would then go to the commander, and he would discuss with me the value of the information they had developed. Being the adviser and sometimes having to take charge of the situation, I'd have to find out what we would really be walking into and decide if it would be better to back off at this point and regroup. Maybe we would gather additional information and go in to hit the target at a later date, or go ahead with what we had. That was the adviser's position, to analyze or evaluate the situation and see if it was really worth the risks.

I had spent Christmas of '68 and Christmas of '69 with the PRUs in Vietnam.

After my second tour I returned to the States in February 1970 and was there less than twenty-four hours! I went from Travis Air Force Base to SEAL Team One in Coronado, California, mustered at eight o'clock that morning, and was on a flight back to Vietnam that afternoon.

On this third tour I was with Delta Platoon in Rach Soi. Lt. Mel Hetzer was the OIC, and Lt. John Shortt was the second in command of the platoon. I spent four or five months with Delta Platoon. In Rach Soi the platoon was split up into two groups. One group was working northwesterly out of Rach Gia, and Lieutenant Hetzer's fire team was located in Rach Soi, east of Rach Gia.

The changing times in Vietnam made it a hard place to operate. It was hard to clear targets. It was hard to gather intelligence. No one would give you any intelligence because everything was starting to come under South Vietnamese control. Everything was being Vietnamized.

Lieutenant Hetzer felt a need for the development of a "Kit Carson" squad to assist the SEALs in Rach Soi. A Navy chief that had been with the PRU program for a long time and who had been an instructor at the Special Operations Training course showed up in Rach Soi. He knew I had advised the PRUs in the past and had worked with Barry Enoch and some of the other advisers on my first tour over in '68. Most of Delta Platoon were fresh, new guys that had just come out of training, formed their platoon, and come to Vietnam to get some experience and work together as a SEAL platoon. The need was there to develop some kind of intel source to assist the SEALs and perhaps develop some targets for them to work on.

We started visiting the *chieu hoi* ["open arms"] centers [for enemy soldiers who wished to surrender] and talking with various individuals and put together a group of six or seven "Kit Carson" scouts [former VC] to use. Two of them were known VC sappers. These were the bomb-carrying, sacrifice-your-body type of guys—the ones that would jump in a bunker with U.S. troops and blow everything up. We recruited them, and they went to work as "Kit Carson" scouts. I think they were also involved with the MACV Phoenix program. One of the scouts was a former NVA lieutenant that helped plan some of the strikes during the '68 Tet Offensive. His whole company was wiped out in the Tet Offensive at Tan Son Nhut Air Force Base. He knew he couldn't go back up north, so he *chieu hoi*-ed. He was an interesting individual.

There were differences between the PRUs and the "Kit Carson" scouts. The PRUs were basically already trained and worked in a larger group. The "Kit Carson" scouts were smaller groups, more of a spin-off of a SEAL group. The SEALs trained the "Kit Carson" scouts on the different weaponry and on various tactics.

We had to watch the scouts a little bit closer because they had not been in a program like the PRUs had. They hadn't been free as long as the PRUs.

The impression I had of the PRUs was that a lot of them were VC that just got fed up with running and hiding all the time. They were either being chased by the U.S. government, or if they didn't cooperate with the VC in their area then they had to deal with them as well. So if they *chieu hoi*-ed and went to work with the PRU program and the U.S. government, then they felt they had it made. They ate three squares a day, their families got to live with them in the compound, and they didn't have to run or hide anymore.

The "Kit Carson" scouts were much different. We had trained them, but they would go out and get drunk, so you could never depend on them. When we planned an operation, we had to be very careful what we told them about where they were going. I think some of them still had some allegiance to their former province or Viet Cong friends. However, once they were in the program for a while there were usually no problems with them.

The seven "Kit Carsons" I received in Rach Soi were fresh out of the *chieu hoi* center. We trained them on the M-16s, AK-47s, and SKSs [Russian assault rifles]. A lot of times we'd have them dress like Viet Cong, and they would go into a village they might be familiar with, and we would stay back a way and support them. They'd tell the villagers they had some "walkees," which were captured Americans, and were sending them north. This was a skin-of-the-teeth-type operation; we weren't working on any kind of intel we had gathered. We'd just send them into a village with this story to see if they could pull out any Viet Cong militia there. If the militia did come out, we'd capture or eliminate them.

We had to get rid of one of the sappers. All he wanted to do was stay drunk all the time, and if he wasn't drunk, he had run off somewhere. We didn't know if he was giving out our intelligence or what, so we considered him a security risk.

My nickname is "Abe," and the "Kit Carsons" pronounced it "Aben."

One time we were out on an all-night operation. After the op we started back along a tree line, and here came one of the local province slicks that fly all over; it was the mail plane or whatever. These "Kits" came unglued. They started jumping behind trees or down on the ground, thinking that a gunship was going to come in on us. I had to convince them to get back up and carry on to our pickup location. Here they were, working with the Americans, and were still scared to death of our helicopters. I guess the gunships had made a distinct impression on them at one time or another in their pasts.

While there were questions concerning the ability and reliability of the PRUs and the "Kit Carson" scouts, there was never a question of a SEAL's operational ability and reliability. When a member of a platoon was injured or killed in action, another SEAL was asked to "take up the slack," and someone would always volunteer to fill the void. One must remember that all SEALs, with no regard to rank, participated in the same training.

When I first got out of the service, I couldn't find a job anywhere. No one seemed to want to hire any Vietnam veterans. My only alternative was to go into law enforcement. With my background in explosives and weaponry, that was about the only position I was able to fit into. I worked in a city police department in northern Texas for several years, then went back to school and later on became a federal agent. Only one-half of 1 percent of all law-enforcement personnel are accepted to attend the FBI Academy. As prestigious as some may perceive that to be, it doesn't mean half as much to me as going through SEAL training and being assigned to SEAL Team One. During that time I developed friendships that have endured through twenty-nine years.

When a SEAL platoon is formed, it becomes a fine-tuned, well-oiled, precise unit. But there is never any hesitation or question concerning a SEAL that volunteers to replace another teammate, simply because all SEALs know that this person has completed every requirement to qualify as a SEAL. Whereas in the other branches of the military, an individual is continually striving to prove his ability and reliability to perform the tasks necessary to gain the trust and respect of his fellow servicemen. Because of this, SEALs will always retain an advantage over other military branches.

SEAL Team One brought together some very special men that had undertaken the most rigorous, demanding, and intensive training any military had to offer. I was extremely fortunate to become a member of SEAL Team One.

My Vietnam experience helped me make some lifelong friends, some individuals that I could turn to at any time and they would be there for me in case of need or support or whatever. That's probably the best part of the whole experience. SEALs become "one" and remain "one" throughout life. Even our spouses and children remain close to other SEALs and their families. We have stayed in close contact by telephone, cards, letters, visits, and our infamous reunions at "Willy's" [Darryl Wilson's] in Colorado.

The men of SEAL Team were and still are some of the most courageous, faithful, loyal, and dedicated men I have ever had the honor of knowing and serving with.

12

Skip "Killer" Crane

Officer in Charge, Kilo Platoon
Seafloat, Republic of Vietnam
Deployed July–December 1969

The year 1966 was a memorable turning point in my life. I was on board an amphibious ship out of Norfolk, Virginia. We were coming back from Vietnam, and at that time you could go through the Suez Canal. It was the midwatch, and I was going to be the junior officer of the deck. At 2330 I came up on deck and reported in to the CO [commanding officer].

"Ensign Crane, ready to relieve the watch."

He said, "Negative, you're not going to relieve the watch."

I asked, "Why, Sir?"

He replied, "You've got the wrong color shoes."

I made a career choice right then to get out of the surface Navy. That was in 1966, on the midwatch, in the Mediterranean.

I made the decision to go to Vietnam. I volunteered for Vietnam, went over and drove PBRs for eighteen months, then finished up in 1967 after working in River Patrol Section 541 in Nha Be. It was during this period in the Delta that I was exposed to SEALs. A number of platoons from SEAL Team One were coming in and out of Nha Be, the base of operations for the Rung Sat Special Zone [RSSZ]. The RSSZ was four hundred square miles of swamps and rivers, just a very dismal mangrove area. The base at Nha Be was on land that was recovered from the river. They used fill and extended Nha Be out another five hundred yards. It was a very barren area and was at the junction of two major rivers. Being a crossroads for that area, it had a very strong tactical value and was determined to be the best site for a naval base supporting operations into the Rung Sat Special Zone.

We had two main missions to accomplish while I was on the PBRs. Our primary mission was to patrol the Long Tau, the main river that came up from Cap Saint Jacques [Vung Tau] in the South China Sea all the way up to Saigon. It was the main water lifeline going into the U.S. effort in Saigon—the main shipping channel. Our mission was to keep it free of enemy traffic and to allow the friendly vessels to safely transit back and forth. We would typically escort merchant-marine vessels and Maritime Sea Transportation–designated vessels from Vung Tau all the way up to Saigon, and vice versa. We varied our tactics; sometimes we'd escort them, and sometimes we ran random interdiction. But during that whole time, patrolling the Long Tau was our primary mission.

Our secondary mission was to support the SEALs. It got to the point that working with the SEALs was more exciting than escorting the merchant ships. The merchant ships were a rather benign assignment; occasionally they would get rocketed, then we would react by closing the source of fire, using our mortars, .50-calibers, and M-60s to saturate the area, then call in an air strike on the source of the ambush. It was reactionary and not very exciting: just another day on the river. Typically, in a month of operations on PBRs we'd get maybe three to five firefights, and the other twenty-five days were spent sunning, eating C-rats, driving up and down the river, keeping our weapons maintained, and reading paperbacks. We looked forward to working with the SEALs because they had a lot more challenging things to do, and it got us off the main river into VC country. No two missions were alike. It took the boredom away, and there was a lot of boredom over there.

The SEALs were a strange lot, very maverick, and they used a lot of unusual methods. Hardly standard Navy: everything was unorthodox, and that captured my imagination and ultimately became my career.

Working with guys like Joe DeFloria and Tommy Nelson caused me to, at first, just admire them, and after a while I asked if I could work out with them. They said sure, so I started doing PT [physical training] with them and got myself in shape. After eighteen months I had pretty well acclimated to Vietnam and felt comfortable driving PBRs, but I just couldn't stay in Vietnam any longer doing that.

I volunteered for SEAL Team and went straight to BUD/S. It was certainly challenging, and I think the instructors were the highlight of it; associating with all those professionals was great.

I went straight from BUD/S into SEAL Team One, assigned to SEAL basic indoctrination, and within six months we formed up Kilo Platoon. Kilo was given another four to six months to train. Chief Diecks, a.k.a. "Deep-diving" Diecks, was with me, and we had an assistant platoon commander, Lt.(jg) David Nicholas, who was later killed in Vietnam.

In July 1969 we landed in Saigon and stayed at the Victoria Hotel for one night. The guys from Det Golf in Binh Thuy sent a representative up to the hotel, and we got our first look at Vietnam from the hotel. Then the next day we flew down to Binh Thuy for the compulsory in-country briefs, area briefs, and everything else.

We were the first team to go to Seafloat, which was located in the unexplored Nam Can province in IV Corps. I didn't learn this until a year later when I was reassigned to NavForV [Naval Forces Vietnam] as the senior LDNN adviser. That's when I discovered the big picture. The entire thrust of our effort to establish a friendly presence in Nam Can was from incursions, which were originally designated Operation Seawave.

Seawave was principally PCFs [patrol craft, fast] operating from the LSTs anchored ten to fifteen miles south of Nam Can province, the very southern tip of South Vietnam. The LSTs would lower their booms, and the PCFs would come alongside and be rigged for both coastal and inshore patrol-craft operations.

The inshore excursions were considered risky. As the PCFs went into the Cua Lon River, they came in locked and loaded, and they just depressed the triggers on their .50-cal. and M-60 weapons and made the transit, in large part, on the offensive, to avoid getting ambushed. They would just lock and load and start randomly shooting during the transits. They virtually kept a constant train of fire to port and starboard during their entire transit. The intent was just to show a presence and start doing some initial reconnaissance, because there were no friendly forces in Nam Can.

That was the first phase, called Seawave. Eventually, the Navy brought in barges that were secured together, tethered, and anchored in the middle of the river. That was the second phase, called Seafloat. In the final phase, Solid Anchor, the Navy moved ashore and set up a semipermanent base on the river. Of the three phases, we were the first SEALs involved, though UDT and EOD [explosive ordnance disposal] elements were initially involved in Seawave, with the mission of blowing bunkers along the river. The mud bunkers were hardened by the sun and had the characteristics of concrete and could deflect a medium-caliber round.

When we got to Seafloat, we were assigned as a task element in Task Force 115. We were part of NavForV's riverine force and were ordered to systematically penetrate the area of operations to gain intelligence about enemy forces, routes, etc. At Seafloat we were brought on board and briefed by the task unit element commanders. We were instructed to penetrate the Nam Can jungle to collect as much intelligence as we could about this big void. Kilo Platoon became the inland extension of the patrol craft with our daily squad-size patrols through the Nam Can jungle.

We had set up security perimeters around Seafloat at five hundred meters, one thousand meters, and two thousand meters. Some of the hardware we introduced included early-warning devices for both water and land, to detect enemy movement. Not only did they give us the advantage of seismic warning, they gave good retransmitting of acoustics [enemy voices and other sounds] that were occurring within their range. The U.S. Navy technicians monitoring these devices were sort of nerd types—the kind that wore Coke-bottle glasses. Their unit was a little shack on the deck of Seafloat. On occasion SEALs would go in there and work with them because we would frequently insert the devices and check on them when they weren't performing. We'd replace the batteries when they went bad and service the devices.

One night some unidentified suspected VC penetrated our perimeter, so the Seafloat mortar team started dropping in 81-mm mortar rounds. Typically, when there was such movement, the team would just shoot in the blind. They didn't know whether they were shooting at a tiger, monkey, or VC. However, because of the listening devices, we were occasionally able to monitor when the VC started panicking at the incoming rounds. We could actually hear them cursing and yelling unflattering comments in our direction when the mortar rounds started falling around them. That was all part of Seafloat's perimeter security.

We divided our fourteen-man platoon into two squads. One of the two squads would go out on an operation virtually every night, even if it was for only a couple of hours.

Given the pressure that was on us, we had to go out and collect intelligence. For that reason, we ran a lot of operations in a six-month period. We also got a fairly sizable number of confirmed kills because most of the Nam Can jungle was a free-fire zone. Any indigenous person seen was assumed to be the enemy.

We became very proficient at setting up basic ambushes in a line along a river, blending in with the nipa palm, the foliage, and the mud. One nighttime SOP we found to be very successful was that whoever was in charge of the squad or platoon would have their first few rounds be tracers. That provided some illumination, and the others could then zero in on whatever the leader decided to shoot at.

That worked out very well except in one instance. On this one op, a sampan with an outdrive [outboard] motor came down the river with two VC in it. One was in the bow, and the other VC was steering, leaning and looking forward. When we opened fire, some of the tracers hit the sampan's gas can, which just exploded, and the guy steering didn't have time to move. He was a burnt marshmallow within five seconds. He remained in that same position, and the boat just kept right on going. We watched it until it was out of sight, still heading down the river with a crispy critter as its coxswain.

Like most SEAL platoons, we were assigned "Kit Carson" scouts. The "Kit Carson" program was an attempt to take former VC that had rolled over and put them to work for the good guys. The intent may have been good, and while the success of some of them may have been positive, it was very difficult for us to interpret the genuineness of the "Kit Carsons."

In spite of our attempts to learn the Vietnamese language, the subtleties could never really be understood without being a linguist. For example, it was often the things that weren't said in an interrogation that were more important

than what was said, or the manner in which they were said or
were not said.

It may have been without justification, but I had an inher-
ent distrust for ''Kit Carson'' scouts and never turned my
back on an armed scout. However, having a ''Kit Carson''
scout worked out very well tactically, as we would dress the
scout up in VC black pajamas, give him an AK and vest, and
he blended well as pointman, or as an extension of the
pointman. Typically, that was the way we used our ''Kit.''
He would be anywhere from five to fifty yards in front of our
pointman. One of our ''Kit Carsons'' was excellent, but
unfortunately he got zapped on point when we walked into a
VC ambush.

Our area of operations in Nam Can was pretty remote;
and even though the VC and their equipment wasn't sophisticated, they were effective—including their use of directional mines. On one of our early missions we jumped down
from the helo during a dawn insertion and did a quick scan
of the perimeter to see what might be there that we couldn't
see from the air. All the overhead photography in the world
sometimes didn't help. We immediately saw a trench line
running beneath the tree canopy. It was apparent the VC
were already waiting for us.

One problem with the Nam Can province was the jungle
canopy was so dense there just were not that many LZs. This
was one of the few LZs in the entire province, and we should
have anticipated the VC being there—like they anticipated
we would eventually use the LZ.

We got hit right there on the LZ within moments after
insertion. The Seawolf chopper had no sooner taken off and
was banking out when the VC fire starting raining in on us.
This mission was a pretty big operation involving all fourteen guys, plus our ''Kit Carsons.'' We were all out there,
exposed in the LZ, and couldn't get the choppers back in to
extract us because of the intense enemy ground fire. The

helos would have come in for us if we could have suppressed the enemy fire.

We were within ten meters of the enemy, but the Seawolf pilots made passes and were literally overhead, shooting everything they had—twenty to thirty meters away from us—including 2.75-inch rockets. They were blowing everything up that they could, but it wasn't enough to suppress fire because the VC were well dug in their concrete-like mud trenches.

Moses Marquez, who was of Indian/Mexican descent, was our pointman and was one of the most heroic men I've ever known. Everyone in the platoon owes that man their lives. We began to flank the VC to get into a better position to return fire. As we were maneuvering around, we saw this monofilament-type, heavy-duty-gauge fishing line running across the field of fire. Moses signaled to me, and I told him to cut the line, which he did. That probably saved our lives

We later discovered it was attached to a 150-pound claymore-type shaped charge made out of a trash can filled with cement and miscellaneous nuts and bolts: a deadly lethal and damned effective weapon. There was a firing device behind it, an old Chicom pull device that was attached to the monofilament line going over to the firing trench.

All during the remaining fifteen-minute firefight I saw the line jerk back and forth, and this little VC kept sticking his head up. I could just imagine him saying, "That goddamn Chinese equipment." You had to empathize with the VC because occasionally their equipment malfunctioned just like ours. Meanwhile, this VC is jerking the hell out of the line, trying to get the charge to fire, not realizing Moses had cut it.

After we flanked the VC and suppressed fire, we discovered some of the VC had leapfrogged out of the area. The way they did it was very impressive. Of the seven left, four guys stayed behind and three withdrew from the trench back so far and laid down a base of fire, then three more leapfrogged out, leaving one behind to keep our heads down with suppression fire. In the end we whacked that one, plus got two others in the exchange of fire as they withdrew.

When it was all over we discovered that they were Cambodians associated with the Khmer Rouge but not actually KKK [Khmer Kampuchea Krom]. They were on the fringe of that whole insurgency inside of the Pol Pot regime in Cambodia. But they were working in Vietnam along the Cambodian-Vietnam border at the time.

Our "Kit Carson" scout was Cambodian, and when we were cleaning things up he went over to investigate the bodies. Our scout took out his knife and cut open the stomach of the Cambodian who made the last stand and took out his spleen. Cambodians generally carried scarves—which was a form of ethnic identification but also had many functional uses. It could be used to carry rice or as bandannas to keep mosquitoes off. In this case our scout took the guy's body part, wrapped it up tight in his bandanna, and threw it in his backpack along with documents and everything else he collected. We then extracted and returned to base.

After our debrief back on Seafloat I went outside and saw our Cambodian scout. He had started a little fire and was cooking the VC's spleen in a helmet turned upside down. This ritual was reserved only for the enemy who showed a lot of bravado, a lot of guts. They didn't bother with the others that had been killed in the firefight, just the one that had stayed behind in the bunker on a suicide mission. In my opinion he was either the dumbest or the bravest, I don't know which. Our interpretation of the ritual was that our scout wanted to share a part of him, his bravery. We all had to take a bite of it, and as the leader of the SEAL platoon I was expected to take a bite. Not to do so would have made me lose face. Actually, with a little *nuoc-mam* [rotten fish] sauce, it wasn't all that bad; it tasted kind of like chicken liver.

In 1969 when my platoon went to Saigon for the trip

home, I stayed behind in Nam Can to break in the platoon that relieved us.

Meanwhile, "Deep-diving" Diecks who was second in command took the remaining guys in the platoon and flew to Guam, then on to Hawaii, where the aircraft developed "mechanical problems." The squadron that flew us to and from Vietnam was based in Hawaii, and every time they landed at their base the planes somehow developed mechanical problems for at least forty-eight hours.

Well, Lenny Horst was anxious to get back to San Diego and didn't want to stay over in Hawaii. At the urging of his teammates, he picked up a phone and called the White House. He got someone's ear on the White House staff and said something to the effect of, "This is First Class Petty Officer Lenny Horst calling from Hawaii, and I've got a bone to pick. I just spent six months in Vietnam, and now I'm trying to get home. The least you could do would be to provide reliable transportation!"

Apparently, the National Security Adviser, who was the president's right-hand military adviser in the White House, got the message within minutes and sent it over to the Pentagon. Shit rolled downhill from there. The Pentagon called the squadron commander and told them they better get the platoon home. Within forty-five minutes the squadron commander showed up at the airfield and personally flew the guys home.

When I flew back to Coronado a few weeks later, I was met at North Island Naval Air Station by the commanding officer of SEAL Team One, Dave Schaible. He wanted to know why my platoon was out of control and why one of my guys had called the White House. Dave didn't even wait to get me back to the team area to reprimand me for my lack of leadership; he proceeded to chew me out right on the runway. Somewhat stunned from this dressing down by the CO, I acknowledged my errant behavior and assumed an appropriate wounded posture.

Dave then changed gears and suggested we retire to the "O" club on base for my formal debrief. After tossing down a few cool ones and hearing several accounts of "special missions" that couldn't be reported in routine after-action reports, we swapped a few more stories and returned to the SEAL Team area to resume our labors.

13

Hal Kuykendall

Radioman, 2d Squad, Charlie Platoon
Ben Luc and Long Phu (Dung Island),
Republic of Vietnam
Deployed December 1969–June 1970

When we first arrived in Vietnam, we were sent up to Ben Luc, which was an established base. You felt very safe there. It was practically like being on a military base in the States.

The Seawolf pilots based at Ben Luc lived right by us, so we got to know the guys. When we called them from an op and said we were in a world of trouble, they'd jump, hardly even warm up their helos, and be out to help us. It was real comforting to have the Seawolf pilots so close.

Way down south on the Bassac River was Long Phu, which was right across the river from Dung Island. When we first went to Long Phu, which we began calling Dung Island also, it was just a sandy area; there was nothing there. We set up porta-campers, slept on cots, and there was no electricity. The heat was absolutely unbelievable. We would go out on operations at night, so we tried to sleep in the tents during the day. They had no ventilation—which made it impossible to get any sleep. You just lay there in your sweat; it was miserable. Another problem was that we didn't have American food. We all ended up with dysentery, worms, and all kinds of dietary problems. I lost a ton of weight.

The only other thing around us was a small Vietnamese Navy base. Calling it a base was kind of ridiculous—they had a little guard shack and maybe a boat or two down there.

When we were at Ben Luc, we had all the boat support and air support we wanted; when we got to Dung Island, we had neither. To get around during operations, we went out on little borrowed junks. For a while we operated in IBSs [inflatable boats, small]. Eventually, we got a Boston Whaler and some boat support down there.

When we needed air support, we had to call Soc Trang and see if we could get them to come help us. My experience was that they weren't interested in helping us out. They would go pick up mail, or even a pregnant Vietnamese, before they would come help us. They just didn't seem to care about us.

The best thing that happened at Dung Island was when the Seabees came down to build a base. They brought food and generators with them—which changed our whole lifestyle. We became really close to the Seabees—which was unusual. I had never been that close to anybody else in the Navy, outside of SEAL Team, except for the Seawolf pilots and the boat-support crews.

The Seabees like having SEALs around because they felt safe. We like them because they had good food, better accommodations, and they brought the generators! We also used them for artillery support. They set up artillery at Long Phu and delivered it over to us on Dung Island.

For security, we put some barbed wire and booby traps around our perimeter. We had a big field around us, and we walked security at night. The Seabees added to our security because we could put their guards out as well.

The first night the Seabees were there, someone crawled up into our camp and threw a grenade in one of the tents. Fortunately, it went off low order. We all came busting out of our tents, and this one Seabee was running around in his underwear, swinging his handgun left and right. It looked like the beginning of the TV show *I Spy*. This Seabee had never been in a combat situation.

One afternoon we got word that there was a meeting of VCI going on over on Dung Island. We got the platoon together, loaded up our MSSC [medium SEAL-support craft], and went cruising across the river.

We got out of the boat, and Rich Solano, our pointman, was trying to find a way to get us through the jungle. But right there on the river the jungle was at its thickest; we couldn't get through it without making a God-awful racket.

We could hear the VC at their meeting; they were just on the other side of the tree line, talking and jabbering. We didn't want them to hear us, so we kept moving around to different places, but Rich just couldn't find a place to quietly get us through. So we called the boat back in to pick us up. We planned to move further downriver to find a spot we could get through, then patrol back up to the meeting area.

We were standing in water about waist deep, and the boat was quietly coming in to pick us up. The operation had been real quiet. We'd used hand signals to communicate. We took great pride in being real quiet inserting and extracting. I can still see that boat gliding in across the river.

About the time it got maybe ten yards out, all of a sudden Mike Lacaze just started screaming—I mean blue, bloody murder. It was so startling, it just scared the hell out of all of us. I'm talking about a man who was just completely in terror. He started running toward the boat. He literally threw his Stoner machine gun, and Mike Thornton caught it. It was almost like he was running across the top of the water;

it was the biggest commotion I've ever seen. He grabbed hold of the cargo net on the boat, lifted himself up, plopped down on the bow of the boat—and he was on his back, just flopping all over the place.

We were all going, "What in the world?" Everyone was looking at the water—we didn't know if there were sea snakes in the water, or crocodiles—we just couldn't figure out what got him.

Mike Sands got up on the boat with him. Lacaze was wearing Levis, and Sands took a Ka-Bar knife and ripped open his jeans to see what had bitten him. I remember Mike Thornton saying, "Whatever it is, don't throw the damn thing back in here with us!"

Well, you won't believe it, but Mike Sands picked it up, and it was a little catfish. But the damn thing had a barb on it about two inches long. While Mike had been standing in the water, waiting for the boat to come in, this little fish swam up his pants leg, something that happened pretty often. But when he went to squish and kill it, the barb went under his knee cap. I mean, it went a full inch to an inch and a half in, and it just hit him at a spot where he went absolutely wild.

After we started to get organized, we couldn't find Nelson, our Vietnamese interpreter, anywhere. We finally found him and figured out what had happened. It's spooky being in the water when somebody is screaming like that. We went from total silence to this blood-curdling scream, and Nelson just went up the nearest tree. We all laughed about that for a long time.

Mike was in such pain that Doc Brown gave him a shot of morphine. Well, Mike then started thinking that he was going to die. He told me, "You tell my wife I love her, I've really been a lousy husband, but I really do love her." He was going on and on, thinking it was all over.

Mike doesn't like that story.

One thing we weren't really trained very well for before going to Vietnam was crossing monkey bridges. The bridges were these little bitty things, and by the time you got to them your boots were all muddy. You had to get up there and balance yourself, and a lot of times you were trying to be really quiet because you were trying to get to a hooch with people in it. Mike Thornton was a big guy, but he had catlike feet. He could always get across those monkey bridges—which amazed me.

On one night op we patrolled toward this hooch, and the last two hundred yards probably took us an hour. Mike got about halfway across the monkey bridge, and all of a sudden you could see him losing his balance. The next thing you know, instead of being quiet, he went, "AHHHHHHHHH" and crashed into the mud. Of course, all hell broke loose then.

Another factor we couldn't plan for was the dogs. The darn dogs there just drove us crazy. We could be quiet enough to sneak up on people, but it's really hard to sneak up on dogs.

One of the few daytime operations we went on took place on Dung Island. We got information that the VC were operating a factory that built junks. We went there to blow the thing up.

Mike Thornton was driving the Boston Whaler, and as usual, we wanted to get in there quietly. We were in this little bitty canal that went right down alongside the junk factory. We were running on a single engine to make less noise. But it was really hard to drive the whaler when you didn't have enough speed—they just didn't go where you wanted them to. We kept running into the brush, and finally, since we were making so much racket, we decided to gas it and get on down there. We gassed it and were just going balls to the walls.

I saw the VC at the junk factory, and they were not running for cover. They were just looking up the canal—like they heard something and they were thinking, "What in the hell is that?" They were shocked when they saw us and started running everywhere.

Before we got out of there, we ended up in a big gunfight. We detonated the explosives we had and just blew the hell out of everything there.

When we were at Dung Island, there was a *chieu hoi* center nearby. We were able to get good *hoi chanhs* there; we found out a lot of intel from them. We would get guys that had just come into the center and take them out on ops with us.

Of course, we never gave these guys a weapon.

One guy really seemed to be a good, fine person. He took us on a rapid succession of great ops. His story was that the VC killed his family, and he wanted revenge. When he took us out on an op, you could see the blood in his eyes.

On one night operation, before we went out, he asked us through our interpreter whether we'd let him have a gun— that he would feel more comfortable carrying a gun. We debated it, and finally Tom Boyhan said, "Well, what the hell, the guy's been proven—we've taken him out, and he's been good." So we gave him a CAR-15.

We put the *hoi chanh* out in front of our platoon, kind of like walking point; he was actually in front of our pointman. There was a meeting taking place in a hooch right under a tree line, and we sent him up to get a closer look. We were standing near a dike line, watching him as he went right up next to the hooch. It was dark, and we were trying to deal with night vision while looking up at the hooch.

I was standing by Boyhan when all of a sudden that damn guy turned around and opened fire on us. You want to talk about shocked!

We opened fire—which really compromised our position. The VC all started running off behind the hooch, through the nipa palms.

We never found the *hoi chanh*. We don't know what

happened to him or the weapon. For me, that was one of the lessons learned in Vietnam. We trusted this guy—we broke one of our own rules—we gave him a weapon.

I often wondered, was it planned from the time he asked us, or did he just get up close to the meeting and decide, "Hey, I could be a hero, I could come in here with one of their own weapons and open fire on them."

Later, we worried whether it had even been a plot all the way back to him going to the *chieu hoi* center. We wondered if he had been put in there to try to lead us into an ambush— except maybe first he had some people he had to get rid of, maybe he wanted revenge for something.

After that we became more suspicious of the guys coming into the center; we were more careful. But we continued to use them; they were our best source for operations. They were far better than any other intel we ever had.

14

Tom Leonard

Pointman, 1st Squad, Delta Platoon
Rach Soi, Republic of Vietnam
Deployed January–July 1970

In high school I was attracted to people who were winners; the MVPs and National Honor Society people—they were the achievers. They were my friends then and still are today. At the time, I had my own kind of achievements. I was an Eagle Scout—which was a program I was in for a long time and did well in. I wasn't a National Honor Society–type person; maybe I was too right-brained for a college-prep high school—more the creative type.

All of my friends went into college, as I did, but I didn't really know why I went. I didn't really have any goal or purpose. My father had not been to college, and he was my central figure, the man I wanted to model myself after. He was a chief in the Navy. He was a good guy.

As a freshman in high school I was four feet eleven inches and weighed ninety-eight pounds. I got stuffed in my half-locker the first day of school because I wouldn't tell some senior upperclassman the combination to my lock. But I did a lot of growing in the course of my four years of high school. By the time I left school I was six feet tall but only weighed 130 pounds—a real string bean. With that kind of growth I felt I was not coordinated enough to participate in sports, even though I was attracted to them. I was the oldest boy in my family and didn't have a brother role model to show me how. I felt a need to do something athletic to prove my manliness.

I had just gotten through high school with a C average, and I needed something else. I needed the ultimate challenge. My one great success in life up until that time was being an Eagle Scout. I met some really nice people in the Scouting association. They encouraged me—which made me realize that if I could succeed in one thing, then I could succeed at other things.

While I was in my three-semester stint at Southwestern College I met some guys that had retired from UDT. These were physically and mentally tough guys. They had come back to the junior college and played sports there. They seemed to be very successful in that environment. I listened to their stories of UDT and how exciting it was. I thought, "I can do that. I'm going to give it a try." By this time I was in a weight-lifting class and up to 170 pounds.

I wasn't getting along very well with my dad at that time, so this notion came to me to join the Navy. Like a lot of nineteen-year-old kids, I was wavering in college, not always going to work, and partying at night. I was as double-minded as a guy could be, and this was infuriating to my dad and mom. Finally, I got an ultimatum from my dad—he wanted me out. Within a couple of weeks I went to the recruiter.

I had already been thinking about UDT because I did not want to go to the fleet, and signed up for the Teams. I passed the UDT screening test while I was in boot camp and was also the honor man in my company.

At the Naval Amphibious Base in Coronado I was processed in and quartered in a little Quonset hut out on the very east end of the base, right on the bay. They had oil-burning heaters, and we had to go get diesel fuel every day or we wouldn't have any heat at night. There was sand, dirt, and shells all around the area. They didn't call it BUD/S then, it was UDTRA [Underwater Demolition Team Training].

Looking back, it seems as if each person that made it through all the rigorous training and made it through hell week all had a personal need to do so. To become a SEAL would fill a void that each of us had in our lives. We all had something to prove to ourselves. Some people just didn't have enough of a personal need or the fortitude to make it through training; they were the ones that dropped out. I was very proud to graduate. Physically, I had never endured anything like that training, and it prepared me mentally for other demanding times that I have encountered since then.

When I arrived in Vietnam, we began running interdiction ops. We were hoping to intercept arms being shipped by Viet Cong and NVA that were down in the delta. We also ran a lot of ambush operations. We did forty-five combat missions in the six months I was there. The missions didn't consist of just picking up your gun and riding in a boat to some operation. It always entailed the full SEAL preparation—which meant we would have a lot of things to do before an operation: planning, warning order, preparation of equipment.

I helped gather intel—which usually meant there was a *hoi chanh* in town with some supervaluable information about where Charlie was going to be or where he was going to have his stuff. We would plan an operation based on this information. The first step was finding a *hoi chanh* we could trust. That was where I felt our platoon was weak; we didn't trust any of them. I'm not sure, but I think that even across language barriers, trust is either transmitted or it isn't. Very early on we had some experiences that created this mistrust.

We operated out of Rach Soi in an area inland from the coast. A series of connecting canals that the French had dug laced the entire area, and eastward toward Saigon. The lieutenant we relieved when we arrived in Vietnam took us out on our first few missions up Sierra Canal. When we went on these first ops the lieutenant was smart; he took us into a place where his intel indicated that there were no enemy around. He only had two missions to go before he was out of the country, so he took us to places where we wouldn't have any contact.

They told us on these first ops that we should experiment with Dexamil. Dexamil is an amphetamine, a stay-awake drug. I popped a cap on the first operation and found out that I didn't tolerate that stuff very well. I was giddy. I would also see things, and I remember falling off a dike in the middle of one of the operations and laughing about it. I didn't take any more of it.

When the other platoon went home, we began to go out and gather our own intelligence. We got info that off of one of the main rivers was a small hamlet where we thought we might be able to snatch some prisoners. Our squad inserted at night from PBRs and patrolled inland about one to two hundred feet to a main trail that paralleled the river, then we headed south on the trail into the hamlet. The NVA cadre were supposed to be gathering there for a local organizational meeting. The purpose of our mission was to kidnap the NVA in this hamlet. That's all the info we had: no photos, no names of the people we were supposed to get, just this vague information.

So here we were, on our third op. We did our bow-touch insertion from the PBRs: we were all clumped up on the bow, and just as the boat touched land, we all off-loaded as one. It all happened so fast; no one even touched the water, so there was no splash to be heard. As we jumped off onto the ground—or clay in this case—the boat backed out and continued on downriver, past the hamlet that we were going to so everything would look normal.

We headed in toward the hamlet. The trail was very dark; it was a double canopy with large palms and such. There was a little bit of cloud cover, and it was so dark that you could just barely see the trail or the guy in front of you. We stopped near the hamlet and prepared to go in. The trail was a raised dike, and both sides of it were covered with pineapple plants. The Vietnamese often planted pineapples along the dikes.

We saw a candle and heard a voice in the hamlet fifty to seventy feet in front of us. A voice called out in Vietnamese, but we didn't say anything. Then the candle started coming toward us, and we all stepped off to the right. We were all completely cammoed out [painted with camouflage] and were lying down in the pineapple plants, watching this candle come toward us. The man holding it started walking right past our whole squad off to the side of the dike. I was the third from the end and could see this guy's eyes in the candlelight, and I was thinking, "He has to see us; there's no way he can't see us."

Mike McCullum was our rear gunner on that op. He was also our senior PO [petty officer] and had already deployed to Vietnam twice. He was the only guy with a lick of sense in our whole platoon since the rest of us were all rookies. The Vietnamese kept walking past the squad, and Mike just stood up, grabbed this guy by the throat, and took him quietly down to the ground, right between himself and me.

He held him on the ground with his mouth covered, and our interpreter came back to where we were. Mike told him in a very low voice to ask the Vietnamese where the cadre was. We had tied his hands behind his back, and our interpreter told him not to yell out or he would die. The guy said he didn't know what we were talking about.

Keep in mind that we were just a bunch of novices; we were floundering. We didn't know what the heck we really had or what to do to operate from there, so we were trusting our senior, veteran guy on how to proceed.

Finally, our prisoner VC told us there was someone visiting down in the last hooch but said he didn't really know who he was. He said he thought the guy had a pistol on him. We were thinking that was good, if all they had was one pistol.

We taped the guy's mouth. I held him by his tied hands, and we came back up on the trail to go toward the far hamlet. We didn't walk but ten steps when someone out on the edge of the hamlet stood right in the middle of the trail and fired a shot down the middle of the trail at us.

These trails were as straight as could be. Before all our missions we discussed in our operation order what our SOPs would be in case we were ambushed. Our SOP on ambushes from the front was for everyone to go to the left. This was our first time ever being shot at, and we all immediately dropped down to the left. The dikes had peaks on them: the middle was raised, and it went down about three feet on either side.

We immediately laid down suppressing fire, and then more candles starting coming on in the hamlet.

This was our first contact. It was insane. We were all novices, frightened to death, and yet we were going to lean into this thing because the Navy had given us the fastest and the biggest and the best guns, and we knew we were going to win. That was our mentality. No one was going to beat us. So we shot the hell out of that whole hamlet. Again, we were nothing but a bunch of frightened men in the dark, letting loose on this hamlet.

The person that fired that fateful shot down the trail— well, that was their last act. I saw him go down: he was definitely hit—I saw the holes in him. Against four Stoners, an M-60, and a bunch of M-16s, he didn't have much of a chance.

The lieutenant called, "Cease fire," and we all stopped.

We heard people running around back in the hamlet and people yelling and screaming. We did a quick role call and got everybody back together.

Then we had the problem of what we should do with the guy we had captured. It was one of those ethical dilemmas. Our novice lieutenant said to just let him go.

We were all going, "Bullshit! This guy's a sympathizer; he could have gotten us all killed; we should take him back or kill him!"

But the lieutenant said to let him go, so we left him there sitting on the dike, and we took off.

We called in the PBRs and extracted. We went to an Army outpost nearby that we had launched out of. It wasn't half an hour after we got there when some injured people started coming in that had been shot in the knees and thighs, probably by us. That was the first time I saw wounded people in Vietnam. They came into that Army base because that was where they knew they could get medical treatment. There was supposedly a kid they were bringing in that was shot in the abdomen, but I never saw him.

I ended up walking point on later ops. I carried a Stoner configured with the hundred-round box, short barrel, and standard stock. I had canvas holders that perfectly held four Stoner ammunition boxes. The plastic boxes inserted right into the holders. They went on the standard web belt with an *H*-harness. These were the magazine pouches that had been designed to hold four thirty-round M-16 magazines. We used them to hold the Stoner boxes, though. They slid right down in it and were covered over by a canvas flap.

Before an operation we received a patrol-leader's order, which consisted of getting all the information about the operation. We would meet in our hooch and lay a map over a bunch of ammo boxes. Our lieutenant, Mel Hetzer, was really gung-ho and very into it all. He'd always say we were going to be a great unit. He always got us fired up, you know, fired and wired, ready to rock and roll. He had visions of us being a highly decorated unit—you know, saving everybody, kicking ass and taking names, that whole thing. He always had great excitement about what we were doing. He was in charge and would run the briefings, and everything was done exactly as the Army's patrol order showed; he followed that to a *T*.

Every particular facet of the patrol-leader's order was discussed for every op; we had that down pat. To this day I think that is still the best way to go because I can tell you the other ways do not work as well. Sometimes, as you became an experienced vet, you might start leaving out things because you just knew what you had to do, so you started abbreviating the process. Future generations, don't do that! Follow every part of the order, every time, because it's your life every time. Don't assume anything.

Our briefings were always spirited and, typical of all the SEAL platoons, participative. The lieutenant did the correct thing: he solicited information such as thoughts, feelings, and perceptions from everyone involved; and although we didn't actually vote, in a sense we voted with our opinions. Often we would make minor modifications, and everyone was aware of and acknowledged those modifications. Everyone had input into the mission before going out. That was the optimum way to fight. Everybody was on the same page.

To keep in shape physically, we tried to do exercises, but that was a real laugh. I went over there at 194 pounds and came back 168. Our diet changed dramatically, and the heat and humidity were just phenomenal—114 degrees was not uncommon, and it just sapped the strength out of you. It was like the whole time you were there, you were constantly, slowly dissolving, deteriorating. All you could do was just operate, operate, operate: get better at it, practice it, and pay attention.

If I were a professional operator today, there are key points I would tell my men. I would say that what you do in your private, personal time has everything to do with when you're at work. You prepare yourself constantly, 100 percent of the time. You focus and you take care of yourself 100 percent of the time. There was a lot of drinking in SEAL platoons. Heavy drinking was condoned; it was a part of the mystique—the image—of the SEALs. We were hard-drinking, hell-raising frogmen. There were many ridiculous things we thought about ourselves, and there were real characters that pumped that stuff. If I were the commander of a SEAL platoon today, I would reach into the heart of my men and encourage them to really be a whole person. There is a need for this.

I think of Dr. Henderson, my old history professor, who always said that history repeats itself, and if you don't protect what you have, someone will take it away. SEAL Teams are just another one of the tools that our country uses to protect what we have. The type of warfare SEALs are trained for can be very effective and at the same time noninvasive. You have to understand its purpose in the greater scheme of things. Surgical strikes like that often surpass a nuclear response.

Most of the guys in the platoon took a pair of camie [camouflage] pants and a pair of Levis to the local tailor and had them sew the camies to the outside of the Levis. They were absolutely the best pair of combat pants you could wear. They were tough as nails, and we could go through nipa palm without shredding the pants. I had some tiger-striped camies, but what I wore sometimes depended on what was clean at the time.

We wore regular camie jackets and web belts with

H-harnesses. Each of us set up our harnesses differently, depending on what weapon was carried. I carried ammo and pop flares, which were always taped and painted. We'd put them on the harness with rubber bands so you could just reach back and pull one off when you needed it. I had a Ka-Bar knife with a smoke flare taped to the scabbard. Our watches had a small compass attached to the band and were always covered so the enemy couldn't see the glowing face at night. We went through a lot of watches because of the stuff we did—we just destroyed them. We wore a floppy hat and always wore a life jacket because we were always in the water in the delta. The life jacket was worn under the *H*-harness. I also had a pistol, a Smith and Wesson Model 39, in a shoulder-holster rig, which rotted in six months like everything else. I carried insect repellent but only used it for removing leeches.

Our face paint was always applied correctly, not like you see in the movies. We put the cammo everywhere: behind the ears, down the neck, even on our hands and arms in case the jacket sleeve got pushed up. If the cammo was applied correctly, the enemy could walk right up to you at night and never see you. When that happened, we started to realize that the cammo wasn't for the movies or the SEAL image; it was for our survival.

When I walked point, I was the eyes and ears of the squad. I could trust myself walking point. It was like tracking in the Boy Scouts, or hunting. Probably the best virtue of a good pointman is to be patient: don't hurry; there's no need to hurry. I'd just listen, move, listen, be patient, watch—use all of my senses. I didn't particularly like being out there on point by myself, but at least I found it more tolerable than having somebody out there that I maybe didn't trust.

I got hurt once on point when I stepped in a *punji* pit. The bamboo sticks could go right through our steel-bottom boots. They were supposed to be *punji* proof, but they weren't. I was walking behind our Cambodian scout that day across an open field. I was stepping in his footprints. He, of course, was a little guy and was not heavy enough to sink into the trap. But I was heavier, and with all my gear on, my left foot collapsed the bamboo mat covering the trap. Luckily, my right foot stayed on solid ground. Three of the sticks went into my left boot, one of them all the way through my foot.

We had two EOD guys with us from Binh Thuy, Ben Rand and another guy named Porter. There I was in extreme pain, and Ben told me not to move because these things were sometimes booby trapped. He wanted to check it out, so they pulled on this bamboo mat, which had about two inches of dirt on it and probably a foot and a half of green grass on top of that: that's how well disguised it was in the field. He got down in the pit to make sure the bottom of it wasn't wired to something, and finally he pushed my foot out of the pit with the stakes still in my boot.

I felt my boot fill up with blood. It hurt pretty bad, but at the same time I was relieved that I didn't blow myself and everybody else up when he took my foot out of there. Basically, they just yanked the stakes out of my boot right there, and that was the end of that mission. I was out of it at that point, so we all went back to the base.

I took my boot off, looked at the holes, and immediately went to see the corpsman. The treatment turned out to be worse than the injury. They put 1,000 ccs of penicillin in one cheek each morning, and another 1,000 in the other cheek at night. They did that for two weeks. That much caused a lump, which caused a bruise, and pretty soon I looked like a disaster area. My butt was black and blue on both sides and just as tender as could be, and I had to endure that for half a month. They also had to scrub out the holes in my foot because the VC had put water buffalo dung on the stakes.

They wrote me up for a Purple Heart for that since I was

injured in the service of our country, but at the same time it was embarrassing.

Walking point had all sorts of intensities involved in it. You were separated from the rest of the squad; they were all behind you, and what was in front of you was the unknown. Walking down trails at night created a lot of environmental worries too. Warrant Officer Fischer told us when we were getting ready to go in-country that 99 percent of the snakes in 'Nam were poisonous, and the other 1 percent could swallow you whole. Walking point, I always saw snakes go across the trail in front of me. When you added the other wonderful layer of paranoia that you get from booby traps, it always made the job of walking point an intense adventure.

Then there was the darkness. It's hard to explain how absolutely black and dark it is on a cloudy night in the jungle, how impossible it is to signal another person. We didn't have the high-tech stuff they do today; no night-vision equipment other than a starlight scope, which hummed and gave you "green-eye," so we didn't like to use it. Those were just some of the challenges of walking point, not to mention actual contact with the enemy!

The most dangerous part of an operation varied, but insertion was probably the most critical. We got ambushed on two insertions. We no sooner got off the boat and it pulled away than we were ambushed. The mission-planning process required that we go through the NILO and in 1970 also the South Vietnamese NILO. When we added that ingredient to the mix, we learned we were basically telling the enemy where we were going to operate. Once we started going through the South Vietnamese NILO, we had to declare an insertion point. After being ambushed twice, we wised up and always cleared two or three operation areas with them. Then we wouldn't tell them which specific one we were going to use. Doing it this way bogged us down somewhat, but we felt it was necessary.

I think a successful op consisted of us going out, encountering the enemy, shooting a lot of bullets, killing a lot of bad guys, and coming back with none of our guys hurt. That would be a win. Of course, it would have helped us to actually have all of the intelligence we received be true, but most of the time that wasn't the case.

Some of our missions were traumatic enough that we never debriefed, we just talked about them forever. The worst op was probably three or four months into our tour. We went up Sierra Canal to the east. The squad was dressed in black pajamas with straw, cone-shaped hats so that we looked like VC. Our Vietnamese, Nu, and Sam, our *hoi chanh,* were on the stern of the boat, and Nguyen, our interpreter, was on the bow. We seized a large sampan with a covered wagon—style top over the center of it that our whole squad plus two indigenous folks could ride in. We were towed behind an MSSC on a two hundred–foot line. About a half a mile before we got to a little canal we were going to release the line and paddle in. We knew we were going to be met by VC sentries who were guarding a small hamlet and a small Buddhist temple where there was reported a large weapons cache. It was a regional cache, and we knew we would probably run into a fair number of VC, perhaps a squad or platoon, and maybe even some NVA.

It was Nguyen's job to take the challenge from the sentries and to answer with the password. We hoped he could bluff his way through. We would paddle in, hopefully looking like Viet Cong bringing in more weapons. Our plan was to just paddle right in past the sentries, go right in to the temple, find the cache, blow up the weapons, kill all the bad guys, and paddle home to victory.

It was an ill-conceived plan. We did not do our homework: we did not look at the tide tables.

We turned up into the canal and paddled about one hundred feet. The canal was about thirty feet wide. It snaked off to the right and then to the left, leaving a peninsula out in front of us. It was about two in the morning, and the MSSC had continued patrolling on to the east as planned. There was almost a full moon up, so we had that kind of blue glow across the land. The thin row of trees on our left were backlit from the moonlight, and there was an open rice field spreading eastward from the trees. I was paddling on the port side; Bob Irwin was on the starboard side of the bow, paddling; and Nguyen was in front of us, ready to interpret. Jim La Vore was in the very back of the boat with Sam and Nu. Jim was on the tiller, steering the boat with an oar. Our lieutenant was inside the covered area behind me. Frankie Gardner and Mike McCullum were in there also. I was lying low in the boat as I paddled because the moonlight was so bright. My Stoner, like Irwin's, was cradled at the ready in my lap.

Nguyen turned around to me and whispered that he saw the VC. I passed the word back to the lieutenant that the VC were up ahead, and he asked what they were doing. I looked up ahead at the peninsula that jutted out from the left bank and saw them hunched over with AKs, walking out on the point. I thought these were probably the sentries that were going to challenge us.

Bob Irwin and I looked at each other. We both had our Stoners up on the gunwales now, and it looked like these guys weren't going to challenge us, they were setting up on us. We decided not to give them the chance. I told Hetzer what was going on. He decided right there to shoot them.

Irwin and I had a bead on these guys, and just about when we were going to shoot, our boat hit the sand. Now here we were, stuck out in the middle of a thirty-foot-wide canal. There were two guys with AKs in cover right up in front of us, and our whole boat had come to a complete stop. This was not good!

Irwin and I put our front sights on the guys and just let go. We let loose with massive firepower right onto that point. We fired maybe all of five seconds, then stopped. The sound was just deafening; my ears were ringing. I was totally pumped, then all of a sudden, not a sound.

Only two or three shots had come out from the point. We knew that because their AKs had green tracers, unlike our red ones. We saw two or three tracers come out of their position, and it was over. Nothing was moving, and I was just waiting for something, anything, to move, but nothing happened. Nobody had said a word in the boat.

About five seconds later I noticed some movement off to my left. Again, perfectly backlit, I saw two more guys with AK-47s, in pajamas, and they were coming alongside of us now.

At this point, I didn't need permission. It was shoot first and ask questions later. Irwin and I both let loose. He was shooting right over my right shoulder, and I don't think my ear has recovered to this day. We shot those two, and they went down.

Then I heard Jim yelling at the top of his voice in the back of the boat to stop shooting, it was Sam and Nu! Sure enough, we had no idea it was them, and we had shot at both of them. That sucked a whole lot.

You can talk about your "best" missions, but that was a nightmare op: a friendly-fire kill. The question we had was why didn't anyone tell us they were getting out of the boat? It wasn't in the original plan for them to get out, but those guys were fighters, and they immediately jumped over the side of the boat when we started firing the first time. We had no idea they were going to conduct a flanking movement. All we would have needed was to have the word passed on to us in the bow. It was a real unfortunate situation. Because of the communication problems, it's my guess now, no one in our boat understood until later what Sam and Nu were intending to do. It was difficult to communicate with them even in relaxed situations.

After we shot them, we called in the MSSC, which came back in on full step [full speed]. It was total insanity. Everybody else bailed out of the sampan and went up into the nipa palm where Sam and Nu were and got them out. Surprisingly, Nu didn't get hit, but Sam did. Sam was shot nine times, from the heel to the head.

We took Sam and put him on the deck of the MSSC. Some of the guys tried to do CPR [cardio-pulmonary resuscitation] on him. I was going to do the respirations, but the minute I put my hand on the back of his head I could feel that half of it was gone—his brains were coming out. In the moonlight I could see his pupils get real big, then stop moving, and his eyes went cloudy; he was gone. I knew it, and I knew that I had done it. Not only did I shoot somebody I knew, but I was also one of the people trying to save him when I knew it was hopeless.

We hauled ass back to the base. It was the darnedest feeling, for a man with my experience. It was just like any other time we were in a fight; but this was different. It wasn't like fighting and killing the enemy.

Up until that point, Nu had been a great Cambodian fighter for us. He believed in us and thought we were great fighters and really squared away. But from that night on he didn't trust us anymore; we had almost killed him, and I didn't blame him for not trusting us.

On my second tour, from 6 September 1971 to 3 March 1972, I was an LDNN adviser. Lieutenant "Whitie" Weir, Bob Irwin, Fred Welch, and I went back together. It was very unusual, very rare that you got to go back to 'Nam with someone that you had gone with the first time.

The reason it happened that way was because in the interim Bob and I went to the SEAL Delivery Vehicle [SDV: small wet submarine used to deliver SEALs to a target] platoon. We really got into the SDVs. We worked on those boats, drove those boats everywhere. I became a primary driver, and Bob became one of the primary drivers, and we were doing our ORI [ordnance readiness inspection] and swimmer attacks on ships off the California coast. We were very good at what we did.

They kept us in that group for a while, then somebody up in admin [administration] was going through records and realized we only had eight months left in the Navy. Someone must have figured that if they didn't send us to Vietnam one more time, we would get out with only having had one deployment.

They sent us to Vietnamese language school and decided to send us to an adviser detachment. I really didn't want to go to the language school, so I played one of my trump cards. I was pretty negative about the whole Team thing at this point and was not real excited about being a Vietnam veteran. America was not at all proud of its veterans at that time. As a matter of fact, we were looked at very suspiciously. So it was very easy for me to not want to go back. To get out of the school, I decided that my wisdom teeth were hurting; I knew I needed to have them pulled anyway. I played my last two wisdom teeth and had to have medication, which excluded me from the rest of the Vietnamese language school.

Two weeks later I got orders to return to Vietnam with the next det that was going over.

Unlike platoons that got together and trained for a number of months, Irwin and I had so little time left in the service that they took both of us at the same time and said we were in the same det going out. It was supposed to be a two-week notice, but it turned out that we left four days later.

In Hoi An we were supposed to train indigenous forces to be a SEAL platoon. Of course, I was supposed to be completely fluent in Vietnamese. After three months in the language school, I still had three months to go when I bailed out, so I could only just get by. "Whitie," Fred, and Irwin didn't speak any Vietnamese.

The Vietnamization of the war had been occurring quite rapidly over the year and a half since I had been there. More and more of the systems and processes had been taken over by the Vietnamese. The entire war operation had become so kicked-back and so unorganized that there was just no way we were going to operate in it.

"Whitie," Fred, Bob, and I sat in our hooch the very first day. We were the only gringos around, and we looked at each other and said, "Well, what do we want to do?"

"Whitie" asked if we wanted to be the last guys to die in Vietnam, and all four of us went thumbs down.

Fred, Bob, and I stayed and were the only three gringos at Hoi An. "Whitie" Weir went to Danang and stayed at the "O" club berthing. Every once in a while he'd show up at the base just to see what we were doing.

For the next six months we only did two different operations. On one op, the Seabees wanted us to do a hydrographic survey out at this little island off of Vung Tau. They needed us to go around the island and do a drop-line survey to record the depth of the water around the coastline; it was one of their projects to build a dock.

The indiginous SEALs were supposed to be a platoon of fourteen men, but you could never tell if there were fourteen men because they never all met together at the same time. They'd float in and float out all the time. They spoke pidgin English, but somehow, between all the swear words, sign language, and goofy stuff we did, we communicated; we got along OK.

Ultimately, we went on this op, and I watched this platoon we were supposed to train, in action. It was amazing. On the way to the island we were going to stop at another small island where it was rumored Thai fishermen were hiding large quantities of narcotics in a cave. They wanted our indigenous SEALs to go onto the island, confirm it, and seize the narcotics. Bob was on this op with me, and we had a visiting full lieutenant with us named "Ace" Sarich. He was running the op from the gringo side.

We were on a Vietnamese LST, an old flat-bottomed American LST renamed *My Tho*—the kind with the doors that opened up in the front. This was the first time I had ever gone to sea on a ship. We were on the back of this boat as we headed out. Bob and I stayed down in the fantail area, but we would go up to the wardroom to visit and eat.

When we left Vung Tau, they told us to batten down the hatches: big typhoon up ahead. I had no idea what we were sailing into. We were going great guns.

This storm that we ran into the end of was unbelievable. The typhoon had already gone by, but the seas were just enormous. By the time it got dark the ship was really tossing and turning, and this was a big ship. The pounding sounds of the waves were incredible. Up on the bridge, the large windows had been closed, and there were small portholes we could look out of. When an LST went into a big sea like that, it would rise on the first wave, and you could see the ship actually bending as it started to go down into the next trough. Then it would just bury itself into the next wave. This wall of green water would come over the top of the ship and slam into the bridge. There was totally green water everywhere. It looked like we were going under—just amazing.

So we had our Vietnamese SEAL team in there running around, and they were just as loosely wound as a group could ever be, and just as goofy. Talk about lackadaisical, the Vietnamese sailors didn't even batten down the hatches. The ship would roll one way, and all the sea doors would go *clink, clink, clink, clink, clink,* open. Then it would roll the other way, and they'd all slam shut, *clink, clink, clink, clink, clink*—just like dominoes.

We got to the island and were standing off the leeward side of the island, trying to stay in the wind shadow of the island. The LST was holding just enough headway to stay in one position. Then the captain said the Vietnamese SEALs would have to go ashore in the IBSs from where we were—which was about a four-hundred-yard paddle. The wind was blowing, there were whitecaps—really terrible conditions.

"Ace" took control and said to get the IBSs out. The LDNNs had kept their IBSs in a conex box [shipping container] back at their SEAL area on land, and they had been invaded by rats. They had put C-rations inside of the IBSs, and the rats ate through the rubber boats to get to the chocolate that was in the C-rats. So here we were, ready to do this operation, and their IBSs had rat holes all the way through them.

We felt like this was some kind of joke. They didn't even have respect for the basic things. Here we had given them a perfectly good $1,000 rubber boat, and they used it to hide chocolate, and the rats ate it.

We got two of the boats repaired by taking parts from others that could not be salvaged. We actually had to cut huge pieces out of some to use as patches on the two that they ended up taking to the island. We had to glue and sew them in place. It was us gringos who actually did the repair work, because if it was left up to them, they would have just said, "Well, we can't do the op now, there's a hole in the boat." We told them, "No, no, you find a way to make it work."

So our operation had started at six in the morning, and we didn't put a boat in the water until almost one o'clock in the afternoon. They took the boat and paddled like crazy for about two hours to get to shore.

Shortly after they got to the island, we heard all kinds of shooting, and we were thinking, "Oh, God, now what?"

On top of it all, they had dropped their radio off the side of the IBS on the way in to the island—it was gone—we had lost radio contact with them. Through my binoculars I couldn't see them shooting.

Then I saw them carry a poncho from the two-hundred-foot-high bluff at the high point of the island facing us. They were careful as they lowered the poncho down the cliff, and three or four of them set it in their IBS and started paddling back. We all thought somebody must have been shot.

They made it back to the boat and threw the tarp up on the deck. We were all there with the corpsman ready to help them out when they came aboard. They got up on the boat, opened up this tarp, and it was filled with seagulls and eggs! They were all saying, "Number-one chop chop!"

So they had gone onto this island on an op and ended up killing all these seagulls and collecting a bunch of eggs. Here we were, supposed to be interdicting drugs, and these guys were out there having an Easter egg hunt.

Then they proceeded to put everything in the oven; they didn't even bother to clean the guts out of them or anything, just put them in this big oven. It smelled so bad when the feathers starting melting. All we could do was go forward on the boat to get upwind from the smell. These guys served these things up just like baked potatoes: they were breaking open their seagulls on a mound of rice, just dumping all the guts and everything onto their rice, saying, "Number-one chop chop!" This was our group, even though we had worked with these guys for six months.

We went on toward the other island, did the survey, and came back. Those were the kinds of ops we did in our last months over there. We never went into combat with the LDNNs. These men couldn't do the simple, nonstress things, so we certainly weren't going to take them into combat with us. No way. Our job of being an adviser at that time was a political job. It really served no purpose, for us or for them.

15

Kirby D. Horrell

*Pointman, 1st Squad, Foxtrot Platoon
Seafloat, Republic of Vietnam,
Deployed March–September 1970*

I was the pointman of the 1st Squad, Foxtrot Platoon. We had made our way down to Seafloat after stopping at the Det Golf office in Binh Thuy. When we arrived, our operating gear was already out.

We went out on a break-in op in the early evening, approximately two or three hours after sunset, and made our way into a canal which was west of Seafloat—or upriver, as we called it.

That night the sky was real clear, full of stars, and the moon was full. We sat there all night, but nothing ever materialized. I got to listen to the jungle and got to understand the noises of the jungle immediately after sunset and how the jungle talked to you in the early morning before we extracted.

The night was uneventful, but we did set up an ambush. We got through the initial anticipation, I think. The early jitters, the early fears of getting into the jungle in Vietnam as a young SEAL—we got through all those things in the first night. We got to learn more about our environment and just exactly what we were there for—learned how to become one with the jungle.

After the break-in op, we shook hands with the people from the platoon we were relieving and said good-bye. We had spent two days going over all the intel they had up on the sit-map [situation map]. From this we knew that there was going to be enemy activity in the area; VC rocket teams were coming up on the Song Cua Lon to attack our patrol boats. We made a calculated guess as to where the next rocket team was going to be, and that's the area we targeted.

I was pretty nervous because I was going to be the guy out in front. It was a little bit of nerves and a little bit of fear, but all that was overcome by the SEAL Team training and all that my mentors had taught me about being a pointman. I was positive and comfortable with my own capabilities. Because I was a hunter as a young man, I knew what to expect. Even though my nerves and my mind were going a thousand miles an hour getting ready for the op, I still felt very confident because of my training. The personal feelings that I had, I dealt with in my own way as we got into the PLO [patrol-leader's order].

Our officer gave a comprehensive PLO, which we all participated in on a regular basis. Everybody in the PLO handled their particular area of expertise. As the pointman, I would take care of all the routes in, the routes out, the E&E [escape and evasion] routes—and what kind of hand and arm signals were to be used. The pointman had one of the largest responsibilities in the whole patrol—he carried on his shoulders the lives of everyone behind him. That he stepped in the right places, that he took the right routes, that he was able to pick up all the sounds out there, that he did not lead them into an ambush. All his senses had to be at their peak.

After the PLO, we all got our operating gear and loaded the MSSC. The squad inserted just after sunset about a klick upstream from the canal ambush site. I patrolled on a predesignated bearing until we hit the canal around 2100 hours. I went up and reconned the ambush site, making sure that we had complete visibility, and checked out the foliage where we were going to set up the ambush line.

Then I patrolled back to the patrol leader and told him what I thought. He brought the rest of the squad up and started placing everyone in position; then we ran out our claymores. The ambush site was long, and we set up a tug line so we could silently communicate with each other.

I was on the right flank, and an AW man with an M-60 was next to me. I had the right-flank claymore clacker [firing device] next to me, as everybody hunkered down and waited. I remember the ground was very muddy. We were on the bank of a canal that had receded; the tidal range this particular night was about seven feet.

We listened to the sounds of the jungle all night long. Practically all you could hear was the mud-sucker fish—we just called them "fuck you fish." You'd hear the streams going, the animals moving through the jungle, and the mud-sucker fish would be making a clicking sound. When we were in the Delta, we used a lot of finger snapping to signal each other because it blended in with the natural sounds of the jungle.

We sat there for about six hours, and I was the first one to notice that the rocket team was heading toward my position on the right flank, but on the other side of the canal fifteen meters away. The glow of the day was just starting to come on, and we could see that our ambush site was not as concealed as we thought—which made us very nervous.

As I spotted the VC on the right, I tugged to the M-60 man, and he tugged to everybody else. Apparently, our camouflage was great: the VC just continued to walk. They were talking and smoking cigarettes, as most of the VC did. All three of them had AKs. I think that rather than a rocket team, they were scouts for whoever was coming later on.

We waited for them to move into the kill zone. They

stopped about ten meters from the right flank—which made me very nervous. I brought my Stoner up and had a sight picture on all three of them. If at any time their weapons would have moved in our direction, I would have done them instantly. But they didn't—two of them were carrying their weapons down at their sides. One of them had his weapon slung over his shoulder.

As any good SEAL Team member will tell you, you didn't look at their eyes, you looked at the weapon. They couldn't kill you with their eyes—they'd kill you with the weapon. If the weapon started to move toward you, you took 'em. That was exactly what my mentors taught me, and that was what I was counting on out there. Because when you trained somebody, as my mentors trained me, you were betting their life on how well you did your job.

I watched and kept my sight picture on the VC. As soon as the officer initiated the ambush by opening fire first, everyone shot to kill. The three VC hit the ground immediately. Everyone had a sight picture, so everyone's first shot was directed at a particular person.

In an ambush, you didn't spray the area down. During the first initiation, you had a sight picture on exactly what you were shooting. After you hit that target, you moved to another target.

Because it was first blood—the first time that we had made a kill—some people in our ambush line were overexcited and just continued to shoot. A normal ambush lasted about ten seconds—no longer. The officer was hollering to cease fire, and I know for a fact the M-60 man next to me fired his whole box of ammo. He and the other M-60 gunner were just raking the area—hosing it. There was nothing wrong with that because they wanted to make sure we had clean kills.

We ceased fire, and then another SEAL and I moved across the canal to check the bodies. It was only about a five-meter swim; everyone covered us going across.

When we got up on the other bank, I saw only two Viet Cong soldiers lying there. We made sure they were dead before we searched them. We could not see the third VC, but we did see a blood trail.

I remembered that my instructors had told me you never chased a blood trail. So I set up on the blood trail to make sure the other Charlie wasn't going to jump up and hit us while the other SEAL finished the search.

He finished searching the bodies, and we called in the boat to extract. We took the weapons and the intel—some maps and documents that would assure that we would continue the intelligence network that had been left to us by the platoon we relieved.

When the weapons and intel were collected, I let loose with a burst from my Stoner down the blood trail to ensure that if anybody was out there, they weren't about to come back as we were leaving and hit us from the rear.

With that in mind, we decided to have the boat come as far as it could into the canal and extract us, rather than patrolling out to the main river. We blew the claymores, rolled up the wires, and got into patrol formation with the captured weapons and intel and headed back toward the main river. We patrolled about three hundred meters and saw the extraction boat coming in. We got aboard the MSSC, feeling elated that all the years of training had actually come to a finalization. We were, in fact, at war, and we were the winners of our first confrontation in Vietnam, our "first blood."

16

Paul Lee Pittman

Radioman, 1st Squad, Foxtrot Platoon
Seafloat, Republic of Vietnam
Deployed March–September 1970

Two platoons of SEALs were living in one of the barracks on Seafloat. We were watching a movie one night when one of the guys, Kirby Horrell, had to relieve himself.

He stepped outside to take a leak between the barges, and there was this guy looking back at him from the water. So he yelled to us, "Hey, there's a guy down there."

Nobody got too excited because there was a good movie on. So we just said, "Well, throw a concussion grenade on him."

Kirby threw out a grenade, and then another face appeared in the water.

After that, everybody was out there throwing concussion grenades all around Seafloat.

In the next three days seven bodies floated up, all wearing explosives. It was definitely a suicidal mission for those guys. They must have known that the guards on Seafloat threw concussion grenades at night to prevent attack by sapper swimmers, because before coming down to attack us, they had taken rags and stuffed them up their rectums. Maybe they thought that would protect their internal organs from the concussion.

At the end of the third day one body floated up that had about 240 pounds of C-4 strapped to him. The charge had seven Chinese time fuses, and one had been set—he'd pulled it before he died. The crew of EOD guys on board took the C-4, went over to the beach area, and blew it. They kept the one time-fuse detonator and put it on their desk. A couple of days later when the detonator dried out, it went off.

It was a good thing Kirby had to take a leak that night. If he hadn't, there's no telling if any of us would be here today!

17

Dodd Coutts

*Pointman, 2d Squad, Hotel Platoon
Sa Dec, My Tho, and Ben Tre,
Republic of Vietnam,
Deployed April–October 1970*

I don't remember the actual number of people we captured while we were deployed, but I know it was in the hundreds. We captured more than we ever shot. Usually, we got them by surprise, set up some good ambushes, or walked into their hooches and got them at gunpoint. We usually didn't have to fight them—just took and manhandled them.

One of the first ops we did was near Sa Dec on Football Island. We went in about two klicks to some hooches where there was a suspected tax collector. Six or seven sampans were tied up by the hooches. Some of the boats had covers over them; people actually lived in the sampans.

We searched the hooches and rounded up all the locals in the area, about twenty of them. I confiscated a lot of the material that I found—maps, documents, local money, and two pouches. As we were coming out, I turned one of the pouches over to our officer and kept the other pouch, just for the ease of carrying it.

We took the individual with us that we suspected was the tax collector. When we got to our extraction point by the river, someone made the decision not to take him back with us. He was being very uncooperative anyway, so we ended up letting him go.

At the time we didn't know for sure, but we found out he indeed was the tax collector. So a couple of nights later we went back in and rounded him up again. Found him in the same place on a sampan, and this time we took him out of there.

About two days later I realized I had forgotten to give the second pouch to the officer. I was going through my gear and noticed I had thrown it under my rack. I pulled it out, opened it up, and found quite a bit of money in it. So it was party time for everybody in the platoon!

Once in the Binh Dai district, out toward the coast, four of us SEALs were asked to help two EOD personnel blow some bunkers. We went in by patrol boat as far as we could, then got into two IBSs and motored in with little fifteen-horsepower motors as far as we could. We had to lift the motors up at times because it got pretty shallow. Then we paddled in and still were about a half mile from shore. The water was only about knee deep at most; at a few places it was only an inch or two inches deep.

We started to walk in, all of us on line, and got maybe fifty to a hundred feet from shore when this one VC stood up in a little bunker. He stood up, waved at us, and started to shoot at us with his little carbine. Here were six of us running as fast as we could away from the beach—running back out because we were getting chased by this one guy with a carbine.

We shot back, but every time we'd shoot, he would get in his bunker, where he had this little hole he could shoot out of. We shot our four LAW [light antitank weapon] rockets and hit the bunker, but he would still come up, make faces at us, and shoot his carbine again. That was the first time we were chased off the beach.

Another time we went in to blow bunkers again near the same area. This was a daylight squad op, and we had to walk in, but we had helo support. We walked in a half mile or so over the beach.

At one point I asked my officer, John Rowe, to take a picture of me. As he was taking a photo, I heard something whiz by, and I spun around—just as he snapped the picture. In the picture I'm spinning around, and you can see an Army Cobra helicopter in the background. Just as he took the picture, about two hundred VC came running out of the tree line about a quarter mile behind us. We went into the instant-flee mode. We ended up running out about a half mile in knee-deep water.

The whole time no one ever shot back—we just ran as fast as we could on line, making sure that everyone was still with us. And all you could see were these little *plunks* in the water around you.

I was asked by an LDNN adviser to go in and help him capture a province-level VCI, who was believed to be in a particular hooch. Supposedly, there were two hooches together. The VCI had been injured recently and was recovering. The way we would know we had captured the right guy was that he would have a Chinese-made K-54 pistol on him or by his side, indicating he was a captain or higher.

I went in with the adviser and six LDNNs. We patrolled—I believe it was—six klicks. During the patrol we had to cross an open field, which was a good mile and a half across. This was at about ten o'clock at night.

As we crossed the field, we heard noises that were off in the distance. Then I heard a noise real close. I was in the rear security position, and the adviser was in the patrol leader's position. I sent the word to hold up, that I heard something. So we got down and waited ten or fifteen minutes just to listen. As we were listening, we saw little campfires being lit all around us, and we heard people talking. We found out we'd walked into the middle of an NVA unit; there were a couple hundred NVA—or NVA and VC—all around us.

We decided to try and sneak out of there as quietly as we could, but as we started to move, we were spotted. The NVA were getting up, and we saw that we were completely surrounded.

They were starting to form a sweep to move in on us, so we called in for air support. The Cobra gunships came in. We signaled our location with an infrared strobe and told them to fire on anything around us. We told them we would keep the strobe light going.

As they started to shoot their rockets and strafe the land, the NVA were running in every direction. In the mass confusion, we headed off on foot in the direction we wanted to go. In the process, I actually bumped into one of the NVA. He was running, and I was running, and we ran into each other. I said, "Excuse me," not even realizing what I was doing.

We got about ten or fifteen feet apart, both stopped dead in our tracks, looked back at each other, then both split and kept running. It was total mass confusion.

We ran on, and I kept thinking, "My God, I could've shot that guy." He probably thought the same thing. But he was running for cover from the air power, and I was running for my life.

We eventually broke contact. I think they were too busy worrying about our air support.

We patrolled about another klick and came across the two hooches where we were supposed to capture this individual. We set up, determined it wasn't feasible to try a capture, and decided we would just ambush the hooches. I had two LAW rockets, and the LDNN adviser had two. I fired one, and it went in one side of the hooch and out the other side. It didn't hit anything, and it exploded in the tree line. He fired one at the same hooch, and it went right through and exploded on the far side.

My second LAW initiated on something in the hooch—which caused some medical supplies to go up and start a fire. The adviser fired his second LAW at the hooch, and it went right through again, so then we just opened fire on the two hooches. Everyone shot until we were about half out of ammo.

We did a search, and indeed, we had killed everybody inside. There were about six people inside, but we knew we had killed the high-level VCI—we captured the K-54 pistol.

On the patrol out we got hit—I'm not sure how many times—by small groups that tried to ambush us. Fortunately enough, they were trigger happy and ambushed us before we got into the kill zone. So we were able to react and move out of the area.

On the way out, being rear security, I was using a Stoner, which I normally didn't carry. I would shoot to where the last fire—the last contact—was, and the Cobras would make a run on that area and try to silence it so we could break contact. We had, I would say, eight to ten contacts like this, where they would try to ambush us and we would run. We got hit more from the side than from the front.

At one point one of the LDNNs ran back to where the Cobras were shooting their rockets. I watched him run by me and figured, "Well, if you want to go, go—I'm not going to risk my life for you." That's when the LDNN adviser told me to go back and get him.

So I ran back—didn't want to—and on the way back one of the Cobra's 2.75-inch rockets landed fairly close and knocked me to the ground.

I got up, collected myself, got my weapon, and grabbed the LDNN, but he was dead. So I threw him over my shoulders, grabbed his M-79, and ran back up to where the adviser was.

He looked at the guy, decided to leave him, and we patrolled out. We were moving too fast to take him with us. We had to leave him for our own well-being.

It was the fastest I've ever patrolled out of an area. It was more of a run because we were heavily outnumbered. It seemed that every time we turned around, we were running into another enemy unit.

We got extracted by boat, and as we left shore, the boat got hit—so it was a good firefight, even on the way out. They were all over the place.

Everybody in the platoon, including our interpreter Ah and our guide Willy, went out to do a prisoner snatch at a VC meeting place. There were three hooches and a bunker. We set up on the hooch in which the meeting was supposed to take place. We watched, basically, the meeting go down, which took about five minutes.

As the individual, a high-ranking VCI, left, two SEALs jumped out and grabbed him. He had no bodyguards, but a couple of VC were over by the hooch. The rest of us shot them. As soon as the VCI was brought to the ground, they put a gun to his head, did a complete body search, and tied his hands behind his back.

You tied them behind the back and took the line up around the neck and then back again. That way, when you held that line, you had him by the neck also. Using the line, you could pull his head back or grab him by the hair. You could manhandle him. Then we took another line and tied it between his feet about six inches apart. So for him to run— well, he couldn't run—he could only take short, choppy steps. Then we gagged him—just put about twenty wraps of rigger's tape around his face to make sure he couldn't talk, then blindfolded him.

We destroyed the three hooches by burning them with incendiaries and destroyed the bunker by blowing it up with some C-4. Then we patrolled out.

On the patrol out, we found that the prisoner couldn't keep up with us, so we cut the line on his feet, but two people were assigned to him—one in front and one behind—and the one behind had physical contact.

On 21 May our squad, Ah our interpreter, and Willy our guide went out in the LSSC. There were only supposed to be eight personnel total in the LSSC, and with the boat crew we had, I believe, twelve total. We were going to do an ambush, and we had to go under a low-hanging bridge. The MSSC wouldn't fit under it because of the radar and the arches. But the LSSC would fit, so we went in at about medium tide.

We passed an Army [ARVN] outpost next to the bridge, and on the other side of the bridge was a small village that was supposedly friendly.

As we went by them, it was just at sunset, and they all waved. We waved back. We went up this little river—more of a canal I would say—as far as we could—which was about a mile, mile and a half—departed the boat, and patrolled almost another two miles up the river and set our ambush. Meanwhile, the LSSC went back out to the main river under the bridge.

We waited probably six hours in the ambush site, and nothing ever developed. So we patrolled back out to where we'd get picked up, but the tide had gone out real low. So we actually walked within a half mile of the village—the "friendly" village.

The LSSC came in, picked us up; and as we came out, knowing it was a friendly village, everybody started to relax. We were standing up in the boat; some guys were starting to smoke.

As we got near the village, the canal was no more than twenty to twenty-five meters wide. The banks were almost ten feet above us. Then we got hit by a four-point ambush—

two on each side of the bank from the front, and two on each side from the back.

As soon as the firing started, everyone got down as fast as they could—a natural response. As I went to duck down, the other guys got down faster than me and pinned my legs in, so I was standing up in plain view against the port-side bulkhead.

I saw that everyone was down except for Ah. He lay down on the bow but decided that wasn't doing him any good.

One of the boat crew up on the bow had the radio, a PRC-77, on. He also had a grenade launcher. We looked at each other and decided, "Well, it's up to us." Nobody else was firing, so I took my CAR-15 and fired on full auto to suppress fire. I ran out of ammo, went to change magazines, and the guy next to me said, "Here" and handed me his Stoner, which I started shooting.

This was the only op that I can actually say that everything seemed to be in slow motion. No matter which direction I fired, I could see tracers go past me.

I fired, emptied one of the Stoner drums, and handed the Stoner back down. Somebody handed me another Stoner. I started firing it and shot maybe twenty rounds when it jammed. I couldn't get it unjammed, so I handed it back down. The first guy handed me his reloaded Stoner. I fired again, then we broke contact.

When we first made contact, the boat driver had just floored it—which ended up getting us stuck in the mud. When the firing stopped, he eased off a bit, leveled out, started to float, then he gunned it slowly, and we patrolled out.

About fifty meters down we got hit a second time. No one else had stood up, so again it was just the three of us.

Once again the fighting seemed like it was in slow motion. I felt bullets whiz by my face—which felt like bumble-bees and was more of a nuisance than anything else. I looked around and could tell it was coming from somebody in a tree. I didn't want to stop shooting at the area I was shooting into because I was trying to suppress firepower.

By this time some of the guys started putting their weapons over the gunwales to shoot. I yelled up to the M-79 man on the bow, "Up in the tree!" He saw where the shooting was coming from and fired back. I saw a leg fall out of the tree, so he must have made a direct hit. The whizzing next to my head stopped.

It seemed like this contact just wasn't going to break when out of nowhere there was this sudden massive sound of firepower. The MSSC had been waiting out on the main river and gotten the word that we were in a world of shit and decided to come in. Driving under the bridge tore the radar dome right off the MSSC—just sheared it right off. The boat spun around, and they hosed the bank with a minigun mounted on the back.

Everything became quiet. Even after we broke contact not one head popped up in the boat.

After we got out, we realized why the Stoner'd jammed. I had held it in front of me at chest level where I could aim, and two AK rounds had hit the drum. I would have taken those two rounds right in the chest if not for the Stoner.

When the M-79 man had been talking on the radio handset to the MSSC, trying to tell them to come in, the cord connecting the radio to the handset had been shot. Later we found three or four rounds in the radio itself—which would have hit him square in the back.

The boat had taken close to 350 rounds. Nobody—not one person in that boat—had been hit. Even though the rounds from the ambush were being fired down into the boat, they just went between everyone and hit the bulkhead. Pretty amazing. Somebody was definitely watching after us that day.

· · ·

On 19 June 1970 we were going to blow up some bunkers on Football Island. All but two of the platoon members went in. I was sent over to the right flank in an area we had been in a couple of weeks before. We knew where the bunkers were and had walked down a path on one of the dike lines.

As I walked up, I noticed that the dike line now had *tu dia* signs on it. I saw where some of the booby traps had been recently put into the dirt. I told everybody, "Whatever you do, don't go down this dike line."

I skirted back around out on the right flank while the others loaded the bunker with explosives. Three people were up at the point position at the *T* of the dike line.

The platoon chief came up to my position to ask how everything was going and if I had seen anything. I said, "No, it's all quiet, I haven't seen anything." I watched him as he walked about twenty-five feet away from me.

I turned around, and not more than ten feet away from me, four VC stood right up on another dike line—but they only saw the chief.

The first VC had his AK-47 aimed at the chief. The second guy was carrying a B-40 rocket. He got down into the kneeling position smack in front of me, but never even saw me. The guy with the B-40 was aiming at the boat, which was still beached on the edge of the island about thirty meters away. I watched as he took it off safe.

I don't know why I did it, except maybe I wanted some camaraderie, or somebody else shooting with me—rather than being out there all by myself—but I turned to the chief and in a low voice said, "Chief . . . guys . . . help!" But he never turned around.

I looked back, and the VC that had been aiming at the chief started to turn, look at me, and at the same time point his AK at me. So I brought my CAR-15 up, and I shot him. I remember this distinctly. My gun was on semiautomatic—I shot him and then shot the guy with the B-40 before he could fire at the boat.

I remember thinking, "Wow! I'm on automatic!" because the rounds came out so fast. My finger—from excitement—was going fast: they were just so close.

The other two VC jumped down over the berm.

I realized my whole platoon was behind me, and I knew their natural response, if they heard firing, was to turn in that direction and fire back. So I jumped backwards, down between the two dike lines into a mud patch.

It was a good thing I did because it seemed the whole world opened up above me. Just as I thought, the platoon, out of natural reflexes, turned and started shooting in my direction.

I heard someone yelling, "Hey, wait a minute. Coutts is over there!" So they stopped firing.

To let them know I was okay, because I certainly wasn't going to stick my head up, I took a grenade, popped it, and threw it over the dike line into the area where I thought the two VC were. The grenade went off, and they knew I was okay.

At the same time all the shooting was going on, the three SEALs in the point position came down the dike line I told them not to walk on. One of them stepped on a toe-popper booby trap buried in the ground.

The explosion blew him ten to fifteen feet in the air. I looked over my left shoulder at him as he was going up. He was yelling, "Mother fuckers!" as he shot his XM-148 grenade launcher at the two VC that were running away. The round from the grenade launcher went off, and before he hit the ground he reloaded and fired a second time. He came down wailing because he'd been hit.

One of the platoon checked on me to make sure I was all right, then went back and checked on the other SEAL and brought him over to my position. The chief came over as the platoon was moving up to give us some support. Two of us carried the wounded SEAL almost all the way back to where the boat was, then the chief said, "I'll take him. You guys go make sure that everything is clear up ahead.'' The chief ended up carrying him to the boat and put him aboard. The corpsman checked his injuries and found that the mine had blown off two of his toes.

We went back to check the area where I shot the two VC. Sure enough, I had killed both of them. We captured a B-40 rocket and an AK.

One of the VC from the berm who was hiding nearby got up and ran. He was only about fifty meters from us when the automatic-weaponsman opened up with his M-60. You could see the tracers hit the VC in the back. He kept running and running, the whole time taking rounds in his back.

Finally, he fell, and we thought he was down for good, but the guy got up and ran again.

So the M-60 opened up, and we knew he hit the VC more than once because his whole back was just covered with the blood soaking through his shirt.

He kept running, but he probably died within minutes.

18

Jim Day

Rear Security, 2d Squad, Hotel Platoon
Sa Dec, My Tho, and Ben Tre,
Republic of Vietnam,
Deployed April–October 1970

My position in 2d Squad was rear security. I carried a Stoner with a total of 700 rounds; four ammo pouches, each with a 100-round belt; and one canteen pouch with 150 rounds. If I needed extra, I just carried it on me, underneath my camies.

Even when both squads operated together, I was always rear security. I was responsible for making sure that no one came up behind us as we were patrolling. I also had to know what route to take to get back out. Sometimes we'd mark trees on the way in, in case we had to go back out the same way.

Actually, there was only one op where I had to lead the squad out. Our officer told me to turn around, and I went back out the same way we had come in. I hadn't gone very far when Ah, our *hoi chanh,* stopped me and told me to get behind him. He wouldn't let anybody else walk in front of him—he always wanted to be first. Ah really knew what he was doing; he was indispensable to our squad. He walked out in front for six months with no problems.

He had been a VC officer and had had some money, land, and a nice house. The VC showed up one day and took it all away. From that day on he hated them. During field interrogations of prisoners he wouldn't take no for an answer. Ah always got whatever information the prisoners had.

One of the shortest ops we went on was when Ah pinpointed a grenade factory to take out. We got a couple helos and went in, almost on top of the place. We just jumped off the helos and ran right inside the factory. We took the molds and forms to make sure the enemy couldn't make any more grenades and left. We didn't blow anything up, just seized it all. It was one of those ops where we were in and out in a few minutes without having any contact whatsoever with the enemy.

One time on Football Field, near Sa Dec, we did a split op, where both squads went out at the same time but to different places. Normally, just one squad would go out, or both would go out but operate together. On this op, we let the other squad off from an IBS, then took the insertion boat in to our objective, which was to blow up a VC meeting place we called the Blue Door.

On the way in we heard a bunch of shooting and thought, "All right! The other squad got a hit."

So we went in and set up a haversack of C-4 in the hooch to blow it up. We found out later that one of the guys put a can of gasoline on top of the charge to make sure it was going to go. We didn't have a good place to hide except down a river embankment, which was only about fifteen feet away from the hooch. When the explosives went off, the concussion knocked us back off the bank, but no one got hurt.

We stayed around to see if anyone would come to see what happened. We split up; four guys stayed on the river embankment, and three of us spread out down in a little gully, but where we could see each other.

We waited thirty minutes or more before some shots were fired from our side of the river.

The next thing we knew, all hell broke loose from behind us on the other side of the river. We all lay down and watched as green and red tracers shot over our heads. Leaves and branches were falling all around us. We called the boat to come get us out of there and called in some gunships to hit the opposite riverbank.

The extraction boat was firing the 40-mike-mike grenade launcher as it came in to pick us up. As soon as we got on board, we opened up on the other side of the river. None of us were hit, and we got out of there and picked up the other squad.

They were all saying, "Neat firefight, guys!"

And we said, "What?" We weren't even shooting; it was the enemy shooting the whole time. We never even fired back until after we were on the boat heading out. We had hoped to be the ones firing. It really surprised us.

A couple of days later the intel people came back and said it was a thirty-man VC strike force that had been shooting at us. We hit some of them when we opened fire from the boat, and the air strikes that came in got more of them.

During the daytime we would just carry on with and do whatever we wanted to do. Sometimes we'd play volleyball or basketball. If you went out anywhere, you had to let someone know where you were going and who was going with you. We never went anywhere alone. We'd check in at a certain time during the day to find out if we were going out that night. If so, we'd find out what extra gear had to be carried and get that ready. We were told what time the patrol order was going to be given, and we'd have to be back then.

Some nights when we didn't go out on an op, we'd sit around and play poker all night long.

We were always aware that our actions could help the enemy predict our movements. We had been frequenting one bar on a regular basis. On nights when we were going to go out on an operation, we went to the bar to have one beer and drink some soda, then we would go back and go on the op. But we didn't want to set a pattern. We didn't want the enemy to notice that we were usually at the bar except for the nights that we were out on an operation. So when we had an op, we'd go to the bar and do what we would normally do, sit there and talk to the waitresses and the girls that ran the bar. Then we'd leave in plenty of time to do our op.

One night op turned out scary, though I didn't even know it until we got back.

We were doing a platoon op, and I was rear security, following the guy in front of me. We were sitting in a field for a rest when all of a sudden he jumped up and took off running.

I thought, "Oh, man, we must really be hot on somebody." It was nighttime, but I could see where he was running because I would catch the glow from his watch now and then; he didn't have his watch face covered.

I followed him, and we ran on for several minutes, then stopped and calmed down. Nothing was happening, so we continued the patrol, with me at the rear.

I found out when we got back to the base what'd happened. I asked him, "What was going on back there; who were we running after?"

He said, "No one; we got left behind. I didn't see the rest of the squad when they got up and left.".

I couldn't believe it! Here we had been running through the jungle, and he was hoping we were going the right way. I told him not to ever let that happen again. It was just him and me out there all alone in the middle of nowhere. Talk about scary!

. . .

When I first arrived in Vietnam, I didn't know what to expect. You know there's a war going on, and you know you have been trained well. So when you first get there, you try to find out what's going on and try to remember everything you have been taught.

The first couple of ops weren't too bad because we didn't hit anything. On the third op we had contact. I felt like I was out in the middle of nowhere, and the enemy could see me even though there were tall bushes all around me.

Toward the middle of the tour you knew what was going on; you knew what you were doing and knew what to do so that the enemy couldn't see you. We had Viet Cong walk up to within fifteen feet of us and not see us. One time we walked right past a guy while he was sleeping in a hooch. He didn't even know it. We sat there and watched him for fifteen minutes to see if he'd wake up and leave, but he didn't, so we just left.

At the end of the tour, you were getting ready to leave and thinking, "This is my last op. Good, I can get out of here." Then you were a little more cautious because nothing had happened to you for six months, and you didn't want it to happen now. So it was a little scary at the end.

But if they called me back right now, I'd go back and do it all over again. Definitely.

19

Bill Noyce

Sea Commando Team Adviser,
Naval Advisory Detachment
Danang, Republic of Vietnam
Deployed April–December 1970

On my first deployment I was with Echo Platoon. I extended my time in service because I wanted one more tour in Vietnam. Once I got over there the second time, I kept extending, because every time I was due to rotate home, I always felt like I had a little more work to do. So my tour was longer than the usual six months.

Camp Fay was the name of the compound just outside of Danang where we were stationed. We were working with the Vietnamese Sea Commandos. My main project there was to make sure that the new guys coming in—and there were sixty in the group—were in shape. We put them through a course similar to a UDT training class. I was the person in charge of that. Once we got them trained, those men were mine to take out in the field and operate with. Thomas McCutchan, from SEAL Team Two, assisted me during the training, and we would share the operations.

At that time our group consisted of two SEALs and two Marine Force Recon guys. Lt. Bill Belding from SEAL Team One was in charge of all of us. His main area of concern was the intelligence we gathered that we needed for our operations.

Originally, I thought that our mission at Camp Fay was an extension of what SEALs were trained for—which was reconnaissance, kidnapping, and assassinations. However, in some of our operations we went beyond that. There were a couple of times that we went into the DMZ [demilitarized zone]. We took the PT boats up, then inserted by IBS. The rubber boats had motors on them—which I wasn't used to. The Vietnamese always found an easier way to do things.

We patrolled in and searched for trails. Later, I figured out that what we had been looking for were trails that the North Vietnamese were using to move American prisoners of war north. While I was there our group never went above the DMZ.

There was one time when a "black shoe" [regular Navy; non-SEAL] captain, who was the commander of the Navy side of Camp Fay, wanted us to go after some people in a certain area, and he wanted me to take all sixty of the Sea Commandos with me. They were still pretty green, and I told him that his idea was ridiculous. I said that I would take only ten and that I would pick the men because I wanted to come out with a bunch of us alive.

The captain didn't like that very much, so he wrote me up for disobedience. That would have resulted in me receiving a dishonorable discharge when I left the Navy. Somehow Lieutenant Belding got it changed so that instead of being written up for disobedience, he wrote it in my quarterly evaluation. He made some good comments such as "conforms to Navy standards," "good shipmate," "helps morale," and "works well on his own." He also added that I had a "high degree of professional knowledge," and "he unquestioningly accepts commands from those directly above him, but is often reluctant to follow orders from those that he feels are less than his equal."

McCutchan and I hardly ever went out together, though it

did happen a few times. A few times I went out as the only adviser on the operation. More often I went out with one of the Force Recon Marines as the second adviser. In the field they were great. It was just like working with one of our guys.

One time when I was on R&R in Australia, McCutchan took the guys out. It was the only time he took them out by himself, and they ended up shooting two of our own men. They were set up on an ambush, and evidently two of the guys were set up separately, got lonely, and came back to the main group. When they came back, they walked into the kill zone of the ambush, and the rest of the guys opened fire. One lost his leg, and the other was killed outright.

Once we had one good intelligence report that a group of VCI in a certain village moved down a river on almost a nightly basis. They were a group of tax collectors and medical personnel that went from village to village. Ten of us, including a Force Recon guy, went in. We inserted by truck at ten o'clock at night and patrolled in about three klicks. It was easy walking because we were moving through an area that was primarily covered with reeds. At eleven o'clock we got to a waist-deep canal, and on the other side was a dike that was covered with grass. Past the dike was a river that was two hundred yards wide.

For the mission that night I chose a pump shotgun as my personal weapon. I wanted an Ithaca shotgun, but we didn't have one in the armory. I had to pick another type that didn't have a duck-bill shot diverter like the Ithaca, but it did have a figure eight type of thing on the end of the barrel so that the shot had a flat spread. Before we left, I had taken the weapon out and test-fired it, and the pattern was straight across.

When I got to the river, my heart sank because we were supposed to swim across to the other side and set up our ambush. The Vietnamese saw how wide the river was and didn't want to go. Finally, I said, ''Let's go,'' and two of the

Vietnamese and I got in the water. I slid the shotgun under my belt and started stroking away. At that time I didn't have my life jacket or Duck Feet swim fins on. The two Vietnamese that were with me had their life jackets and Duck Feet.

When I got about fifty yards out, I stopped and looked back, and the rest of the guys were still on the bank. That was a mistake—the weight of the shotgun and ammo started taking me down.

I didn't know if I wanted to drop the shotgun, which would have made the swim back easier, or keep it and try to make it back without going under.

Finally, I was to the point where I knew I wouldn't make it, and I quietly spoke the Vietnamese word for ''help.'' The two guys that were with me came over and helped me get back to the dike.

The commanding officer of the Vietnamese, a green lieutenant, wanted to call the mission off. At that point I figured that my weapon was no good because I thought the bad guys were going to come down on the other side of the river. The rest of the guys had weapons that would be effective at that range, and there was enough starlight that we could see movement on the other side. I was able to talk the commander into setting up the ambush right where we were.

We were sitting there shivering, facing the river, and had our weapons up in front of us because the water was at chest level.

For some reason I looked back over my shoulder and saw sampans in the little canal twenty yards behind us. The first sampan was coming right through the kill zone, and behind it was another one. I looked farther up the canal and didn't see any others. By this time the first sampan was beginning to head out of the kill zone, and the second was just entering it. The first boat had two VC in it, one in the back and another three feet in front of him.

I fired one round from the shotgun, and when I looked

up, both of the VC were gone. Then everybody to my right opened up on the other sampan.

When the firing stopped, we left the ambush site, and I called the Marines. They went in later and checked the area. They found that we had only killed two in the ambush and that both of them had been taken out with that one shotgun round.

We did a lot of other missions, but one that comes to mind is when we went out in the PT boats and inserted one klick from the northern edge of the DMZ. We went in through three-foot surf—which surprised me because it was much easier than the rough water we had been through during training. We took the boats in and hid them under some vegetation and marked the location.

We were patrolling through the sand, and all of a sudden, artillery shells started coming in on us.

At a distance the flash is red and yellow. When they get closer, they are white; and when they land right next to you, the flash is blue. We saw a couple of yellow flashes when the rounds first hit. Then we started to see white flashes. Finally, they started dialing in on us, and we saw two blues. We didn't catch any of the shrapnel because the soft sand absorbed it, but at that range the blast was deafening.

We waited there for what seemed a half hour, and they finally stopped the shelling.

We got up and went on with the patrol. Mainly we were looking for paths. We went three to four klicks in without finding anything, then came back, found our boat, and got out.

Whenever there might be a serious confrontation with the enemy, we, as advisers, did get to say who we wanted to go on the mission. Usually, the Vietnamese officers agreed with us, but they made the final decision.

The Vietnamese commandos were divided into squads, each commanded by a Vietnamese officer. The officers were really slipshod. As an adviser, sometimes I had to make the decisions when the officer just couldn't make up his mind. One Vietnamese officer was so bad that it got to the point that, when anything had to be done, he turned around and looked at me. I ended up being his crutch, which is not what I should have been.

Another Sea Commando Team [SCT] officer was a real good man, and he also spoke very good English. He would tell me what he wanted to do, ask my advice, and then make his own decision. I went right along with him.

When I was with Echo Platoon, I worked a little bit with the LDNNs and liked operating with them. A couple of times "Espi" [Gilbert Espinoza] and I went out with the LDNNs. Most of the time they were our scouts. These guys were real good operators.

The people that I was operating with as Sea Commandos were a cut below. It was very frustrating for me; I almost got in trouble because I was expecting too much out of them. I was gung ho as hell and was expecting the same attitude from them. It just wasn't there.

During training I had to set up a competition based on them competing against me. I'd ride them until they all wanted to beat me. That's the only way I got the training accomplished. I couldn't get them to be like we were in UDT training. If they didn't like what was going on, they would just turn around and walk away, with a "we don't need this" type of an attitude. They had no desire to be there because they were kind of like draftees. They were either just out of boot camp or off some of the Vietnamese Navy boats.

We provided physical training for them. Some of the guys couldn't even do one pull-up. That just drove me right up the wall. We worked them into shape and took them out on swims. I felt like a lot of them started coming along with me when, one day, we did an ocean swim out off the beach. I took a Vietnamese as my partner, and we swam about two miles with fins. Coming back, we swam right through a mass of jellyfish. They were everywhere, but the trainees didn't give up. This was near the end of their training, and it was just like training a dog—all of a sudden things just started clicking. At that point, I knew most of them were coming along. We had welts all over our bodies.

After they were physically in shape, we got them mentally motivated to where they wanted to do something. From there it was just strictly time spent on ambushes and learning sneak-and-peek tactics.

They weren't always reliable. About 20 percent of them really didn't want to be there. It showed in the way they reacted. They were just a strange group of people to be in a special forces–type unit.

Camp Fay was set up with one side being the Navy contingent and the other the Army contingent. The Vietnamese Sea Commandos were down the road in their own barracks. Our Vietnamese mechanics were situated toward the back of the camp.

Our vehicles were embassy licensed, and it was always interesting when the embassy couldn't get us all the vehicles we were supposed to have. We would go out and *cumshaw*—"borrow"—a vehicle that we needed, bring it in, and have it repainted and licensed. In fact, one of the times I came closest to getting shot was when I decided to look at a Vietnamese general's jeep. I was sitting in it, and out came a "white mouse" [Vietnamese military police] with his gun trained on me.

Down the beach from Camp Fay was the admiral's cove. His house was on a beautiful beach, and he had a great sailboat. We'd "borrow" it every now and then and go sailing. I remember going sailing one day with Lt. Bill Belding. Being the commanding officer, he'd try to talk me into letting him take over the rudder. While sailing around Danang Bay he almost ordered me to give it to him. Finally, I let him have the tiller, and then he lost control and accidentally rammed the hospital ship that was anchored out in the middle of the bay. The sailors were out there looking over the side, just laughing at us.

It may sound amazing, but we did a lot of operations from trucks. Some ops we did from helicopters and PT boats, but most of them were from trucks. We'd just drive up a road, park, jump off, and go in. Once in a while we'd use boats, but nothing like when I had been with a SEAL platoon and used LSSCs and PBRs.

We did use some PBRs, but in our operation we usually cross operated the Sea Commandos with other units. One thing that did concern me was when we went out with Echo Platoon, it seemed like we had a little bit more backup when we got in a "dick dragger." With the SEALs we were always lining up fire support from helos or our boats. With the Sea Commandos, it just felt like we were stuck out there by ourselves. It was something that we didn't get very often with the Commandos.

It was different when I was with Echo Platoon. One time I was operating with an LDNN unit, and 1st Squad of Echo Platoon had gone in the night before and made a hit that morning. While they were being extracted, our LDNN group was inserted just about a klick away. We stayed there all day, and in the evening we decided to go down to where 1st Squad had made the hit earlier that morning. There were two advisers, myself and an officer, and eight LDNNs.

We patrolled down, and our pointman sprung the ambush that the VC had prepared for us. I was carrying a Stoner on that op and a 9-mm sidearm. While "Espi" and some of those guys loved the Stoner, I never quite trusted it.

When the point sprung the ambush, all hell broke loose. They started firing and throwing grenades, and I started sweeping with the Stoner. It was just starting to get dark; and I could see muzzle flashes coming from one area, so I started moving the Stoner up and down as I fired into that area—and the last thing I saw was some green enemy tracers going up in the air. I ripped him, and his AK-47 must have been on full automatic because the rounds just went up in the air.

I had fired all of the rounds in the drum. I ripped off one of the long belts of ammo that I had looped over my shoulder and around my waist. I fed it into the gun and fired about twenty rounds when the Stoner jammed. It was a tough jam, and I couldn't clear it. It stayed jammed until we got back to the base. So I was basically out there with a 9-mm—which was a lonely feeling.

Under the circumstances, with all the adrenaline flowing, I maybe yanked on something I shouldn't have and made the jam worse. I normally carried the M-16 with an XM-148 grenade launcher under it.

The firefight was still going strong, so we motioned for the LDNNs to break contact. We crossed the canal behind us and went over the dike and down the other side. I grabbed the radio handset from the Vietnamese radioman, keyed it, and nothing happened. The water had infiltrated the radio, so we had no comm.

We started out on the run, and I was the second man from the rear. One of the Vietnamese was supposed to bring up the rear. The VC were still looking for us by firing toward us. This Vietnamese kept running up, and I was much bigger than he was, and he would run up in front of me. Every time he would do that, I would grab him and pull him back behind me. So I kind of ended up watching the back as we were running out.

Then all of a sudden, I heard the helicopters coming in, so I brought out a blue strobe light with the protection around the side and pointed it at them. They keyed in on us and came right down. I was pushing all our guys in, and just as I got the last Vietnamese in, the helicopter took off.

I grabbed the skid and got about five feet in the air and thought, "This is stupid," and I let go. I hit the ground, and the helicopter went on out.

All of a sudden, no gunfire, nothing—just silence. The VC must have figured that the helos had pick up all of us.

I got out my poncho, flashlight, and map, threw the poncho over me, and got down on the ground. I turned on the light and, using the map, got a compass bearing on where I was. I figured I was only about ten klicks away from friendlies. There was no doubt in my mind that I would make it back.

I was just putting everything away when I heard the helicopter coming back in. I pulled out my strobe light, flashed it on, and they came back in and picked me up.

I thought, "This is great!"

20

Joe DeFloria

Officer in Charge, Detachment Golf
Binh Thuy, Republic of Vietnam,
Deployed September 1970–April 1971

I returned to SEAL Team One from the Experimental Diving Unit in the summer of 1970. Dave Schaible, Team One's skipper, said he needed someone to take over Det Golf in September. I told him I would do it. Since I had been gone a few years, I went back through SEAL Advanced Training and began operating with a couple of platoons out in the desert near Niland, California. A couple of people from my old platoon were instructors there. Talmadge Bohannon was one of them.

In September 1970 I deployed to the large Navy base at Binh Thuy. It was the home of Commander, Task Force 116 [CTF-116], which was known by the code name "Game Warden." Det Golf was responsible for all of the SEAL Team One direct-action platoons in the delta. Sometime between the time I left in 1968 and 1970, SEAL Team One took over the delta, and SEAL Team Two took over at Nha Be in the Rung Sat Special Zone; they just exchanged roles.

While I was in command of Det Golf, I had a number of SEAL platoons under my command. Zulu

Platoon arrived at Solid Anchor in August 1970, led by Lt. Grant Telfer and Ens. Tom Richards. Subsequently, we split this platoon up and sent Tom Richards's squad up to the Dam Doi area, where there was good operating. Telfer's squad continued operating from Solid Anchor.

Golf Platoon, led by Lt.(jg) Richard Dill, had been there since May and departed shortly after I arrived in September. Whiskey Platoon, led by Lt. Dick Couch, with assistant platoon commander John Sandoz, arrived 3 November 1970. Yankee Platoon arrived 22 September 1970, led by Lt.(jg) Mike Horst and his assistant, Lt.(jg) Malcolm Campbell; they ended up operating in Bac Lieu.

When I arrived, Lt. Bruce Dyer was acting Det Golf Seafloat coordinator; he was stationed down at Solid Anchor. Chief Clarence Betz deployed with me, and at his request I sent him down to do intel work on Seafloat. Chief Leon Rauch and John Rowe, an intel specialist, were working in intel. At this time, SEAL Team One was generating a lot of its own intelligence. All these guys had previous tours in Vietnam and were really good at putting it all together.

On 21 October 1970 X-ray Platoon, led by Mike Collins, arrived to relieve Al Todd's Hotel Platoon at Ben Tre. Chief Frank Bomar was Mike's assistant. It was one of the few platoons that didn't have an officer as an assistant platoon commander.

Juliet Platoon had been down at Dung Island since 20 June 1970. Lt. Joe Quincannon and Lt. Nick Walsh had that platoon. In December 1970 Quincannon and Walsh were relieved by Victor Platoon, which was commanded by Roger Clapp and Jim Young.

In July of 1970 Kilo Platoon was at Rach Soi, commanded by John Marsh and Gary Stubblefield. Marsh was later evacuated when he got shot up pretty bad. Kilo Platoon was relieved by Romeo Platoon, Tom Boyhan and Lt.(jg) Stephan Dundas, in January 1971.

The commander of Det Golf was responsible to CTF-116

for special-warfare operations. If CTF-116 gave me a task-ing, I would assign platoons to it. I was also responsible for the support of the direct-action platoons, wherever they might be. The commander of Task Force 116 was stationed at Binh Thuy, and I was designated CTU [Commander, Task Unit] 116.0.1. I reported directly to the commodore for special-warfare activities. I was also responsible to SEAL Team One for the administrative work of the platoons.

I supported the platoons—made sure they had everything they needed. If they were having a problem with the commander where they were stationed—which happened frequently—I stepped in. Many of the base commanders resented having SEAL platoons running their own ops in their area. A lot of times the base commanders tried to influence the operations of SEAL platoons—which they weren't supposed to do. Some of the SEAL commanders worked it out pretty well with their base commanders. The base commander would usually be a full commander in rank, and the SEAL platoon officer in charge would be a lieutenant (jg) or a lieutenant. Although I was only a brand new lieutenant commander, I had the commodore (CTF-116) behind me.

Occasionally, we had problems at Solid Anchor and at Rach Soi, but John Marsh and Commander Brown worked it out; they had a good relationship.

Occasionally, I would go out and operate with a platoon. I operated with the platoons in Rach Soi, Bac Lieu, and Solid Anchor a couple times each so that I had a good feel for what the platoons were doing. I wanted to make sure they were operating the way SEAL Team trained them to operate. On one occasion I had to talk to a platoon commander about the fact that I thought he was using one particular method of insertion too much. They were always going in by boat. So whenever he left his base in a boat, it was perfectly obvious he was going out to operate and the general direction that he was heading for. This made them more likely to be ambushed. I advised them to use helicopters more often.

Depending on the geographic layout, if we left the area in a boat, we'd have to travel so far in a certain direction before it was possible to branch off. So it was pretty easy for the enemy to keep track of us. With a helicopter, it was harder for the enemy to tell where we were going.

I got some intel from Saigon once about an operation involving the tracking of a radio transmitter. The daughter of a Viet Cong leader in the U Minh Forest was going down from Saigon to see her father. She was traveling by boat and carried a typewriter with her that had a transmitter covertly placed in it so she could be tracked to where she would meet up with her Viet Cong family.

I went over and talked to John Marsh and Gary Stubblefield with Kilo Platoon at Rach Soi, and we lined up all the assets, which were slicks, gunships, fixed-winged aircraft, and artillery support.

We took off every day from Binh Thuy in a helicopter that had a receiver in it, and we would overfly the area where we thought the girl would be. We could pick up the transmitter from three thousand feet and could tell exactly where she was. When she stopped, we could even tell what house she was in; it was that sensitive. We followed her all the way down from Saigon until she got to the U Minh Forest— which took four or five days. When we picked up the signal from the same place two days in a row, we figured that was it—that was where the family was.

Kilo Platoon was standing by, and all the other assets were ready to go. One problem we had was that the slicks we used to fly down to where the girl was and insert could only carry enough gas to give us eight or ten minutes on the ground. Hardly enough time to do anything.

Because the area was a large swamp laced with dikes, the

helos had to hover while everyone jumped into the goddamn waist-high water. We inserted in broad daylight, within fifty yards of the target, and worked our way over to the building the signal was coming from. A bunch of bunkers were nearby, and we began to exchange fire with the people in them. We made our way up to the building, which sat on one of the few high and dry spots in the area. The building was wood and glass, very light construction.

We had picked up the signal on our receiver in the helo, and when we got on the ground, we were trying to pick it up on our radio. We picked up the signal coming from a bunker, so we sent in a couple of ''Kit Carson'' scouts—but nothing was in there! I don't know what the hell happened.

We all moved up to the building, and by that time people were scattering out of it, and a firefight took place. I remember a couple of fixed-winged OV-10s [armed spotter aircraft] coming in and taking these guys under fire with fléchette rounds.

We never found the typewriter or transmitter; we didn't get anybody. We quickly picked up some intelligence from the building and had to get right back in the helicopters because they were low on fuel. It was an interesting op, but anticlimactic.

One time I assisted Mike Horst down in Bac Lieu. He was having a hard time getting certain supplies. I said, ''Well, damn it, if you need them and you need 'em tomorrow, I'll get 'em down to you.'' So I got ahold of a six-by [six-wheel-drive truck], got in the truck, and drove down there myself. It was quite a trip; it took me all day. The route went from Binh Thuy to Can Tho, Fung Yip, Can Hung, Soc Trang, Con Tre, Bac Lieu, which was also known as Vinh Loi.

I also put together the biggest SEAL Team party in the delta. The story ended up in *Reader's Digest* and a couple of other magazines; it was one hell of a night. When I took over Det Golf, there was some money in the recreation fund. So I decided we should have a Christmas party with the rec fund money. That was Christmas of 1970. We wanted all the platoons in Det Golf up there, but of course we couldn't get everyone up at one time, so we planned to have the party over two weekends. One weekend would be for half the platoons, including the MST boat-support people, and the following weekend we would get the other half up there. We rented a hotel in Can Tho. We had all the food and drink and rooms for the guys who were coming from everywhere: Seafloat, Rach Soi, Dung Island. We let them stay there and party for the whole weekend. We even had a bunch of Navy Seawolf, OV-10, and some Army dust-off [medical evacuation] pilots join us. We were a very close group.

The part that made the news occurred one weekend when there also happened to be a Vietnamese wedding going on. Somehow, the activities of the wedding and our activities got intermingled, and everybody just had a great time. It was a good break in operations for everyone.

I was also responsible for determining the best locations for SEAL platoons, and we moved platoons around while I was there. Even during a single tour we would move some of them around. I moved Mike Horst from Seafloat up to Bac Lieu, where he had excellent support from the U.S. Army, including an OE-1 Bird-dog reconnaissance plane that was available to him whenever he needed it. I moved half of Grant Telfer's platoon to Dam Doi.

When Frank Bomar with X-ray Platoon got killed in an ambush, Chief Betz, who was at Solid Anchor for intel purposes, wanted to go help out Lt. Mike Collins in Ben Tre. I thought that was a good idea since Mike didn't have an assistant platoon commander. So I sent the chief up there, and just a few weeks later he got nailed in an ambush, shattered one of his femurs, and had to be evacuated.

At that point, Ed Jones was a warrant officer in Danang. He was with a small SEAL detachment doing admin duties, and he wanted to see some action. He told me he'd give Mike Collins a hand, so I sent him to Ben Tre. Shortly after that, one of their boats got ambushed, and Clint Majors, Mike Walsh, Paul K. "PK" Barnes, James MacCarthy, and Don Barnes all got hit. "PK" and McClaren of MST-2 each lost a leg in the attack. MacCarthy lost half of his ass. Walsh and Don Barnes were with Victor Platoon at Dong Tam and were just visiting one of the guys in X-ray Platoon when this happened.

Just a few days later, Mike Collins's boat [MSSC] got hit. He was killed, and the rest of the men with him, including Ed Jones, were wounded. That was the last operation for X-ray Platoon.

I'll never forget Father McMahon. He was in Binh Thuy, and he sort of adopted the SEAL Team guys. He came aboard as a forty-something-year-old, brand-new Navy guy, and he was a Jesuit priest. He was the chaplain, and he loved special warfare; he really wanted to get into combat.

The weekend he arrived at Binh Thuy, we were in the officers' club, and he was there dressed in his brand-new greens. He had his cross on and his lieutenant bars. Three or four of us were there having a couple of beers with the Seawolf pilots.

This little ensign guy who also just reported aboard was in there, reading a book, and we went over to him to do a skivvy check.

We walked up and said, "Hi, Ensign, how ya doing?"

He said, "Oh, fine, Sirs."

We said, "Would you be wearing skivvies by any chance?"

Now, nobody wore skivvies back in those days; they were uncomfortable because of the environment we operated in. The SEALs didn't wear them, and the Seawolf pilots that hung around with the SEALs didn't either.

We said, "How about getting on your feet, Ensign."

So he stood up, and somebody looked down his pants and said, "Yeah, he's got skivvies on."

All of a sudden about fifteen sets of hands went down there, trying to rip them off.

Father McMahon was at the bar, watching this whole thing, and said, "You guys are great. Damn it . . . my kind of people."

So we said, "Well, how about you, Padre, do you wear skivvies?"

He said, "You wouldn't . . . you wouldn't . . . I'm a man of the cloth!"

Well, we got ahold of him and just shredded his skivs.

Dave Del Giudice, the first CO of SEAL Team One, was down from Saigon for the weekend. We looked at Commander Del Giudice, and he said, "No, no, no," and dropped his pants right there; no skivvies on, so he got off OK.

I remember going to the hospital with Father McMahon to see "PK" Barnes, who had lost his leg, and McClaren, the boat-support guy that lost his leg. We walked in, and these two guys were arguing over who had the shortest stump.

Father McMahon said, "Look at these guys. Aren't they something, arguing over who has the shortest stump!"

He told all the nurses and doctors, "These are my people."

21

Jim Berta

LDNN Adviser
Dung Island, Republic of Vietnam,
Deployed November 1970–April 1971

In 1969 I was in SEAL Team One, Golf Platoon, stationed at Ben Luc, seventeen miles south of Saigon on the Vam Co Dong River. I was an automatic-weaponsman and backup to the pointman. I carried a short-barrel Stoner with a 150-round drum, and I carried additional belts that I'd slap in when needed. Gary Gray was our platoon officer, and Mike Horst the AOIC [assistant OIC]. We deployed in July or August and came back in December.

After we had been in Vietnam a few months and had done a couple of operations, we were feeling pretty bully. One day we went out on a cache operation. We had some intel, and we were going to meet a PBR unit on the docks at My Tho. A *hoi chanh* was going to take us in on this daytime cache operation.

We were standing on the docks when these "old guys" came up to us. One of the old guys was Hershal Davis. When I say old—they might have been in their late twenties or early thirties, but all of us were just maybe eighteen to twenty years old. To this day I can see Hershal Davis standing there on the pier with this handlebar mustache; he looked like a walrus, his mustache was so thick. He carried a Stoner with a long barrel, and I remember thinking, "Look at these old guys with their long-barrel Stoners."

I found out later Hershal was thinking to himself, "Look at these kids with those short-barrel Stoners." We were the first platoon to deploy after Stoner had come out with the short barrel.

That day we didn't discuss that fact because it was like—hey—"Those guys are SEAL Team Two," and they were thinking, "Those guys are SEAL Team One." So it was just, "Hi, how ya doin'," and a little small talk, then we went on with our operation.

The intel we had indicated that this was going to be a really big cache. That's why we went in during the daytime: we thought if it was that big, we wanted the benefit of the daylight to remove all the weapons. I think the SEAL Team Two guys were a little miffed because they weren't included in the op.

An Army light company provided security, cordoning off the area where the cache was located. We got a few weapons: I think two SKSs that were in fairly good shape and maybe a little bit of demo [demolitions], but it was nothing compared to what the *hoi chanh* had led us to believe. We thought we were going to have to bring tracked vehicles in to haul off all the stuff we were going to get; but it just didn't pan out that way. We got a few things, so it was a success, but we were kind of disappointed.

About twenty years later I was on my two weeks of active duty in a SEAL Reserve unit, and I went to the training cell at SEAL Team Three. Hershal Davis was, I think, the senior enlisted of the training cell. We were out at Niland, and I was helping Hershal teach combat pistol, combat rifle, and combat shotgun. We worked all day, and we were in the hooch that night, cooking dinner, and started talking about old times.

He said, "Berta. Now I remember you."

And I said, "Yeah, I remember you, too." He pretty much looked the same as he did twenty years before. I told him he was pretty old at that time in Vietnam, according to my standards, since we were all so young.

He said, "Yeah, you guys were just young snot-nosed kids with those short-barrel Stoners."

When we started our six-month predeployment training, Gary Gray decided I would be an automatic-weaponsman. We had three automatic-weaponsmen in a SEAL squad at that time. Two carried Stoners, and one had an M-60. I was a little too small for the M-60, but I could shoot the Stoner well. Before we deployed, I and one other guy went up to Cadillac Gage in Warren, Michigan, a suburb of Detroit, to the Stoner weapons school. I liked the weapon before I went up there, but after I went through the school, I liked it even more.

The last time we went out to Niland before we deployed, Gary Gray told us we could take our wives or our "squeezes," or favorite lady. I wasn't married to my wife at the time, but we were dating. I took her out there, and she shot very well; to this day I am amazed at the way she handled the Stoner. She could have gone to Vietnam with us and shot it. You wouldn't think it to look at my wife; she doesn't even like weapons or anything like that, but she was a natural.

I think the Stoner was the best weapon we had. I can't believe that SEAL Team let it out of their weapons system.

Once we got to Vietnam, we changed the way we carried our ammunition from how we did it in predeployment training. It actually changed daily and nightly.

The web gear I set up in training was the standard web gear with the *H*-harness, belt with two canteens, two or four ammo pouches, a first-aid kit, a Ka-Bar knife on the *H*-harness, and a compass case.

By the third or fourth operation in Vietnam, it had completely changed, and by the end of the tour I wasn't even wearing the *H*-gear. I carried 150 rounds in the drum of the Stoner, and I carried two 150-round belts crisscrossed over my upper body. When I needed it, I just broke the detachable link, opened up the feed tray, and slid it in. The only thing that remained from the original setup other than my knife was the morphine. I stopped carrying the first-aid kit, but through both my tours I carried a morphine Syrette in my cut-down floppy bush hat. I kept it in my hat because it usually didn't get muddy or wet.

When I first got to Vietnam, we all wore the issued jungle-leaf-pattern camie uniform. They were fine in the States, but it only took a week or two in-country to realize that the mosquitoes and leeches could go right through that camouflage material like it was tissue paper. That's why we started wearing Levis: mosquitoes couldn't get through the denim. The leeches could crawl up the legs, so we'd put rubber bands around the bottom of the pant legs. The mud didn't cling to Levis like it did to the cammo pants, and there were no large side pockets on the jeans, like there were on the cammo pants, that would fill with water when you came out of a river or canal. Some guys wore the tiger-stripe camie shirt with blue jeans.

When we left Ben Luc and returned to the States, I became a SEAL cadre instructor. At that time, when you graduated from UDT training and went to SEAL Team One, you had to go through eight more weeks of SEAL cadre training. It taught more of the specifics regarding weapons handling, patrolling, and insertion/extraction techniques. After that, I went through special-operations training, which lasted for about three months. It taught the basics of how advisers worked. I must have done a pretty good job on my first tour because all of the people in the class were senior to me in rank. I found out later that my platoon officer had highly recommended me to go back to Vietnam as an adviser.

I deployed with a platoon for the trip over and was probably the first SEAL to deploy on a second tour to Vietnam— with a surfboard. The first time I made the trip we all had to go through a five day EOD booby-trap school in Hawaii. Since I had already been through that training, I knew I would have five days with nothing to do in Hawaii. The morning we arrived in Hawaii, the platoon began their training, and I rented a car and drove to Waikiki and surfed for six or seven hours.

Once in Vietnam I relieved Ray Hollenbeck at Dung Island. He took me on three or four operations before he departed for the States.

My LDNNs and I ran one op with Roger Clapp, the OIC of Victor Platoon. This was just after they had relieved Juliet Platoon and gone on a few break-in ops. The intel we had indicated that a meeting would take place in a certain hooch. That night we set up an ambush around the hooch. At first light a VC came out carrying a weapon, and we opened up.

When the shooting stopped, we found several wounded VC, and Roger wasn't sure what to do with them. They were badly wounded and in so much pain that we couldn't interrogate them. It was clear that they would not survive their wounds, so I told Roger that I would handle it and put a bullet in each of their heads.

When we returned to Dung Island after the op, Roger said that he thought I had been very calm while shooting the VC. I told him it had been easy only because it was the humane thing to do; it was necessary because they were suffering.

I was the only LDNN adviser at Dung Island, and I worked with one officer and twelve or thirteen enlisted men. I enjoyed it and was proud to be an adviser and the only U.S. personnel working with this group. This gave me the incentive to do well and to show the senior advisers that I could do the job as well or better than they could. But it was a big change going from a SEAL platoon to a group of LDNNs.

When we went out on ops I was the only American with the LDNNs. Up in Ben Luc on my first tour we ran into a lot of enemy and got into some pretty good firefights. We had good luck up there; Golf was the first platoon to deploy with fourteen men and bring all of them back. In that same platoon the other squad had the highest-ranking hit of the war effort up until that date when Mike Horst's squad killed three COSVN-level VCI—which were equal to three of our senators.

There were more enemy down at Dung Island than there had been up at Ben Luc. It was a real hot area. One night—it must have been on the first or second operation by myself— we were going to a hooch to meet someone who was going to take us in on an operation. We didn't know that this guy was a double agent. What saved us was that we got there early and showed up at the same time as the VC.

When we started taking fire, I first thought it was from my other fire team, which could have gotten in front of us and was coming in the other side of the hooch. As it turned out, we were coming in the front door and the VC were coming in the back. My pointman realized what was happening and initiated on them.

We got in a pretty good firefight, and my radio operator was hit bad. He went down not very far from me, and I knew the only way I was going to get out of there was to get to the radio and call for support. He was lying there making gurgling noises and couldn't move. I could only speak pidgin Vietnamese, just enough that I could get a point across very crudely, so I knew I had to get over to him and the radio.

Our *thieu-uy* [Vietnamese lieutenant junior grade] was named Hew. He spoke excellent English, but in a firefight, when the adrenaline was pumping, you could hardly hear anybody. I finally made it to the radio, but it seemed like it took me two hours. In reality it was only about eight minutes. Once I got to the radio, I called and got some fire support and requested extraction.

After we extracted that night, I was sitting in the boat, and *Thieu-uy* Hew came over to me and asked me if I was cold. I was sweating heavily and shaking because everything was so different from when I had operated with a SEAL platoon. Then, we had control all the time. But that night, if the Viet Cong had had more fire power and used a flanking movement, they probably could have wiped us out.

Another thing that bothered me was that in the order of march my pointman was first, I was second, and the radioman was behind me. I should have taken the round that got the radioman. I couldn't figure out how it had missed the pointman and me and hit the radioman, because we were in such a small space.

On operations, I usually had to go through Army channels for my air support. They would support me, but they were always kind of reluctant. They would do anything to get me out of the field, but once they had me in the chopper and knew I was safe, they weren't real concerned about the rest of my men.

When I had relieved Ray Hollenbeck, I got what was called an adviser kit that included a jeep, a refrigerator, and some other items. There was also a box of morphine Syrettes that I kept in my medical lockup.

On my first operation, I issued everyone in my platoon a morphine Syrette. During the operation my radioman was gut-shot. I got to him, and we got out of there.

As we where leaving on the boat, I wanted to shoot him with a morphine Syrette to relieve some of his pain. I knew I couldn't use the one I had in my hat because when we were opened up on, me and the guy behind me got knocked back into a benjo ditch. The Vietnamese put all their human waste into ditches right around the hooches. I was stinking bad, and my hat had gotten wet, so I knew I couldn't use mine because it had to be filthy from when I was in that shit ditch. I told the *thieu-uy* to give me his Syrette, but either the needle was already bent or I bent it pulling off the plastic protective cap. So I told him to get one from someone else. I couldn't believe it, but out of fourteen people, the *thieu-uy* and I were the only ones that had our morphine Syrettes. Investigating further, I found out they'd either sold them in town or shot up with them. So I learned a lesson on that one. After that, only the *thieu-uy* and I carried the morphine Syrettes; I didn't issue Syrettes to any of the other men.

The LDNNs were very good to work with, as long as you could keep them together and get them in the field. Once you got them in the field, they were as good, or better, than the SEALs.

22

Bill Hill

LDNN Adviser
Hoi An, Republic of Vietnam,
Deployed February–August 1972

Prior to going to Vietnam, I went through SEAL advisory training in addition to SEAL cadre training. We went up to Cuyamaca, California, for part of the training. We learned about intelligence gathering and talked about the human side of intelligence—how to deal with and talk to the LDNNs and work with foreign indigenous personnel. They taught us how to grade the intelligence we would get, and that you needed at least two sources of info, and the more you got the better. They showed us how to set up a card file of the intelligence we got and how to set up a map in coordination with your card file to show different trends—using the information gathered.

One of the most important things they taught us was how to do MedCAPs [medical civil action patrols]. Doc Johnson, a corpsman, was supposed to go over with us, but just before we left, they canceled him. This happened during a time when all corpsmen going in-country on operational status were canceled.

I had to take a crash course on how to start IVs, how to deal with wounds, and other basic medical training.

I arrived in Vietnam at the Tan Son Nhut Air Force Base just outside of Saigon. Someone from the advisory group picked up Eddie Farmer and me at the airport. From there we drove down to the headquarters building, where we met Cdr. Dave Schaible and Lt. Cdr. Tommy Nelson, who were the CO and the XO of the American side of the LDNN program. They briefed us on who our OIC was, where we were going, and who we were relieving—Bob Irwin and Tom Leonard.

The next day we met the CO of the LDNN program, Thieu Ta Hiep, Schaible's Vietnamese counterpart.

In the evening we went to the ammo bunkers, loaded up our magazines, and got our gear ready for departure to the Danang area.

For about three days prior to going up to Danang we did in-processing in Saigon with our pay and service records. We got our NILO cards, which were written in English on the front and Vietnamese on the back. The card gave us authority to go into villages that Americans normally were not allowed to go into—for instance, in a situation where we needed to collect information. Americans were normally limited to safe areas, otherwise the MPs [military police] could pick you up and haul you in. If questioned, we just showed them the card, which said the person couldn't be detained for more than five minutes. Another NILO card gave us authority for whatever vehicle we were driving at the time. It was kind of like a universal military trip ticket, so you didn't have to have specific trip tickets for the vehicle.

About the fourth day after we arrived in Saigon, we got on a C-130 [cargo aircraft] to Danang. The OIC, Lt.(jg) Ed Cahill, and one of the MST personnel met us at the airport. We proceeded to Camp Tien Sha on the other side of Danang and picked up some stores there—the lieutenant advised us we could only go to pick up supplies at certain times. Because the coastal group was located on an island, it was difficult to get out, whether by boat or vehicle, during low tide. Either way, you couldn't set up any patterns going in or out since there was a good chance of getting ambushed.

The next morning we drove down to the Army base in Hoi An, where we would get our Army intel and helicopter assets, when available, for visual reconnaissance before our operations. We also met our Vietnamese NILO counterpart at the base that day.

We unloaded our supplies and gear from our vehicles onto a junk and a PBR, then took them out to the coastal group. On the way out Lieutenant (jg) Cahill pointed out some of the AOs [areas of operation] we'd be operating in. One area was right next to our coastal-group compound. The compound was camped on an island that was VC held; no one else was on the island besides the enemy and us. We unloaded our stores and took them into our hooch. We got an indoctrination from the lieutenant—where we would get our information, what our AO was, and where the free-fire zones were.

The next morning we were introduced to our LDNN counterparts. The LDNNs we worked with changed about every two or three months. Lieutenant (jg) Can was the OIC of the fourteen-man group there at the time. The OIC of the next group was Lieutenant (jg) Binh, and his AOIC was Ensign Huy.

We usually only took seven LDNNs out in the field at one time. Two advisers would always go on an op in case one of the advisers went down. One talked on the radio or communicated with the Army base in case we needed a medevac or anything else. The Army would not react to a Vietnamese voice on the radio. Eddie Farmer, Gary Chamberlin, and I were the three advisers.

During our base indoctrination we learned where the different bunker areas were and saw where our assigned positions were if the VC tried to overrun the base. The E&E routes were basically to head out into the ocean and try to get picked up. We were right on the South China Sea, and that was the quickest way to get out. There were only one hundred yards of beach between our compound and the ocean. We usually saw an American vessel out on the horizon every day, or at least every other day.

We had a twenty-one-foot open boat called a ski barge. It had an eighty-five-horsepower engine that didn't work very well. We could barely keep that thing running because we had a hard time getting parts for it. We had one fifteen-foot and one twelve-foot Boston Whaler, each with a forty-five-horsepower motor. We used them for insertions, as well as the PBRs, junks, and sampans. The junks were kind of like Vietnamese fishing boats. They were about thirty feet long, almost the same size as a PBR, but solid wood. There was a covered area for the coxswain, and there was a lower hold. They were armed with mounted .50-caliber machine guns and M-60s. The Vietnamese used them as patrol boats. They could get into a lot of different areas with them.

The next day we went back into Hoi An on an intel run. The lieutenant took some of the side canal areas to show us some other parts of the AO we would be operating in. We transited some of the PBR patrol areas. The PBRs could pass only as far as an area called the Parrot's Beak, an island shaped like the bird, before it got too shallow. At high tide a Boston Whaler could get through, but at low tide it was by sampan only. There were two VC training camps in the area, as well as a couple of VC-oriented villages.

When we first got in-country, we met with the corpsmen that were up in the Danang area. One spoke Vietnamese, so we brought him down to our area and visited different villages. He would help the locals by treating some of them and at the same time ask them questions about what was going on in the area. Because we were helping the people out, they were open to giving us a certain amount of information, but they didn't want to put themselves too far out on the line because the bad guys always lived right there by them.

In Hoi An we met the Army intel officer and got some information from him, and some from the Vietnamese Navy intel officer. We made a third stop at the *chieu hoi* center to coordinate an operation we were planning to go on in a few days. Back at our base we compiled the info we had and made one more check the next day to verify a few things from the intel reports. Then we had the Vietnamese plan the operation.

The plan was for seven LDNNs and two advisers to go on a one-night operation. A VC training area was located outside one of the ARVN camps. The Vietnamese were having trouble with the VC coming out of their training area and hitting the Vietnamese compounds and villages. We planned to leave from the ARVN camp in the middle of the night, patrol parallel to a road, head inland across from some rice paddies, then cross a stream near an area where VC were going in and out of the training camp.

From the information we had, it wasn't advisable for us to go too close to the training area because it was heavily booby trapped and had a lot of guards in and around the area. We planned to pick up one of the villagers to guide us to a certain point, then we would be on our own.

We patrolled two or three hours before we crossed over into the rice-paddy area and patrolled another hour and a half through the rice paddies. We got into the jungle, going toward the camp—at which time the guide said he would go no farther, so our pointman took over.

We patrolled another two hundred yards to a bend in the trail. It was the best area to take advantage of anyone coming and going, so we set up our ambush. Since this was our first op with the LDNNs, they wanted to go on a mission they thought was easy to set up.

We went in, laid up, and waited pretty much all night

until early the next morning, when we heard people talking back in the jungle. The plan was to grab a VC, get more information on where the camp was; but nobody came out of the jungle.

It was almost dawn when we left the area and headed back to the ARVN compound. We loaded our vehicles, headed out to the boat area, and went back out to the coastal group.

I was impressed with the LDNNs after that first op. They were very conscientious about their noise discipline. Every time we stopped, we'd do a head count to make sure everyone was accounted for. Their pointman was exceptional—he made sure everything got passed back. When we made crossings in danger areas, he always made sure everything was checked out. He always marked the booby traps we encountered so the next person to pass by knew right where they were.

The Vietnamese did the operational planning phase to a point, then came to us for review. We went over their patrol-leader's order and plan of action for the op before they briefed the people going out. That way we could input our advice regarding any aspects of the operation. With Lieutenant (jg) Can's operations, nine times out of ten we didn't have to change anything because he was very thorough.

We usually took a minimum of two M-60s out in the field. The pointman had his prerogative of what to carry. Generally, he carried either a CAR-15 or an AK-47, depending on how thick the terrain was. The AKs could penetrate the bush a little better. The advisers would carry either a CAR-15 or an M-60. Whoever carried the CAR carried the radio. The guy with the M-60 just carried that—and a lot of bullets. We had a machine shop in Danang shorten the barrels of the M-60s. We used the springs designed for aircraft-mounted M-60s to increase the cyclic rate of fire. We only had the M-79 grenade launchers at that time—no XM-148s or M-203s.

After an op we'd put in our post-op report, a sit-rep [situation report], a spot-rep [spot report], and a cas-rep [casualty report] if needed, whether friendly or enemy—and sent that information through the Army base. Our radio at the coastal group was in contact with both the Army compound and Danang. Once every three days we reported in to the Navy base in Danang so they knew that everything was OK. We always used authentication codes before coming on line to talk, and standard spot-rep format.

We did one op on Cam Tanh Island to find out exactly where some other camps were so we could call in helicopter gunfire on them. Every day you could pretty much go outside, and there'd be either a helicopter or an aircraft dropping ordnance on Cam Tanh Island.

There were some mountains fifteen to twenty miles from us by air. At least every three days there was an Arc Light [B-52 bomber] strike there. Sometimes it would wake us up early in the morning. It felt like a 5.1 on the Richter scale and would vibrate our beds across the room.

We did one operation on an island using the twelve-foot Boston Whaler to get us in as far as it could. From there we patrolled down a canal through waist-deep water until we got to within fifty to one hundred yards of a camp. We heard VC troops talking, and the Vietnamese with us translated.

The VC said that their North Vietnamese advisers had just received their refresher training with their Russian communist adviser in North Vietnam and were coming down within the week to give them some training.

We went back and reported the information, again with no enemy contact made. A lot of our missions were strictly intelligence gathering for the ARVNs and the U.S. Army.

After being at the base for a couple of months, we had gathered quite a bit of information on a compound campsite in the mountainous area at the edge of the Dien Ban and Dai Loc districts. The information was that the VC had Vietnamese POWs at the camp and also ran American POWs through there. We had several sources of info, some from a couple of our agents and some from a couple of *hoi chanhs* that had come out of that area. The *hoi chanhs* were from different *chieu hoi* compounds, so the info was pretty well corroborated. They knew there were at least twenty POWs in the compound at any one time.

We gathered additional information and did a lot of coordination for the mission. Two groups of Vietnamese LDNNs planned to use both of their platoons for the operation. One group was to hit the forward element just in front of the compound area, and the other group was to hit the back compound. We laid on the aircraft assets and vehicle assets to get in to a certain point. From there we would take helicopters in and make the hit. We were to have some UH-1H [Hueys] insert us, and Chinooks or CH-46s would be waiting to pick up the POWs. The POW camp had five guard towers, fifteen to twenty people guarding the compound; and approximately 1,500 meters down the road from the POW camp was a Regular VC Army compound that provided assets to the POW camp. So we had to have air-strike coordination to hit them and keep them off of us.

The people we talked to said they had seen Americans in there at least four different times. They were usually there for a maximum of two or three days. They only came through sporadically. There wasn't a regular pattern. The maximum seen at any one time was three, and generally there would just be one. The *hoi chanhs* giving us the info weren't part of the guard unit in the camp but had been part of the VC unit that was in the area, during their indoctrination process.

The whole op was coordinated, all the way up through our assets in Hoi An. When we tried to get the helo assets coordinated out of Danang, the op got shot down. The Army didn't want to take any chances because they figured it was getting close to the end of the American involvement in Vietnam. They didn't want to chance going in there even though they had similar information about the camp. After spending three or four weeks working out the details, the whole op got shot down.

The majority of our missions in and around the Hoi An area were information-gathering intelligence ops. We would also try to do some direct action and ambushes. On one op we tried to find this VC unit that had a 57-mm recoilless and a mortar. A couple of other VC supported this unit, going into areas, shooting at the different bases, and then taking off. We didn't find them on that op.

Just prior to the op we got our HSSC—heavy SEAL support craft. It was kind of like an LCU [landing craft, utility] with a lot of armament on it. It had an 81-mm mortar, four .50s, two M-60s, plus heavy armor around it. It had a deck built over the well deck, which is where the 81-mm mortar was. The M-60s were in the rear, and the .50s were all along the sides. The boat was Vietnamese run, coordinated by an MST adviser. Later on they got in a Mark 19 40-mm grenade launcher, but it was the hand-crank type, and they had a lot of problems with it. Sometimes it would work, and sometimes it wouldn't work.

We did another op against the VC with the recoilless. We had inserted and patrolled about one hundred yards when we got a radio call from the HSSC. They said they spotted some people following us—which we knew could be the unit we were looking for. We patrolled another hundred yards, did a fishhook to backtrack around, and set up a hasty ambush.

We sat in a nipa-palm area, laid up for about fifteen or twenty minutes, but didn't hear anything. We were just about to get up and leave when we started taking fire, but it was a recon by fire—we knew they didn't know where we were. The rounds were kind of going off away from us, then they tracked over toward the area we were in. Some of the rounds came over our heads. You could hear the cracking sound the bullets made—they were obviously AKs. We knew they were shooting just to see if we would fire back, so we just lay there and didn't do anything.

We could tell what area the fire was coming from, but we couldn't see them. The AK fire stopped, and they fired two rounds out of their 57-mm recoilless—which sounded like a freight train going over our heads. You'd be surprised how tall nipa palms look when you were trying to hide behind them! We lay there a little longer and didn't return fire, hoping they would come toward us.

They fired some more AK rounds, again not close enough to show they knew exactly where we were. They were still guessing. There wasn't any more fire after that, and we were there for probably another forty minutes.

Because they had been firing at us, we knew our op was compromised, so we patrolled out a different way, and the HSSC picked us up. We never did see those guys—and we really wanted to see them bad!

During the April 1972 Easter Offensive, the NVA took over Cua Viet and Quang Tri. We were asked to go in and see what the NVA had done to it, but we felt the op was too dangerous and turned it down. Once the NVA took over that area and moved down closer to Hue, the South Vietnamese made a plan of action to move all the Vietnamese SEAL groups up to a coastal group. I think it was Coastal Group 16 at Tanh Mi. It was outside of Hue on the South China Sea, in the Phu Vang District.

We made plans to pack up everything and move out. Eddie Farmer and Gary Chamberlin went with the advance party and met Lt. "Whitie" Weir, Bill Bradburn, and J.J. Adams, who had already gone up to that area.

I stayed at Hoi An to hold down the fort and coordinate the load-out. It was a rather trying time—being there by myself. One evening the base was put on red alert because the ARVN compound across the river was taking hits—the

VC were trying to overrun it. An AC-130 gunship worked out for an hour and a half before they squelched the attack.

When the guys came back, we packed up everything we could out of the base and went to Danang. From there we got everything loaded on a Vietnamese-run Navy boat for the trip up to the Hue area. Bill Bradburn, Eddie Farmer, and I rode up with the gear. Everyone else flew up in helicopters to get everything set up at the American compound, which was supported by a nearby Army Cobra helicopter compound and a Coast Guard station that coordinated the B-52 Arc Light strikes.

We made a couple of trips with the Vietnamese junks up toward the Quang Tri area. We were just offshore, getting a feel for things. On one operation Gary Chamberlin, Eddie Farmer, and "Whitie" Weir recovered an OV-10 pilot who had been shot down. He was presumed dead, and it turned out he was. They recovered the body and brought him back.

It was decided that more information was needed about our area of operations. Our responsibility was over-the-beach reconnaissance ops. These were the first over-the-beach ops by the LDNNs up in the Quang Tri province. We also went a little bit north of there along the river.

Eddie, "Whitie," Gary, and I conducted the first op with four of the LDNNs. We launched from one of the junk boats via two motorized IBS rubber boats. We went in close to the beach but never actually landed the boats on the beach. Gary, "Whitie," and the four LDNNs went in for a two-hour visual recon of an area where NVA were suspected to be.

We knew the location for extraction and coordinated references using our starlight scope. After the insertion, we moved the IBSs down, anchored off the beach, and waited for the guys to call us for pickup.

It got a little tricky at that point. OV-10s were in the area, spotting targets for Navy gunfire as well as for "fast movers" [jets]. While we waited in the boats, an OV-10 circled

three or four times. We decided to break radio silence and
called back to the junk to make sure everything had been
coordinated and that the area was clear. They said it was.

In the meantime, the guys called for pickup. We used the
starlight scopes to see them, recognized their signals, and
picked them up on the beach. They said they hadn't found
much of anything.

We got to the junk and went back to the base, then to Hue
to find out what the aircraft were doing in the area since we
had cleared it for our operation. We found out that they had
forgotten to send out a clearance. So actually, they were
spotting us—we were lucky we weren't fired on.

During August 1972 we conducted numerous operations but
didn't run into much of anything. "Whitie" Weir had already been relieved by Lt. Doug Huth, who came in as the
OIC. Later on Ryan McCombie came up—Huth, McCombie, and Ed Cahill were all officers from Team Two.

Our last op was a break-in for Lieutenant Huth. Since we
knew the area, Eddie, Gary, and I, along with five LDNNs,
took Lieutenant Huth to do a recon. We were lying off the
beach, waiting for them to call for pickup.

About twenty minutes before the time they were supposed to call us, we heard them on the radio, not real distinctly, calling for emergency extraction. They needed
pickup right away. We didn't know what was going on; we
just knew where to pick them up. We recognized their authentication code, picked them up, and got briefed on what
had happened.

They didn't see anything on the way in, but on the way
out the pointman noticed a guy smoking a cigarette. They
watched him until he finished smoking, then all of a sudden
he just disappeared. They couldn't figure out where he went
since it was a sandy area with not much vegetation around.

Upon investigation they saw a couple of barrels from the

Russian tanks used by the North Vietnamese. The NVA had buried the tanks under the sand so they couldn't be spotted in daylight. The guys saw at least three tanks and possibly one tank retriever. The NVA moved the tanks down from North Vietnam at night—no one ever saw them moving during the day. When it got close to daylight, the tank retriever would dig revetments for the other tanks to drive into. They used netting and other things to cover the top. The tanks would be semiburied to where only a six-to-eight-foot barrel section was left out of the sand—just enough so that the barrel wouldn't get sand in it.

After discussion with the lieutenant, Gary and one of the LDNNs decided they would mark the position, patrol out, and call in naval gunfire or "fast movers" on the area.

Gary and one of the LDNNs went in to mark the position, using a tierra grenade with a time fuse on it. When this type of grenade exploded, it put a chem-light [chemical light] effect on the whole area. It would glow in the dark—real nice. They positioned the grenade, set the fuses, and moved to where the rest of the patrol was laid up. They exfiltrated from there, and we picked them up. On the way to the junk we coordinated fire with the OV-10. We told them what we had seen in the area and the approximate time the tierra grenade was supposed to go off.

The only report we read was the one we got from the Army. They had spotted the tierra signature and coordinated a naval-gunfire strike on the area. We never heard what the actual end results were.

It came time for Eddie and me to leave the country, so we flew down to Saigon and linked up with our replacements, Mike Thornton and Steve Jones. We left country and not long after that found out that Mike Thornton and Tom Norris [Medal of Honor recipient] were doing an over-the-beach op and got compromised. Mike Thornton ended up with a Medal of Honor for saving Norris's life on that op.

During the time I was there, it just so happened that the

NVA had taken over the area. Overall, the LDNNs didn't really get into many firefights with the VC, and they didn't do a lot of ambush setups. They were able to get in and out of areas and get the information needed. Somebody was needed that could get in and out without being compromised and then set it up for others to go in and stop the NVA if at all possible. Firefights weren't always the most important ops. It was just as important to be able to get in and out without being compromised—the bad guys never knew we had been there.

The group of LDNNs we worked with were good. They were conscientious about getting information coordinated. They did some rehearsals prior to ops, although they weren't as extensive as some of the rehearsals we did. We had to be as tactful as possible when advising the LDNNs how to, or how not to, do their operations because they got a little uptight if we put too much into what they were doing. A lot of times the LDNNs wouldn't seek our advice, so we would say, "We think this would be a little bit better way to do it" or, "Don't you think it would be better if it was done this way?" Kind of make it sound like it was their idea.

It worked out pretty well. They knew to do what we suggested because our hold over them was, "Well, OK, go ahead and run the op, we don't need to go tonight." They always wanted us to operate with them in the field because they knew we had the radio link with the American bases for support.

The LDNN program, especially at the time we were doing the over-the-beach ops in the Quang Tri area, was very well coordinated. They had all the LDNNs up there, and we had all the boat support we needed to conduct the operations. We did a lot of rehearsals on the beaches close by.

The LDNNs conducted some riverine ops in areas south of Hoi An. That was kind of limited because invariably every night we also had an op that we were conducting up above the new DMZ. When the VC and NVA took over

Quang Tri, the DMZ was moved south a bit. It was the NVA's area—they owned it—so the DMZ was moved. We had as much support as could be given to us by the Vietnamese.

If we got into a bad situation, we had the American Cobra helicopter's call signs and frequencies, and they would come help us. Shortly after we left, they moved that squadron out because everything was being turned over to the Vietnamese. American involvement was winding down.

Personally, during my Vietnam years I made a lot of good friends as far as the Vietnamese we worked with were concerned—real close friendships with those we went out in the field with. I also gained a lot of experience as far as how to work with foreign nationals. Since then it has helped me know how to approach and coordinate situations when working with people from foreign countries because there are certain cultural differences where if you are not careful you could ruin the situation.

I really enjoyed the operations. We had a free hand in how we wanted to run our ops. They were usually never turned down once we coordinated and put in for them. I saw firsthand the difficult situations you can run into, especially when you have limited gear, equipment, and assets. That experience has helped me out immensely in the twenty-seven years I've been in SEAL Team.

Glossary

ADM: Anti-Disturbance Mechanism.

Air America: The airline owned and operated by the Central Intelligence Agency.

AK-47: Assault weapon of the communist forces.

Arc Light: Massive B-52 air strike.

AW Man: Automatic-Weaponsman.

B-40: Chinese-made antitank rocket.

BDA: Bomb Damage Assessment.

Black Shoe: A fleet sailor.

Boston Whaler: A small boat used by SEALs for insertion and extraction.

BSU: Boat Support Unit.

BUD/S: Basic Underwater Demolition SEAL training.

C-4 Explosive: Moldable high-explosive well suited for general and underwater use.

Canister Round: Cartridge for the 40-mm grenade launcher, containing twenty-seven pellets of 00 buckshot.

Cas-Rep: Casualty Report.

***Chieu Hoi* Program:** The "open arms" program for enemy soldiers who wished to surrender.

Chinese *Nungs:* Ethnic Chinese living in Vietnam who worked as mercenaries for U.S. forces.

CIA: Central Intelligence Agency.

Claymore mine: Directional antipersonnel mine capable of delivering seven hundred steel pellets over a sixty-degree fan-shaped pattern, two meters high, fifty meters wide, at a range of fifty meters.

CO: Commanding Officer.

COBRA: U.S. Army attack helicopter.

COSVN: Central Office for South Vietnam; headquarters for the Viet Cong.

C-rats: Also called combat rations. Food in green cans packaged in cardboard boxes.

DMZ: Demilitarized Zone between North and South Vietnam.

Duck-Bill Shot Diverter: A device fitted over the muzzle of an Ithaca Model 37 12-gauge shotgun that caused the shot pattern to spread horizontally.

Duck-Feet Swim Fins: Rubber swim fins used by UDT and SEAL Team members.

EOD: Explosive Ordnance Disposal.

Fast Mover: Jet attack aircraft.

Fléchette: Small metal darts loaded into 12-gauge rounds, 40-mm rounds, and artillery rounds, as well as rockets fired from aircraft.

HE: High Explosive.

Hoi Chanh: Enemy solider who surrendered under the *Chieu Hoi* Program.

HSSC: Heavy SEAL Support Craft. A converted landing craft.

IBS: Inflatable Boat, Small. A seven-man rubber raft.

Intel: Abbreviation for intelligence.

Ka-Bar: The standard-issue knife made by the Ka-Bar company.

KIA: Killed in Action.

Klick: One kilometer (one thousand meters).

LCM: Landing Craft, Mechanized.

LCPL: Landing Craft, Personnel, Light.

LCU: Landing Craft, Utility.

LDNN: *Lien Doi Nguoi Nhai:* Vietnamese SEALs. Later changed to *Lien Doan Nguoi Nhai* when the Vietnamese EOD, salvage diving, boat-support unit, pier security, UDT, and SEAL personnel were consolidated under one command. The Vietnamese word *doi* means team. The word *doan* means group.

LSD: Landing Ship, Dock.

LSSC: Light SEAL Support Craft.

LST: Landing Ship, Tank.

LZ: Landing Zone.

MACV: Military Assistance Command, Vietnam.

Marine Force Recon: Marine personnel trained for deep reconnaissance missions behind enemy lines.

McdCAPs: Medical Civil Action Patrols.

Mighty Mo: Nickname for a converted LCM used to insert and extract SEALs.

Mike Boat: Another name for an LCM.

Minigun: Electrically driven, rotary-barrel machine gun with a high rate of fire; it used the same 7.62-mm NATO (North American Treaty Organization) round and link as the M-60.

MP: Military Police.

MSSC: Medium SEAL Support Craft. Designed to carry a SEAL platoon of fourteen, plus crew.

MST: Mobile Support Team.

MTT: Mobile Training Team.

M-16: The standard U.S. military assault rifle.

M-16/XM-148: M-16 rifle with an XM-148 40-mm grenade launcher mounted underneath the barrel.

M-60: Belt-fed, general-purpose machine gun used by U.S. forces in Vietnam.

M-79: Single-shot 40-mm grenade launcher fired from the shoulder.

NavForV: Headquarters for Naval Forces, Vietnam.

NCO: Noncommissioned Officer.

NILO: Naval Intelligence Liaison Officer.

NVA: North Vietnamese Army.

OIC: Officer in Charge.

OV-10: Bronco. A twin-engine, high-wing aircraft that could be armed with miniguns, bombs, and rockets. Also called a Black Pony.

PBR: Patrol Boat, River.

PCF: Patrol Craft, Fast.

PIC: Provincial Interrogation Center.

PLO: Patrol-Leader Order.

POW: Prisoner of War.

PRU: Provincial Reconnaissance Unit.

***Punji* Pit:** A camouflaged hole in the ground containing bamboo spikes that had been hardened in fire. Many

times these spikes were dipped in human or animal
excrement.

Quonset Hut: A metal half-moon-shaped building.

Regional Force: The South Vietnamese national guard–
type unit.

RSSZ: Rung Sat Special Zone.

R&R: Rest and Recreation.

Sapper: A highly skilled soldier who would infiltrate U.S.
and Vietnamese bases to plant explosives.

SAS: Special Air Service. In this case, Australian Special
Forces.

SCUBA: Self-Contained Underwater Breathing
Apparatus.

Seabees: Personnel of the Navy Construction Battalion.

Sea Commando: Vietnamese personnel trained in Danang
for missions in North Vietnam.

Seafloat: A group of nine ammi-barges anchored together
to form a floating base of operation on the Cua Long
River.

SEAL: SEa, Air, Land.

Seawave: The first military incursion of the Ca Mau
Peninsula conducted by U.S. Navy patrol craft.

Seawolf Helos: Navy gunship helicopters.

Sit-Map: Situation Map. Map used to show the position of any friendly and enemy forces.

Sit-Rep: Situation Report.

SOG: Studies and Observations Group.

Solid Anchor: The land-based extension for Seafloat.

SOPs: Standard Operating Procedures.

Spot-Rep: Spot Report.

Starlight Scope: A device that magnifies ambient light so the user can see at night.

Stoner: Belt-fed light machine gun firing the same round as the M-16.

The Strand: The road running in front of the SEAL Team One area in Coronado is called the Silver Strand, abbreviated to the Strand.

Swift: Another name for Patrol Craft, Fast.

Tierra Grenade: A grenade developed for use in Vietnam that spread a phosphorescent powder when it exploded. Used for marking targets at night.

Toe Popper: A small mine or booby trap designed to cripple by blowing off several toes.

Trident: The gold insignia worn over the left breast pocket of SEAL-qualified Navy personnel.

UDT: Underwater Demolition Team.

UDTRA: Underwater Demolition Team training.

UNODIR: Unless Otherwise Directed.

VCI: Viet Cong Infrastructure.

Vietnamization: The program under which responsibility for fighting the war was turned over to the Vietnamese as U.S. forces were withdrawn.

Warrant Officer: An officer with a high degree of technical skill in a particular area.

White Elephant: Local CIA headquarters in Danang.

White Mice: Vietnamese military police.

WIA: Wounded in Action.

Willie Peter: White Phosphorous.

XO: Executive Officer.

About the Author

In 1984 Dennis J. Cummings left a ten-year career in law enforcement to work in the import business. Three years later he helped form Actionpacked Visual Productions and has produced four documentaries on the Navy SEALs. These include *Navy SEALs: America's Secret Warriors* and *The Stoner Machine Gun: A Navy SEAL Remembers*.